WAR AND THE STATE

War and the State

The Transformation of British Government, 1914-1919

Edited by
KATHLEEN BURK
Department of Humanities,
Imperial College of Science and Technology

London
GEORGE ALLEN & UNWIN
Boston   Sydney

George Allen & Unwin (Publishers) Ltd,
40 Museum Street, London WC1A 1LU, UK

George Allen & Unwin (Publishers) Ltd,
Park Lane, Hemel Hempstead, Herts HP2 4TE, UK

Allen & Unwin, Inc.,
9 Winchester Terrace, Winchester, Mass. 01890, USA

George Allen & Unwin Australia Pty Ltd,
8 Napier Street, North Sydney, NSW 2060, Australia

First published in 1982

British Library Cataloguing in Publication Data

War and the state.
1. Great Britain—Politics and government—1910-1936
I. Burk, Kathleen
354.41'0009 JN231
ISBN 0-04-940065-7

Library of Congress Cataloging in Publication Data

Main entry under title:
War and the state.
Includes bibliographies and index.
1. Great Britain—Politics and government—1910-1936
—Addresses, essays, lectures. 2. World War, 1914-1918
—Great Britain—Addresses, essays, lectures.
I Burk, Kathleen.
DA577.W34   940.3'1   82—3989
ISBN 0-04-940065-7   AACR2

Set in 10 on 11 point Press Roman by System 4 Associates Ltd,
Gerrards Cross and printed in Great Britain
by Billing and Sons Ltd, Guildford, London and Worcester

Contents

Editor's Introduction

The origin of this book lies in my first year of postgraduate research, when I felt the lack of a single book describing how the British government had developed during the First World War. It was clear that the period had seen fundamental change: the central government had increasingly taken on responsibilities which had before been left to private initiative, especially in the fields of industry and food distribution; further, the Cabinet, with its attendant secretariat, and the Treasury acquired in this period the powers and developed the procedures which subsequently enabled these two institutions to oversee and to control the central government machine itself. It seemed that an attempt should be made to answer the following general questions: What was British government like in 1914? How and why did it change? and What permanent changes remained thereafter? To provide some answers to these questions is the purpose of this book.

Deciding on how to begin and to end the book was relatively easy. First, it seemed that there ought to be an essay setting out the background to the extension of controls which was such a mark of the war. What were the changes in political perceptions which made economic planning seem necessary? Symmetry demanded that the book end with an essay analysing just why so many of the wartime controls disappeared so quickly. The central chapters of the book, however, which deal with individual departments, presented a problem of selection. It seemed clear that essays on the Cabinet and the Treasury should be included, both because of the importance of the war to their development and because of their central importance to the government machine. It also seemed obvious that the Ministry of Munitions, the first and most famous of the 'mushroom ministries' which seemed to spring up overnight, should also be considered. The other two ministries discussed, those of Labour and Food, were ministries established during the war which had a major domestic impact. Their separate births provide interesting contrasts. The idea of a Ministry of Labour was not a new one, although in the event its establishment awaited the political pressures generated by the war. The Ministry of Food, conversely, was more akin to other wartime ministries (of which at least seven were born between 1916 and 1918) in that it owed its establishment purely to wartime requirements. The Ministry of Food is notable in that it interfered more than other ministries with the daily lives of non-combatants by means of a nationwide system of rationing. Altogether, the seven essays go some way towards providing a picture of a government responding as best it could to the unexpected and unfamiliar requirements of a long and destructive mass war.

Within months of the beginning of the First World War, it became evident that the plans which had been made for government intervention in the economy were woefully inadequate. In the first essay, David French shows that this was due not so much to devotion to *laissez-faire* precepts on the part of prewar planners as to a false expectation of the nature of the war. Those concerned with anticipating the disruption likely to be caused by a war worked on the assumption that Britain would follow a strategy organised on the following principles: the army would be small and manned by volunteers, and the greater part of the British effort would be concentrated on controlling the oceans and blockading Germany. There would thus be no need for the government to organise manpower or industry, and business as usual in the domestic economy was a reasonable expectation.

It was the decision by the Cabinet to raise a mass army which upset the prewar calculations. It took some months for the Asquith government to face the implications for administrative change which the need to supply a mass army implied − such as industrial mobilisation − and Dr French describes the reluctant confrontation with reality. The essay ends with the setting up in May 1915 of the Ministry of Munitions under the leadership of Lloyd George, the first ministry created during the war to exercise economic control.

In the second essay, C. J. Wrigley considers the activities of the Ministry of Munitions, asking whether it was as new, exciting and different as myth makes out. Was the allegation which led to the setting up of the Ministry of Munitions, that the War Office was incompetent, justifed; or was it true that the Ministry of Munitions reaped the benefit of the War Office's plans? Was the ministry as innovatory in its activities as has been claimed? Dr Wrigley argues that although the War Office did fail, it did so not through placing insufficient orders but rather through not ensuring that its suppliers had the necessary labour, machinery and other scarce resources. Once the ministry was established, it was organised differently from the rest of Whitehall, in that its separate sections were nearly autonomous, rather than centrally controlled within the ministry. (This, however, changed in the later years of the ministry.) It further challenged estab- lished patterns by the widespread introduction of businessmen in policy- making positions, and by the large percentage of women employed in the bureaucracy. These innovations, however, were merely the means to the end, which was to mobilise British industry to produce the munitions and supplies needed for the mass armies. The Ministry of Munitions was in- volved in every sector of industry. It encouraged the expansion of capacity in engineering firms, and promoted purpose-built state munitions factories; it fostered new manufacturing techniques, and pressed firms to specialise. The ministry involved itself in industrial relations, alternately coaxing and coercing both management and labour. It used the Defence of the Realm

Act to house munitions workers. However, such activities were considered to be specific to wartime, and unlike the other two wartime ministries discussed in this book, the Ministry of Munitions was closed down as soon as possible after the peace treaty was signed.

The question of the central direction of the war was one which exercised the informed public. The responsible institution was of course the Cabinet, and in the third essay, John Turner describes the evolution of the Cabinet and its attendant secretariat in response to wartime exigencies. Dr Turner demonstrates that the central feature of wartime Cabinets was the practice of reserving critical decisions for inner committees. These committees were, successively, the War Council, the Dardanelles Committee and the War Committee; subsequently the War Cabinet subsumed the powers and functions of both the Cabinet and the War Committee. He also argues that the time necessarily devoted by the Cabinet to military matters meant that it had little time available to investigate the activities of individual departments. This led to the establishment of standing sub-committees of the Cabinet to co-ordinate department functions. However, the major problem of Asquith's war premiership was the Cabinet's inability to agree on war policy, and administrative change alone could not resolve these conflicts. When Lloyd George became Prime Minister in December 1916, he established a new, small War Cabinet representing a balance of political power. Lloyd George's War Cabinet has been represented as concentrating authority in one small committee, but Dr Turner argues that this was not in fact the case. Rather, responsibility was devolved upwards or downwards to inner committees which determined strategy. The War Cabinet's principal and most time-consuming role was to act as a supreme court which arbitrated between these committees.

The Cabinet in both its functions – development of strategy and executive supervision of the departments – was aided by the Cabinet secretariat under the direction of M. P. A. Hankey. The establishment of the secretariat was perhaps the most long-lasting of the innovations stemming from the war: the essential routine of the Cabinet Office has continued to be that laid down in late December 1916. But the war destroyed the Cabinet's unity as an executive body. It remained as a political committee to give coherence and discipline to the government.

That other government institution with responsibilities for central control, the Treasury, also experienced a transformation in its powers and duties as a direct result of the war. In my own essay, I suggest that in 1914 the Treasury was wholly unprepared to administer a great and unexpected war, beyond coping with the immediate financial crisis. Further, even in its traditional duties, those of overseeing public spending and the staffing of the Civil Service, it was perceived as weak, with neither the manpower to investigate nor the powers to enforce its will. During the years of the war, the Treasury did not have the political support necessary to overcome departmental reluctance to submit to Treasury strictures. Military necessity was the only imperative, and if this meant that public spending shot up and departments multiplied their staffs, there was little that the Treasury could do about it. In the end, of course, the war provided the Treasury with an extremely useful horrible example, since the size of the government and the huge sums involved in public spending appeared to demonstrate the results if effective Treasury control were lacking. By 1919 political pressure supported the efforts of the Treasury and its Chancellor to gain the powers needed to control spending and Civil Service staffing; and in the end it was reorganised, enlarged and strengthened.

A major reason the Treasury pushed for increased powers was that it wanted to curtail the activities of the new interventionist ministries. Rodney Lowe, in his essay on the Ministry of Labour, in fact ascribes in part to the Treasury the short-term failure of the ministry. It was established in December 1916 essentially as a political gesture by Lloyd George, designed to win the parliamentary support of the Labour Party. The original intention was to co-ordinate policy on labour matters under a ministry which had the confidence of organised labour. Unfortunately, the ministry seldom had enough political support to enable it to win in administrative or political conflicts. Its main administrative weakness was external; logically, it should have controlled manpower policy, industrial relations and the planning of demobilisation and industrial reconstruction, but there were rivals for its authority in each of these areas.

In the immediate postwar years the ministry experienced little but failure. There were political constraints on its operations, and a lack of industrial consensus, including a consensus as to what industry and labour wanted and needed from the ministry; but most important, the ministry was beaten down by the Treasury, in that the services which the ministry might have offered were severely restricted by the lack of finance. Dr Lowe, in fact, asserts that the formal strengthening of Treasury control was the most important administrative change to come out of the First World War, and the Ministry of Labour, as he demonstrates, was one of those ministries which most suffered from this control.

The Ministry of Food was established in response to a widespread clamour for some control of food prices and distribution. The question which bedevilled the ministry was the nature and scope of this control. José Harris looks at this debate, and considers the contributions made by Whitehall civil servants and businessmen drawn into government by the war. She describes the factors undermining the prewar assumption that, because of the Royal Navy's command of the sea, the supply and distribution of food would not be unduly disrupted. Prewar planning, however, did not anticipate the depredations that would be made by the German submarines, nor the closure of the Dardanelles Straits (which prevented access to Russian wheat). After the poor harvest of 1916, political pressure forced Asquith to appoint the first Food Controller, Lord Devonport, but it was not until the accession of Lloyd George in December 1916 that the Ministry of Food was set up and Devonport was appointed minister. Yet Lloyd George was no more prepared than his predecessor for drastic measures of food control, and Devonport himself preferred moral exhortation to coercion. The ministry was viewed as such a disappointment that Devonport was forced to resign in May 1917.

The ministry only began to fulfil the hopes of its supporters when Lord Rhondda took over in May 1917 in the wake of strikes. Rhondda was given much wider powers than Devonport, and he used them to develop an ambitious and all-embracing economic policy. (Nevertheless, it should be noted that he, too, adhered as far as possible to the principle of maintaining existing channels of trade.) Rationing was first introduced (for sugar) in December 1917, and a virtually complete local and national rationing machinery was in existence by July 1918. In no other area of civilian life was bureaucracy imposed with such meticulous detail and comprehensiveness – and it was not achieved without controversy and conflict. This conflict raged within the ministry as well as without. William Beveridge, one of the permanent civil servants, claimed that the conflict was essentially between career civil servants and temporary civil servants, the businessmen. Dr Harris disagrees, however; she argues that the clashes were quite personal and did not follow the permanent/temporary line: there were 'adventurers' and 'mandarins' from both camps.

In the final essay, Peter Cline considers the problem of the origins and growth of reconstruction policy during the war. He begins by describing the Tawney thesis, the theory which many later scholars took as their starting-point: during the war the government failed to develop a general view of controls which accepted that they could be useful in the postwar period; thus when peace came the government were pushed down the road to precipitate decontrol by the Treasury, bankers and others who disliked the state's playing an interventionist role. Professor Cline disagrees. He argues that reconstruction policy must be seen in the light of wartime assumptions about the difficulty of defeating Germany, and the possibility that even after the war Germany would launch an economic offensive which would render an Allied military victory nugatory. Until the summer of 1918 it was not wholly clear that the Entente would beat the Central Powers. In the case of a stalemate, it might be necessary for Britain and her Allies to resort to economic weapons in order to beat the enemy after the war, or to use Allied controls over raw materials to gain at the peace-table what Allied armies could not win in the field. Even as the German danger receded at the end of 1918, the Foreign Office began to fear world-wide shortages of raw materials, a shortage which could only be overcome if the Allies acted together and rationed those materials which were in short supply. The implication of all of these apprehensions, he argues, was that coping with them would require the government to plan the economy after the war. But because the postwar situation was not as threatening as the government had feared, the need for controls quickly vanished. In other words, 'The defeat of the 'British revolution' of social and economic reconstruction was only secondarily the result of the reassertion of ortho- dox economic thinking in 1919: the primary cause was the unexpected collapse of Germany in 1918.'

The First World War caused striking changes in the organisation and procedures of British government. With the possible exception of the strengthening of Treasury control, it is probable that few of the changes would have happened during this period had it not been for the war. Some changes and innovations persisted into the interwar period, most notably the strengthening of Treasury control and the Cabinet secretariat. Some veterans of the wartime Whitehall experience — Viscount Addison was one — emerged from the experience convinced of the efficacy of controls imposed by central government as the most efficient means of changing society. However, the extensive system of government controls was very rapidly dismantled after the war. Yet the precedent had been set. The interventionist ministries were consciously chosen as models when controls were once more needed in the Second World War, and that time, controls survived the war for a much longer period.

1

The Rise and Fall of 'Business as Usual'

The economic plans and policies for war of Asquith's Liberal government have received scant attention from historians. The little work which has been done on them has tended to be highly critical of the government's supposed unpreparedness to meet the economic problems the war produced. The government's failure to make adequate preparations has been attributed to their adherence to *laissez-faire* principles. It has been argued that these principles made them reluctant to plan for widespread state controls over economic resources and manpower. Writing in 1924 E. M. H. Lloyd, formerly a senior civil servant at the War Office and the Ministry of Food, argued that the Liberals had been too deeply committed to the doctrines of free trade and individualism to make proper economic plans for war or to take decisive action during the first few months of the conflict. 'It is not surprising [he wrote] that the necessity of State intervention was only gradually admitted by Ministers who had spent the greater part of their political careers in exploding the fallacies of Protectionism on the one hand and Socialism on the other.'[1]

Lloyd's interpretation of the government's inability to cope with the problems the war created at home has now become an orthodoxy. It is the purpose of this essay to show that this explanation requires serious qualification. The government's policies were not determined solely, or even in large part, by an economic ideology. Most planners recognised that the outbreak of war would dislocate the economy and if total collapse was to be averted the government would have to interfere in parts of it. By 1914 it was recognised that unless the government took control of the entire railway network and supported the shipping insurance market the economy would collapse and social order would be endangered because the populations of the great conurbations would be starving. More important than ideology in determining the government's courses of action and inaction was their decision about the correct strategy to pursue in a war against Germany. Largely for political reasons, before 1914 they rejected the idea of raising and dispatching a continental-size army to France. Instead they intended to fight the war using the existing small volunteer army and the Royal Navy. This decision had important results for the government's economic policy. It meant that there was no need to draw on and, therefore, to organise manpower and factories normally devoted to civilian consumption to support the war effort. 'Business (almost) as usual' was possible.

However, Kitchener's decision to raise and equip an army numbered in millions upset all prewar calculations. Within a few months of it having been taken it was becoming increasingly apparent that the economy could no longer be left largely to run itself. Shortages of men, machines and raw materials and production bottlenecks meant that the government was eventually compelled to intervene to determine the proper distribution of increasingly scarce resources. By May 1915 a growing number of ministers accepted the need in principle for such intervention. But effective action was delayed, especially in the vital engineering industry, because Kitchener and Lloyd George could not agree on how the process should be organised.

Naval and military plans for a war with Germany had been formulated in outline by the time of the Agadir crisis in the summer of 1911. The result was two incompatible plans. For their part the soldiers had firmly embraced the continental commitment. They were determined that the British Expeditionary Force (BEF) should be sent to France to co-operate with the left wing of the French army on the Franco-Belgian frontier. The British General Staff hoped that the six divisions of the BEF would be just enough to tip the scales of the land war in the Entente's favour and stop the German advance through Belgium and northern France. Then the Germans would be faced by a stalemate and so would be forced to sue for peace.[2] The Admiralty, however, rejected the continental commitment in favour of their own maritime strategy. Their war plans had been prepared by the Ballard Committee in the winter of 1906–7. This committee had recommended that Britain could best bring about the defeat of Germany by means of a naval blockade. The German merchant marine could be swept from the seas and her Baltic coastal towns could be bombarded. This would bring about the collapse of her economy and so she would be unable to continue fighting. To assist them in this plan the Admiralty wanted the War Office to lend them part of the BEF so that they could employ it to seize islands off the German coast for use as advanced destroyer bases. The Ballard Committee were tremendously impressed by Germany's supposed vulnerability to a naval blockade, although in their report they merely asserted this fact and produced no evidence to support it.[3]

These plans were mutually exclusive: the BEF was just too small to be committed to northern France *and* to the Baltic coast at the same time. But when the plans were discussed by a Committee of Imperial Defence (CID) sub-committee investigating the military needs of the Empire in 1908–9 the sub-committee was unable to decide between them. It simply concluded its report by saying that 'In the event of an attack on France by Germany, the expediency of sending a military force abroad, or of relying on naval means, is a matter of policy which can only be determined, when the occasion arises, by the Government of the day.'[4]

The reason why the sub-committee was unable to resolve these conflicting plans was made explicit in the late summer of 1911. On 23 August a carefully selected group of ministers assembled at the CID. They were treated to a full exposition of the General Staff's plans and a much more vague and 'puerile' account of the Admiralty's.[5] But although the former was accompanied by much well-reasoned argument Asquith recognised that it would still be extremely difficult to persuade the majority of his Cabinet colleagues to accept the army's ideas.[6] Only Asquith, Grey, Haldane, Lloyd George and Churchill knew anything of the army's plans to send troops to France. The rest of the Cabinet had not been told of them in the expectation that they would not agree to them. This small group thought that even if Britain did go to war with Germany their colleagues would insist that only the navy and not the army should be sent to aid the French. Their fears were well founded. Writing only a few days after this meeting Walter Runciman, the President of the Board of Education, told Lewis Harcourt, the Colonial Secretary, that 'The sea is our natural element and the sooner they [that is, the French] realise that we are not going to land troops the better will be the chances of preserving Europe's peace.'[7]

In writing this Runciman was only echoing ideas which were common currency in the Liberal Party both within and without the Cabinet.[8] Most Liberals, however reluctantly, were prepared to go to war, but they were not prepared to fight a major land war. Like the Admiralty they wanted to avoid committing a large army to the Continent and to fight the Germans by attacking their trade.

Reliance on the navy was, therefore, fundamental to the success of 'business as usual'. It would protect Britain from invasion, it would strangle the German economy and thus by obviating the need to send a large army to the Continent, it would ensure that Britain would win the war at the least possible cost to herself. Even more than this, safe behind her Dreadnoughts, Britain's economy could continue to function smoothly and this in itself could become a potent weapon in defeating Germany. This argument was expressed most cogently by the secretary of the CID, M. P. A. Hankey, in a memorandum he sent to the Secretary of State for War, Colonel J. E. B. Seely, in March 1913. Hankey, previously the secretary of the Ballard Committee, was an uncompromising navalist. In his memorandum he rehearsed the usual navalist arguments in favour of relying on the fleet and then began to develop a powerful new line of argument. He stated that if imports continued to come into Britain her industries would continue to function and she would thus be able to supply her allies with all the supplies they needed to fight the Germans on land. But the *sine qua non* of Britain becoming the economic powerhouse and paymaster of the Entente was that the economy must not be deprived of manpower by futile attempts to raise a large army. If that were attempted the economy would be ruined and Britain would be pitched into a costly land war. At home, 'The transport services would be demoralised, [and] the mills, mines and agriculture would all be short of labour at a time when it was specially required.'[9] The burden of this argument was that there was simply no point in Britain paying the blood tax of a land war if the navy and the French and Russian armies, equipped with British-made supplies, could win the war alone. Indeed it might be disastrous for Britain and her partners if large numbers of men were taken from the factories and put into uniform, because 'This might result in a general and universal destitution and starvation and the Government would be subjected to heavy pressure to bring the war to an end at all costs.'[10]

The internal logic of these arguments was quite sound. The notion behind them was not. Hankey never contemplated what would happen to the Entente if the French and the Russians were not strong enough to checkmate the Central Powers and bring them to the peace-table quickly. Nor did he ask himself how long Britain's allies would be prepared to fight alone whilst Britain enriched herself supplying them with arms. A cash nexus was not a stable basis for a wartime alliance. Navalists like Hankey were fond of looking back to the Royal Navy's successes during the Napoleonic War, but they had forgotten or misunderstood one of the lessons of the war. In a war with a great continental power British naval and economic strength alone had not been enough to ensure victory. She also needed powerful military allies. Between 1793 and 1815 Britain spent nearly £66m. subsidising various continental allies but money alone could not give them the will to resist the French. Only in 1813, when they had found that will from within themselves, could they make effective use of British aid and it was only when Napoleon had been defeated on land that he surrendered.[11]

The belief that naval and economic power would suffice to defeat the Germans was one of the fundamental premises on which 'business as usual' was based. The other was that raising a continental-scale army was impossible. Before the war voluntary recruiting left even the small British regular army undermanned, and political prejudices against conscription were such that the government never seriously contemplated introducing it. In August 1910 Lloyd George frankly recognised that compulsory training even for home defence was beyond the bounds of practical politics 'because of the violent prejudices which would be excited even if it were suspected that a Government contemplated the possibility of establishing anything of the kind'.[12] The truth behind the Chancellor's remarks was made evident by the hostile reception given to a bill of

March 1913 introducing compulsory service for the Territorial Army. So hostile was the opposition from the Liberal and Labour benches that its sponsors withdrew it before it was put to a vote.[13] One of the consequences of this was that the War Office did not think they would be able to raise many more men on the outbreak of war and so made no plans to do so.[14]

Thus the rejection of the continental commitment by all except the General Staff and a handful of ministers and a belief in the efficacy of a maritime strategy were the fundamental premises on which 'business as usual' rested. As long as they were put into practice 'business as usual' could survive. If they perished 'business as usual' would perish too. The implications of this for economic planning were crucial. Britain planned to rely on the navy to do most of her fighting and the Cabinet refused to contemplate raising an army numbered in millions. Hence there was no need to plan for the kinds of collectivist measures which the government increasingly adopted after 1915. Nor was there any need to set up the elaborate administrative apparatus to run the war at home which was established piecemeal during the war. Adherence to *laissez-faire* principles seem to have played little or no part in deterring the government from making plans to mobilise the economy in wartime. Because, for the time being, they shunned the continental commitment, the government failed to recognise that there was any need for them to organise the redistribution of resources between the needs generated by the war and the normal requirements of the civilian population.

This argument can most easily be illustrated in detail by examining the engineering industry. During the war it underwent considerable redirection. But before the outbreak of war in 1914 the government's policy had stemmed directly from the experience of the Boer War. Early in that war the inability of the Royal Ordnance Factories and the handful of specialised munitions manufacturers to supply enough shells for the army in South Africa had meant that Britain had been denuded of nearly all stocks of artillery ammunition. The Unionist government then tried to rectify this dangerous situation by increasing reserve stocks of ammunition. By 1914 each field gun had 1,500 rounds compared to only 300 in 1899. Five hundred rounds per gun were kept in a reserve at home, ready to be sent abroad when required. By all previous standards this represented a prodigal supply of ammunition and Haldane, the Secretary of State for War in 1910, believed that it was 'amply sufficient'.[15] It was estimated that these stocks would be sufficient to maintain the army in the field for six months, by which time munitions manufacturers would be able to take their reserves of machinery out of mothballs and take on new hands to operate them. Once this had been done it was expected that they would be able to meet all the army's requirements. In an effort to reduce production overheads reserves of machinery were reduced from 1907[16] but the remainder proved to be sufficient to meet the needs of the original BEF cal-culated at the prewar rate of ammunition expenditure. Before the war the War Office expected to order 162,000 rounds of 18-pdr. shrapnel ammuni-tion in the first six months of a major war. In practice, by the end of that period, the trade and the Royal Ordnance Factories between them were delivering that many shells in only one month.[17] But by then all these calcu-lations had been overtaken by events. No one had anticipated the advent of trench warfare and its attendant demands for enormous quantities of ammu-nition. Similarly no one had anticipated that Lord Kitchener would try to raise his New Armies or that they would need to be equipped from scratch.

The government's reliance on a small circle of suppliers before the war has been characterised as a policy of *laissez-faire* and condemned as being inadequate. On closer examination this is not so. The trade and the Royal Ordnance Factories did what was expected of them and before 1914 no one had anticipated that they would have to do more. Assumptions about the military nature of the coming war, rather than economic ideology, lay behind the government's planning. In 1935 Hankey highlighted most of the govern-ment's omissions and the reasons behind them when he wrote that

> the Government had no national plan for an expansion of the army, or for its armament. None of the problems had been worked out or thought of at all — exemption from military service of skilled or un-skilled labour, machine tools, raw materials, and national industrial mobilisation generally. Consequently, and in particular, there was no basis for programme making or for estimating future requirements and supplies, no warning was given to the armament firms of what would be expected of them.[18]

'Business as usual' could only succeed if the economy did not collapse completely on the outbreak of war. Considerable time and effort was spent in devising plans to prevent this from happening. In April 1903 Balfour's government established the Royal Commission on Supply of Food and Raw Materials in Time of War. In 1905 it reported on Britain's major strategic weakness, her heavy dependence on overseas trade for vital imports of food and raw materials for industry. Unless the Royal Navy kept the sea-lanes around Britain open the population would face starva-tion and mass unemployment within a few weeks of the outbreak of war. Seaborne trade could be disrupted in several ways. The Royal Commis-sion's most pressing fear was that British shipowners might be reluctant to allow their ships to put to sea because Lloyd's would refuse to give them insurance cover against war risks. Consequently the Royal Commission recommended that a small committee of experts should prepare a scheme whereby the government could provide the insurance.[19]

The war risk insurance question became a significant issue. The struggle between supporters and opponents of state intervention was fought over it and by 1914 the former had gained a victory. Permanent officials of the Board of Trade, the Admiralty and the CID supported a state insurance scheme. The Board of Trade had few scruples about the state crossing the dividing line between public and private business. If private insurance brokers refused to sell war risk insurance except at prohibitive rates which would have the effect of pushing up prices charged to the consumer to famine levels, then, the Board argued, the state had a right and duty to act. The state was bound to take control of the war risk insurance market for the sake of the whole community.[20] Admiralty and CID officials accepted the Board's arguments. In addition their attitude to the question was also governed by their departmental concerns. Their job was to prepare Britain's defences for war. The likely state of the war risk insurance market appeared to pose a danger to those defences and they felt that they had to act to meet it.[21]

Treasury officials took a different view and one which was much less sympathetic towards state intervention. Their interest in defence was dominated by their concern to limit government expenditure. In July 1905 the Unionist Chancellor of the Exchequer, Austen Chamberlain, insisted that CID minutes should be circulated to the Treasury so that his officials could examine them to ensure that any expenditure they called for was consistent with Treasury policy.[22] From that date onwards hardly any CID inquiry was without a senior Treasury official, whose purpose was to protect his department's interests. They had two related objectives, to preserve free trade and, partly in order to do so, to keep the defence estimates as low as possible. Free trade precluded the government from placing a large share of the tax burden on commerce, and so they were forced to raise their revenue from taxes on income. These gave a strictly limited yield, and it was feared that if they were raised too sharply they might harm trade and industry. But in the first decade of the century rising expenditure on defence and the social services conspired to increase the pressure on these sources of revenue. Defence expenditure also accounted for a slightly higher percentage of total government spending in 1913 than it had done in 1890.[23] The total rise in expenditure seriously perturbed orthodox Gladstonian financiers. As one senior Treasury official, then attached to the Board of Inland Revenue, wrote in May 1911, 'The present House of Commons' indifference to increasing expenditure is, as the Speaker remarked the other day, a new feature, and it is most alarming. People quite forget that public money is, after all, only private money.'[24]

Many senior officials at the Treasury regarded the rising defence estimates and the Liberals' social policies as dangerous because they required a constantly rising level of expenditure. Their fear was that sooner or later protective tariffs would have to be introduced to pay for them. They were also afraid that the rising burden these costs placed on the income tax would undermine Britain's ability to pay for a major war in the future.[25] Because of this, on the question of war risk insurance they took their stand on the principle that it was 'undesirable, too, to increase the scope of the State's activities and responsibilities if such a course can be avoided'.[26] They refused to concede that intervention would be for the benefit of the whole community. Instead they contended that it would constitute a state subsidy to shipowners and, therefore, would provide them with an unfair advantage which was not shared by other traders. And in 1906–8 they were in an excellent position to make their opposition effective. The whole issue of a state insurance scheme was handed over to a Treasury committee. It debated the question for two years and then decided that there was no pressing need for a scheme and that the whole thing should be dropped.[27] Government interest in the whole problem then lapsed and it was not awoken until the middle of 1911.

In the summer of 1911 the government was beset by problems both at home and abroad. Abroad the Agadir crisis threatened war. At home a series of strikes culminated in a threat by the Transport Workers' Federation or 21 July to paralyse the conveyance of food. By 11 August a number of large towns, including London, were seriously short of food and so the Cabinet decided to use troops to safeguard the passage of essential supplies. By the middle of September both crises had passed their peak but they had left behind them at least one positive legacy. They had awoken the Home Secretary, Winston Churchill, to the possibility that a similar crisis could occur on the outbreak of war. During the crisis Churchill had been in communication with Sir Frederick Bolton, a shipowner and former chairman of Lloyd's. Bolton had infected him with the fears shared by many shipowners that unless the government supported the war risk insurance market they would be unable to send their vessels to sea. Churchill passed on this news to the Prime Minister and added some disquieting conclusions of his own. If Bolton's fears were correct, when war came the government would have to act to ensure that food continued to arrive in the cities. If it did not, the result would be widespread food riots, and if the army had been sent abroad they would be difficult, if not impossible, to suppress.[28]

The Admiralty and the War Office had already given some consideration to related problems. In September 1908 the Director of Naval Intelligence had begun to worry that if the Germans blockaded the east cost, ships normally using east coast ports would have to be diverted to the west coast and the population of the east coast would then have to be supplied across country by rail. This possibility alarmed the War Office. They were afraid that these movements would block the railway system just when they wanted to use it to mobilise the BEF and the Territorial Army. In February 1910 they persuaded the CID to examine the whole matter.[29] But it was not until after the crises of the summer of 1911, when Churchill began to show an interest, that any sense of real urgency was given to their work. From late 1911 onwards a series of CID sub-committees was set up to investigate how to transport food to feed the civilian population in the event of war. By August 1914 the government had decided to take control of the railways on the outbreak of war, and it had devised a practical war risk insurance scheme, but it had not firmly decided to put it into practice; and it had turned its back on rationing or price fixing.

In August 1912 a sub-committee chaired by Seely recommended that on the outbreak of war the government should assume overall control of the railways to ensure that the best use was made of them in the national interest. In return for their co-operation the government promised to maintain the railways' profits at their prewar levels. The Treasury opposed this offer, again on the grounds of expense to the public purse and because they were convinced that it would confer an unfair advantage on railway shareholders. Other traders would suffer from the wartime depression, but they would prosper. The way in which state control would be exercised was to be of great significance for the future. The actual day-to-day runnning of the lines had to be left in the hands of the existing management, who, in effect, became temporary civil servants for the duration of the war. The government was well aware that it had to work with and through these people if it was to do anything at all. It simply did not have anyone else to run the industry on its behalf.[30]

The same pattern was to be followed in industry after industry during the course of the war. Numerous businessmen were co-opted into government departments or committees in need of their particular skills, or else they were left in their existing jobs but made responsible to a government department. The outstanding example of this was to be the Ministry of Munitions, but other examples, such as the Royal Commissions on Wheat Supplies and Sugar Supplies, abounded.

Seely's 1912 report was followed by a second report from another sub-committee presided over by Runciman. Its main task had been to discover the likely consequences if Britain's trade across the North Sea had to be suspended and to recommend how the dislocation could be mitigated. It reported that Britain would suffer shortages if the trade was suspended but it immediately rejected price-fixing by the government as a way of keeping down the cost of goods in short supply. Instead it hoped to make good the shortages by drawing on fresh supplies from neutrals, but the only way to attract them was to let prices in Britain rise. The operations of the world economy would in time put the deficiency to rights. For, as the report commented, 'If prices were kept low by artificial means the principal stimulus to enterprise in bringing supplies to this country would be withdrawn and an actual shortage might result.'[31]

In view of the Treasury's known reluctance to subsidise foreign purchasing of food and raw materials, this was sensible advice. Effective rationing and price-fixing across a wide spectrum of goods was only made possible in 1918 by America's entry into the war in April 1917. It was not until then that the Entente controlled both the world's disposable food and raw material stocks. Before the outbreak of war the Runciman Committee did not think that 'business as usual' in the literal sense of the words would be possible. They recognised that the war would produce shortages, higher prices and unemployment and the closure of some former markets and sources of supply. But if the Royal Navy performed its proper functions near-normal conditions of trade would soon reassert themselves. If Germany was blockaded British traders would be able to penetrate into former German markets and draw on sources of supply the Germans had once used. Safe behind the Royal Navy Britain would be able to pursue her proper strategic role as the economic powerhouse of the Entente.

The task of preparing a practical war risk insurance scheme was begun late in 1911 by Churchill. But progress on his sub-committee was hampered by a continual rearguard action mounted by the Treasury and supported by Runciman and the Home Secretary, Reginald McKenna. Runciman did not think that shipowners would be so craven as to keep their ships in port and McKenna thought that Churchill had exaggerated the danger to merchant ships posed by German commerce raiders. However, eventually a scheme was produced by Sir Hubert Llewellyn Smith, the Permanent Under Secretary of the Board of Trade. Lloyd's underwriters were no longer interested in financing war risk insurance themselves because after the Agadir crisis they considered that it would be too costly. This made it possible for Llewellyn Smith to devise a scheme which would be financed by the Treasury and which the professional underwriters agreed to administer on the government's behalf in return for a small commission.[32] But in the meantime Runciman and McKenna were successful in preventing a decision being taken definitely to implement the scheme. McKenna was a former First Lord of the Admiralty and Runciman was a shipowner. Both, therefore, could pose as experts on this problem. But it is doubtful if their opposition would have been so successful but for Asquith. As so often happened this was another occasion when he was reluctant to impose a decision on warring ministers. Asquith was never a particularly effective chairman of the CID. He possessed considerable skills as a political mediator and these were often valuable in peacetime, but in wartime his propensity for postponing decisions was to prove to be a dangerous liability. Sir Charles Ottley, Hankey's immediate predecessor as secretary of the CID, often had difficulty in gaining access to Asquith to discuss CID business.[33]

This was partly so because defence planning, and in particular economic defence planning, was accorded a low priority by the Liberal government. Ministers were often too busy to attend CID meetings and so decisions often had to be postponed. In the spring of 1914, for example, the Irish question was such a pressing issue that Asquith could spare little or no time for CID work. The Liberal Party's interest in defence hardly extended beyond keeping the estimates as low as possible. The prewar Cabinet contained, at any one time, about twenty ministers, but Hankey considered that only five ever played an active role in the CID's work.[34] Hence it is unlikely that before the war more than a minority of them ever considered the rights and wrongs of the state's interfering in private businesses in the name of national defence. From the limited evidence available Churchill, Seely and Buxton seem to have supported state interference on the railways and in the war risk insurance market on the grounds that it was dictated by the needs of national defence. There is no evidence to suggest that they recognised that any far-reaching principles were at stake. Runciman and McKenna opposed government interference in the insurance market because they believed that the actual danger from German cruisers was exaggerated and because they thought that the scheme Churchill proposed was unsound and would open the Treasury to massive frauds from unscrupulous shipowners. Only the permanent officials of the Treasury appear to have grounded their arguments on points of ideology. Lloyd George, who was 'rather out of the picture in the detailed work of preparation for war',[35] seems to have shared the general indifference of most of his colleagues to these questions.

Indifference towards the CID's work, amounting in some cases to hostility towards the CID as an institution, was indirectly responsible for one of the government's most serious omissions in the field of war planning. This was their failure to create a unified central planning staff to co-ordinate the work of the naval, military and civil departments. Hostility towards the CID came from two sources. Ministers who were excluded from its deliberations were jealous of it. They believed that it was usurping the Cabinet's function to decide on naval and military matters. Meetings such as the one held on 23 August 1911 served only to confirm their suspicions. The second source of hostility came from senior officers of the army and navy. In 1903 the War Office Reconstitution Committee had planned that the CID's secretariat should become a joint general staff to co-ordinate the strategic policies of both services. But the two service departments were, by turns, very loth to surrender power to this new creation.[36] The CID failed to win their willing co-operation and Ottley and Hankey were only too painfully aware that this left their committee in a precarious position. It had lost most of its original rationale, and they dared do nothing to excite the jealousy of other, more powerful, departments. As Ottley explained, 'the most serious danger that besets this Committee is the jealousy of the great Departments, if its members or secretariat seek (or unwittingly contrive) to trespass on their prerogatives'.[37] His plan to ensure the committee's continued existence was for it to provide itself with a new purpose by dealing with problems which were the responsibility of no one department. The major result of his initiative was the numerous sub-committees preparing plans for the war at home which began work in 1910–11. Ottley was determined to proceed stealthily by securing the appointment of *ad hoc* sub-committees to investigate particular questions. They could be made into *de facto* permanent sub-committees by giving them work to do which would require two or three years to complete and then would need to be updated constantly. Ottley chose to concentrate on the home front because of 'the terrible question of the "feeding of the people" and of "employment" in war. That [*sic*] alone will take the patience of angels and the strength of giants to unravel and provide for.'[38]

Hankey's contribution to this work was to ensure that all of these tasks would be properly co-ordinated on the outbreak of war. In January 1911 Asquith agreed that there was a need for this to be done and so Hankey and another assistant secretary, Major Adrian Grant Duff, began to prepare the War Book. Although the War Book was in itself a great achievement its inception marked the final defeat of the CID as a central strategic planning staff for the whole Empire. Indeed when Hankey was arguing that there was a need for the War Book he made it quite clear that in preparing it the CID had no intention of interfering in 'such questions as the policy, strategy or plans of the Admiralty, War Office and Foreign Office...'[39] The task of the War Book was to co-ordinate the administrative actions of the civil departments with the mobilisation plans of the army and navy. The final edition of the book was divided into eleven chapters. Each chapter was devoted to a single department and listed the various tasks it had to perform on the outbreak of war.[40] So, for example, once war had been declared, the book noted, the War Office would be called upon to submit a bill to Parliament to control the movements of enemy aliens, and once the bill had become law the Home Office had to obtain an Order-in-Council to enforce it.

The War Book did not even attempt to co-ordinate larger questions of naval, military and foreign policy. The ambiguities in them remained. Nor was it a plan for national industrial mobilisation. This, of course, was only a reflection of a lacuna in the government's plans as a whole. An equally significant omission which was also reflected in the War Book was the government's failure to look beyond the first few days of the war and to consider the need to establish some special machinery to ensure that the plans of the army, navy and civilian departments were co-ordinated during the war. The measures tabulated in the War Book did not extend beyond the outbreak of war. After that everything was left to chance and to the deliberations of the full Cabinet. No steps were even taken to ensure that the CID's secretariat remained in being in its role as a *de facto* economic general staff. This was to prove an extremely serious failure when

war came, because there was no organised body of experts present to warn
the Cabinet that by December 1914 their naval, military and economic
plans were increasingly out of step.

In August 1914 the plans for 'business as usual' proved to be enough
to meet the immediate crisis. The most urgent facets of this crisis were the
collapse of the mechanisms of international finance and exchange and the
war risk insurance market. These were coupled with a very sharp rise in
both unemployment and food prices. The Cabinet threw to the wind any
ideological scruples they may have had against interfering in the mechanisms of the market economy and acted to save the situation. Lloyd George
coined the phrase 'business as usual' on 4 August to reassure businessmen
and bankers that they had nothing to fear except their own fears. If they
did not panic, hoard gold and refuse credit, all would be well.[41] But what
the government actually did made nonsense of this slogan. They intervened in the insurance and financial markets on a massive scale. Between
mid-August and the end of 1914 they pledged their own credit behind
almost the entire financial system in order to re-establish confidence and
to restart foreign trade.[42] These steps were successful and the immediate
crisis was overcome and so the Cabinet was soon able to implement some
of the more aggressive aspects of 'business as usual'. The Royal Navy kept
open Britain's sea-lanes and swept German merchant ships from the seas,
and on 18 August the Cabinet launched what they hoped would be a
concerted trade war on Germany's overseas markets. They ordered government departments to encourage British businessmen and exporters to
produce and export 'the class of goods which Germany has up to now
been supplying to overseas markets'.[43] To assist them the Board of Trade
organised a number of trade exhibitions and suspended patents taken out
by German companies in Britain. Britain also began to act as the banker
of the Entente. By the end of March 1915 she had lent nearly £52m. to
her Allies and Dominions.[44]

But food, and in particular grain imports, remained a serious problem.
The railways were successfully taken over on 4 August so that chaos in
the distribution of food was avoided. But rising world demand pushed up
prices and by 1 January 1915 the retail price of food had risen 18 per cent
since the start of the war. The Cabinet tried a number of more-or-less
high-handed expedients to reverse this trend. On 3 August they established
the Cabinet Committee on Food Supplies. Its chairman, McKenna, told
the Commons that their policy 'has been not to interfere with ordinary
trade at all, but to leave the traders to conduct their own business'.[45]
This was far from being the truth. In an effort to increase stocks in Britain
and to stop food from reaching Germany the committee at once began to
order all British ships carrying grain to European ports to land their
cargoes in Britain. They only desisted when the American owners of the
grain threatened to cut off all supplies to Britain. So dependent was

Britain on American grain that the committee had to take the threat seriously and comply with the American demands.[46]

By February 1915 public opinion was pushing the committee in two directions. The organised labour movement wanted the government to fix maximum prices and to take control of Britain's whole food supply.[47] But the Treasury's opposition to spending large sums of money on relief measures made this impossible. Lloyd George and his Permanent Secretary, Sir John Bradbury, hoped that high prices would be one inducement towards persuading men to enlist or to undertake well-paid war work.[48] On the other hand grain merchants were very hostile to state interference. Because of Runciman's announcements of 11 and 17 February reassuring businessmen that there would be no state intervention, it has always been supposed that the government had rejected state trading and were in favour of complete *laissez-faire*.[49] This was not so. Runciman deliberately hid the truth from the public. Even as he spoke the government was buying wheat so that if the retail price rose too steeply it could be released on to the market at less than cost price, undercutting the grain merchants and forcing them to lower their prices. But it was vital that the merchants remain in ignorance of this. If they ever learned of it they would strike.[50] The committee's fears proved to be justified. In March the merchants did learn of the government's wheat stocks and immediately suspended their operations. The committee had no option but to suspend its operations as well. Now all they could do was to hope that the Dardanelles would be opened and that Russian wheat would reach them.[51]

By the spring of 1915 it was becoming apparent that 'business as usual' was not winning the war. The events of the war had falsified too many of the assumptions on which it was based. Neither the blockade nor the dispatch of the BEF to France had forced the Germans to the peace-table. By May 1915 the Restrictions of Enemy Supplies Committee, which supervised blockade measures, had to admit that the blockade would not produce the swift collapse of the German economy.[52] Furthermore neither the French nor the Russians were ready to do all the land fighting without major British help. On 17 December 1914, for example, Sir John French's liaison officer at French Headquarters reported that the feeling was rife amongst the French that the British were not bearing a fair share of the fighting.[53]

The British had already gone some way towards meeting this criticism by raising the New Armies. They were the brainchild of Lord Kitchener, who became Secretary of State for War on 5 August 1914. They represented an alternative and competing strategy to 'business as usual'. Instead of relying on her naval and economic power Kitchener wanted Britain to become a major military power as well. He was intent on transforming Britain into a 'nation in arms' on the prewar continental model, but with one exception. His 'nation in arms' was to be recruited by voluntary methods. Numbed by the outbreak of war and preoccupied with the economic crisis the Cabinet gave him a free hand and until Christmas 1914 failed to recognise the economic implications of what he was doing. By December 1914 he had raised over 1 million men, thereby more than doubling the total strength of the army. In doing this he destroyed the foundations of 'business as usual' more effectively than anything the Germans could have done. The New Armies swallowed men and industrial resources on a huge scale and made the normal functioning of the economy impossible. By the spring of 1915 nearly one-third of the total employed male labour force had left their civilian occupations to enlist or to work in war-related industries.[54] Kitchener's decision to raise these forces was correct. Without them the Entente could not have gone on fighting in 1917–18. But the manner in which they were raised, by voluntary recruiting, caused economic chaos at home.

Until December 1914 men were taken as and when they were prepared to enlist. On 25 August the Cabinet decided that conscription was still politically impossible,[55] and without conscription it was impossible to fill the army and to ensure that vital sectors of the economy kept the men they needed. The immediate result was that the early wartime unemployment was replaced at the end of 1914 by growing labour shortages in many sectors of the economy. It was not until the end of the year that the Cabinet recognised that uncontrolled recruiting had created almost as many problems as it had solved. The export industries and munitions manufacturers were particularly badly affected. During the first nine months of the war the deficit on the visible trade balance increased by between £160 and 170 million. Most of this deficit was due to a sharp fall in the value of manufactured exports. This happened at the very time when imports were increasing because, as Runciman explained, 'we have to purchase enormous quantities of supplies for the army and navy as well as for the civilian population from America'.[56]

After men the most urgent need of the New Armies was equipment. But recruiting bit deeply into the labour force of the munitions industry at the very moment when they needed more not fewer men to meet the demands of the war. Their failure to meet these demands quickly was the main reason why the government took its first steps towards controlling manufacturing industry. In October 1914 the Cabinet decided that the New Armies should be ready by June 1915. A Cabinet Committee on Munitions Supplies tried to extract promises from the main suppliers to produce the weapons needed by then. All the manufacturers would do was to promise to do their best. They knew that they were faced with two difficulties. Importing the necessary machinery from America took a long time and when it arrived it was very difficult to find men to operate it. By June 1915 it was estimated that the industry required at least another 12,000 skilled men.[57]

But hardly had the manufacturers begun to prepare themselves to equip the New Armies than new and even greater demands were made on them. By February 1915 Lloyd George was bitterly disappointed with the lack of progress shown in the war. On 22 February he circulated a lengthy memorandum to the Cabinet that asked them to pursue a new, and much more ambitious, national strategy. He wanted to abandon many of the aspects of 'business as usual' and to refine Kitchener's drive to create a 'nation in arms' by putting the whole nation on a total war footing. Alarmed at the reverses suffered by the Russians and despairing of swift victory on the western front, he wanted Britain to place another 1–1½ million men in the field and at the same time to supply the Russians with the munitions they needed. Victory demanded that the Germans had not only to be outfought but out-produced as well.

I do not believe [he told the Cabinet] Great Britain has even yet done anything like what she could do in the matter of increasing her war equipment. Great things have been accomplished in the last few months, but I sincerely believe that we could double our effective energies if we organised our factories thoroughly. All the engineering works of the country ought to be turned on to the production of war material.[58]

Lloyd George imagined Britain becoming not only an even more powerful economic powerhouse for the Entente than she already was but a major land power as well. Much of the subsequent debate over economic policy, particularly under the Asquith coalition, revolved around the question of whether she could afford to do both. But for the time being, although he was a little surprised at Lloyd George's boldness and vision, Asquith allowed him to proceed and to introduce the Defence of the Realm (Amendment Number 2) Act. This gave the government powers to control the engineering industry. It was the first legislative step towards setting up an economy geared to total war. In introducing the bill the Chancellor made clear his repudiation of 'business as usual'. 'Instead of business as usual', he told the Commons, 'we want victory as usual.'[59]

But although the Act was on the statute-book by 16 March 1915 it was not immediately implemented in the manner in which Lloyd George intended. The War Office's first concern was to supply their own troops. When Lloyd George castigated them for not recognising the magnitude of the war, he was really blaming them for not sharing his concern for supplying Russia. Kitchener wanted Lloyd George to confine himself to helping to organise a supply of skilled labour for the existing manufacturers by persuading the trade unions to relax many of their normal trade practices.[60] But on 23 March the Chancellor persuaded Asquith that he should be given control of a committee charged with mobilising the entire engineering industry to meet the needs of Britain *and* her Allies. The committee was to work in consultation with the War Office and Admiralty, but it had powers to take all necessary steps 'to ensure the promptest and most efficient application of all the available productive resources of the country to the manufacture and supply of Munitions of War...'[61] This marked the start of a bitter struggle between Lloyd George and Kitchener for the control of munitions supply. Kitchener objected to the Chancellor's interference because he thought that it was part of an effort to remove him from the War Office and because he was afraid that Lloyd George's proposals would delay the delivery of supplies to the New Armies by diverting men and machines working for them to work for Russia. To prevent this he insisted that the Chancellor's committee must not interfere with the work on existing War Office contracts. He wanted the Chancellor to confine his activities to finding more labour for existing contractors who had idle machinery and no hands to operate it. The New Armies and the BEF wanted munitions immediately. Kitchener's first concern was to develop the sources of supply he already had. He had no pressing concern in the development of new sources which might only be able to deliver orders in, as Lloyd George admitted, nine months' time.[62]

Until the fall of the government in May 1915 the struggle between them revolved around whether to spread contracts to new manufacturers, as Lloyd George advocated, or to concentrate labour with existing contractors, as Kitchener wanted. Since December 1914 the War Office and the Board of Trade had been trying to do the latter, but with only limited success. Many engineering firms objected to their efforts which threatened to drive them out of business. Many ostensibly working on private contracts were, in fact, sub-contractors for munitions manufacturers, and many of those that were not believed that by pooling their resources of men and machines they, too, could produce munitions. In the first week of February the Board began to exhibit certain types of shells in each of the major engineering centres in the hope that manufacturers would see what was wanted and then tender for contracts. But the War Office wanted to use the exhibitions simply to discover firms with suitable labour which they could then siphon off to work for existing manufacturers. In March the War Office went further and wanted to use the powers given to the government by DOR (Amendment Number 2) Act to close firms working on private contracts so they could then transfer their labour. On 16 March Kitchener appointed the Liverpool shipowner G. M. Booth to head a committee to carry out this policy. Booth himself actually preferred the Chancellor's policy of spreading orders but he did as Kitchener asked.

This was the very opposite of all that Lloyd George wanted and on

continuous watch on the progress of the war. The Cabinet remained a collection of departmental ministers who were increasingly submerged by a growing volume of work. It kept no minutes, nor even a formal record of its decisions beyond the Prime Minister's brief letters to the King. This lack of system bred confusion and ignorance. Lord Emmott, a newcomer to the Cabinet on the outbreak of war, described some of its shortcomings thus in January 1915:

> My chief disappointment in Cabinet work is the difficulty of obtaining a hearing and the insufficient time given to consideration of questions brought before us. The Prime Minister writes letters and weighs in at the end with very sound and weighty opinions; but the rest seem to worry things out as best they can among themselves. Were it not for Winston and L. G[eorge] asking Kitchener questions we shd. [sic] have precious little enlightenment on military questions.[69]

Discussions of purely economic issues were confined to the full Cabinet or to a handful of *ad hoc* committees. All the discussions of Lloyd George's DOR (Amendment Number 2) Act took place in the Cabinet. But these discussions did not take place as part of a continuous and wide-ranging review of national policy. Naval and military policy was decided apart from economic policy. In November 1914 a War Council was established. Its work was dominated by the concerns of the Admiralty and War Office. Problems of economic policy did not come within its purview, even when they were affected by economic factors. So, for example, there was no discussion of how the Dardanelles operation would be affected by the growing shortage of merchant tonnage in the spring of 1915 or how the operation would affect British trade by diverting merchant ships into war use.[70] Much of the responsibility for failing to recognise that economic policy had to be considered side by side with military and naval policy must rest with Asquith. For too much of the time he was content to believe that war was too serious a business not to be left to the generals and admirals and their immediate political chiefs. He was content to leave the direction of the war in their hands, allowing the Cabinet to discuss problems at length, but relying himself on the advice of Kitchener, Churchill and, in the spring of 1915, on Lloyd George. It was difficult for other ministers to put forward alternative policies if one of these three objected to them.[71] The composition of Asquith's inner Cabinet goes a long way towards explaining why, by May 1915, 'business as usual' was being overtaken by Kitchener's plans for a 'nation in arms' and was itself being challenged by Lloyd George's strategy of total war. Runciman did not have the Prime Minister's ear on major strategic questions as Kitchener or later Lloyd George did.

These administrative and personal shortcomings contributed significantly to the Cabinet's failure to impose a single coherent strategy on the nation. But that does not imply that these faults could have been rectified in the circumstances of 1914—15. The history of the Liberal Cabinet's economic policies was one of administrative muddle, but, above all, of confusion of purpose. Recent studies of the Liberal Party in the House of Commons have indicated that MPs were divided between Liberal fundamentalists who wanted to preserve the traditional liberties the party had always been associated with, and those who recognised that some of these would have to be sacrificed for the sake of victory. Between them sat a mass of un-committed Members who did not know quite which way to turn.[72] The Liberal Party in the House of Commons may have been divided between the proponents of *laissez-faire* and state control. The members of the Cabinet were not. The major lines of division within the Cabinet were between supporters and opponents of different strategies. When Britain went to war in 1914 the government had few plans to impose widespread state controls over the economy. This was not because they were addicted to *laissez-faire*. Only the Treasury expressed any real ideological scruples against the state interfering in the economy at a time of national danger. The government was prepared to take control of the railways to ensure that the civilian population was fed. Runciman and McKenna objected to state interference in the war risk insurance market because they con-sidered that the danger to merchant ships from German cruisers was exaggerated by the Admiralty and so a state insurance scheme was un-necessary. The absence of any plans to control manufacturing industry was a product of the naval and military strategy the government intended to pursue, not of their economic ideology. They intended to rely on the Royal Navy to blockade Germany and contribute to her collapse by destroying her overseas trade. At the same time the British economy would be protected from outside interference. It would be able to func-tion almost as normal and to supply Britain's allies with the money and supplies they needed to fight the land war. There were no plans to expand the army and so there was no need to plan to impose widespread state controls over the civilian economy to mobilise it for the coming war. The machinery of government could, therefore, continue more or less as it did in peacetime.

By May 1915 'business as usual' still had its supporters, but in reality the foundations of this policy had been undermined by the war. The blockade had not crippled the Germans; nor were the French and Russians content to rely on British money and supplies. They wanted large numbers of British troops as well. Kitchener's attempt to come to their aid by raising the New Armies diverted men and economic resources from their normal occupations and made 'business as usual' untenable. Setbacks on the Eastern and Western Fronts and production bottlenecks in producing munitions finally convinced Lloyd George that in order to win the war the state would have to take direct control of the engineering industry. He was in the process of urging his case upon the Cabinet when the government collapsed and the opportunity presented itself for him to establish the Ministry of Munitions, the first ministry created during the war to exercise state control over the economy.

Notes: Chapter 1

1   E. M. H. Lloyd, *Experiments in State Control at the War Office and the Ministry of Food* (Oxford: University Press, 1924), p. 21.
2   John Gooch, *The Plans of War* (London: Routledge & Kegan Paul, 1974), ch. 9 *passim*; Col. C. E. Callwell to Capt. Ballard, 'British military action in case of war with Germany', 3 October 1905, WO 106/46E2/1, War Office Papers, Public Record Office (PRO), London.
3   P. Haggie, 'The Royal Navy and war planning in the Fisher era', *Journal of Contemporary History*, vol. VIII (1973), pp. 118–21; P. Kemp (ed.), *The Papers of Admiral Sir John Fisher* (London: Naval Records Society, 1964), Vol. II, pp. 315ff.
4   'Report of the sub committee ... on the military needs of the Empire', 24 July 1909, CAB 4/3/1/109B, Cabinet Papers, PRO.
5   S. Williamson, *The Politics of Grand Strategy* (Cambridge, Mass.: Harvard University Press, 1969), pp. 169–91; Asquith to Haldane, 31 August 1911, MS 5909, Haldane Papers, National Library of Scotland.
6   M. V. Brett (ed.), *Journals and Letters of Reginald Viscount Esher* (London: Nicholson & Watson, 1938), Vol. III, pp. 61–2.
7   Runciman to Harcourt, 4 September 1911, Box 63, Runciman Papers, University of Newcastle Library.
8   A. J. A. Morris, *Radicalism Against War, 1906–14* (London: Longman, 1972), pp. 10, 33; H. S. Weinroth, 'The British radicals and the balance of power, 1902–14', *Historical Journal*, vol. XIII (1970), pp. 653–79.
9   Hankey to Seely, plus enclosure, 'Some new aspects of the national service question', 15 March 1913, Box 12, Mottistone Papers, Nuffield College, Oxford.
10 ibid.
11 P. M. Kennedy, *The Rise and Fall of British Naval Mastery* (London: Allen Lane, 1976), pp. 146–7; J. M. Sherwig, *Guineas and Gunpowder. British Foreign Aid in the Wars with France, 1793–1815* (Cambridge, Mass.: Harvard University Press, 1969), pp. 345, 352.
12 Copy of Lloyd George's memorandum to Balfour on basis for possible coalition government, 17 August 1910, C/3/14/9, Lloyd George Papers, House of Lords Record Office, London.
13 51 *House of Commons Debates* 5 s., 11 April 1913, cols 1533, 1591–3.
14 Minutes of Evidence, Dardanelles Commission, Q. 4045 (Sir Reginald Brade), CAB 19/33.
15 Haldane to Elizabeth Haldane, 12 January 1910, MS. 6011, Haldane Papers; see also the author's article, 'The military background to the shell crisis of May 1915', *Journal of Strategic Studies*, vol. II, no. 2 (September 1979), pp. 192–6.
16 Murray Committee, 'Report of the departmental committee on government factories and workshops', 1907, WO 33/163.
17 *Statistics on the Military Effort of the British Empire* (London: HMSO, 1922), p. 471.

18 Sir M. Hankey, 'Notes on private arms manufacture in the Great War', May 1935, Appendix V, T.181/50, Treasury Papers, PRO.

19 *Parl. Papers 1905* (Cd 2643), *Report of the Royal Commission on Supply of Food and Raw Materials in Time of War.*

20 F. J. S. Hopwood, Remarks by the Board of Trade on CID 46B, 4 April 1905, CAB 4/2/69B.

21 G. S. Clark, 'National indemnity or insurance of the war risks of shipping', 5 December 1904, CAB 4/1/46B; Evidence by Sir A. K. Wilson to the Treasury Committee on National Insurance, 2 July 1907, CAB 16/24.

22 Minutes of 75 meeting of the CID, 13 July 1905, CAB 2/1.

23 B. R. Mitchell and Phyllis Deane, *Abstract of British Historical Statistics* (Cambridge: Cambridge University Press, 1976), p. 398; A. T. Peacock and J. Wiseman, *The Growth of Public Expenditure in the United Kingdom* (London: Macmillan, 1967), p. 168; H. Roseveare, *The Treasury: The Evolution of a British Institution* (London: Allen Lane, 1969), p. 187; H. V. Emy, 'The impact of financial policy on English politics before 1914', *Historical Journal*, vol. XV (1972), pp. 103–27.

24 B. Mallet to Lord Cromer, 23 May 1911, FO 633/20, Foreign Office Papers, PRO. (I am grateful to Dr P. M. Kennedy for drawing my attention to references in the Cromer MSS. on this subject.)

25 Since the days of Pitt the Younger Britain had always *tried* to pay for her wars from current taxation. See Olive Anderson, *A Liberal State at War* (London: Macmillan, 1967), pp. 194–201.

26 'National insurance of the war risks of shipping', 8 May 1905, CAB 4/1/56B.

27 *Parl. Papers 1908* (Cd 4161), *Report by the Committee on a National Guarantee for the War Risks of Shipping to the Lord Commissioners of His Majesty's Treasury.*

28 F. Bolton to Asquith, 19 January 1909, CAB 17/26/B27 (1); Churchill to McKenna, 13 September 1911, 3/21, McKenna Papers, Churchill College, Cambridge; R. S. Churchill, *Winston Spencer Churchill, II, Companion, Part II, 1907–11* (London: Heinemann, 1969), pp. 1296–7.

29 E. W. Slade, 'The defence of commerce with proposals for its defence in peacetime', 16 September 1908, microfilm (one reel), National Maritime Museum, London; Minutes of 105 meeting of the CID, 24 February 1910, CAB 2/1.

30 'Report of a sub-committee … on the internal distribution of supplies in time of war', 20 June 1912, CAB 4/4/33/152B; Minutes of the 119 meeting of the CID, 1 August 1912, CAB 2/2/1.

31 Report of a sub-committee of the CID, 'Supplies in time of war', 26 January 1914, CAB 16/30.

32 Report and proceedings of the standing sub-committee of the CID, 'Insurance of British shipping in time of war', 12 May 1914, CAB 16/29; see also Runciman to Hankey, 18 December 1912, CAB 17/82.

33 G. S. Clarke to Esher, 3 January 1906, 10/38, and Ottley to Esher, (?) March 1910, 5/33, both Esher Papers, Churchill College, Cambridge; C. Hazlehurst, 'Asquith as Prime Minister, 1908–16', *English Historical Review*, vol. LXXXV (1970), p. 506; J. P. Mackintosh, 'The role of the Committee of Imperial Defence before 1914', *English Historical Review*, vol. LXXVII (1962), pp. 495–6.

34 Lord Hankey, *The Supreme Command*, 2 vols (London: Allen & Unwin, 1961), Vol. I, pp. 147–8.

35 ibid., p. 148.

36 N. D'Ombrain, *War Machinery and High Policy* (London: Oxford University Press, 1973), chs 1 and 2 *passim.*

37 Ottley to Esher, 16 October 1909, 5/32, Esher Papers.

38   Esher to Ottley, 18 October 1909, 5/32, Esher Papers.
39   Hankey, *Supreme Command*, Vol. I, p. 119.
40   Sokolov Grant, 'The origins of the War Book', *Journal of the Royal United Services Institute*, vol. CXVII (1972), pp. 65ff.; War Book, 1914, CAB 15/5.
41   Conference between the Chancellor of the Exchequer and Representatives of the Bankers and Traders, 4 August 1914, T.170/55, Treasury Papers, PRO.
42   D. French, 'Some aspects of social and economic planning for war in Great Britain, c. 1905–15', London University PhD thesis, 1978, pp. 139–47.
43   Asquith to HM the King, 18 August 1914, CAB 41/35/32.
44   *Parl. Papers 1914–16*, vol. xxxviii, *War Charges*, 14 September 1915.
45   65 *H.C. Deb.* 5 s., 8 August 1914, col. 2217.
46   CID Historical Section, 'Report on the opening of the war', 1 November 1914, CAB 17/102B; see also Attorney-General to the Board of Trade, 20 August 1914, BT 11/7, Board of Trade Papers, PRO; Department of State, *Papers Relating to the Foreign Relations of the United States, 1914, Supplement: The World War* (Washington, DC: US Government, 1928), pp. 304–6.
47   R. Harrison, 'The War Emergency Workers National Committee' in A. Briggs and J. Saville, *Essays in Labour History* (London: Macmillan, 1971), pp. 227, 231.
48   [Sir John Bradbury], 'The relief of distress in relation to finance', 7 September 1914, T.171/93; Deputation by the War Emergency Workers National Committee to the Rt Hon. David Lloyd George, MP, 6 October 1914, T.172/142.
49   See, for example, 69 *H.C. Deb.* 5 s., 17 February 1915, col. 1178.
50   Board of Agriculture and Fisheries, 'General outline of the special war activities of the Board of Agriculture and Fisheries', n.d. but c.1919, CAB 15/6/28; Note by Lord Lucas, 10 April 1915, Box 92, Runciman Papers.
51   Wheat Prices – Appendix by J. M. K.[eynes], 26 January 1915, CAB 37/123/51; R. H. R.[ew], 'Note on the wheat position', 26 April 1915, CAB 17/118.
52   Restriction of Enemy Supplies Committee, 'Shortage of foodstuffs in Germany', May 1915, CAB 17/118.
53   G. French, *The Life of Field Marshall Sir John French* (London: Cassell, 1931), p. 267.
54   Sir G. Mallett and C. O. George, *British Budgets, Second Series, 1913–14 to 1920–21* (London: Cassell, 1920), p. 57.
55   Gainford diary, 25 August 1914, Gainford Papers, Nuffield College, Oxford; Emmott diary, 25 August 1914, Emmott Papers, Nuffield College, Oxford; E. David (ed.), *Inside Asquith's Cabinet: From the Diaries of Charles Hobhouse* (London: Murray, 1977), p. 184.
56   'Effects of diminished exports on foreign exchanges', 2 June 1915, Box 89, Runciman Papers.
57   Board of Trade National Clearing House, 'Demands for labour', 1 June 1915, MUN 5/8/171/29, Ministry of Munitions Papers, PRO.
58   D. Lloyd George, 'Some further considerations on the conduct of the war', 22 February 1915, CAB 37/124/40.
59   70 *H.C. Deb.*, 5 s., 10 March 1915, col. 1460.
60   Lord Kitchener, 'Remarks on the Chancellor of the Exchequer's memorandum on the conduct of the war', 25 February 1915, CAB 1/11/33.
61   Munitions of War Committee, 8 April 1915, MUN 5/8/172/3; see also Asquith to Kitchener and enclosure, 23 March 1915, PRO 30/57/82, Kitchener Papers, PRO.
62   Hankey diary, 16 April 1915, 1/1, Hankey Papers, Churchill College, Cambridge; Kitchener to Lloyd George, 26 March 1915, PRO 30/57/82, Kitchener Papers.
63   Munitions of War Committee, 8 April 1915, MUN 5/8/172/3; Lloyd George to Balfour, 8 April 1915, C/3/3/4.

64   Minute by G. J. H. Lloyd plus enclosure, 4 May 1917, MUN 5/8/171/18; Mr
     Davison, 'Contracts for shells and fuses', 27 March 1915, MUN 5/8/171/22;
     G. M. Booth, 'General instructions for officers visiting districts suitable for
     providing labour for armament work', 30 March 1915, MUN 5/6/170/12;
     D. Crow, *A Man of Push and Go: The Life of George Macaulay Booth* (London:
     Hart-Davis, 1965), pp. 106–7.
65   Llewellyn Smith to Lloyd George, 21 May 1915, C/7/5/21, Lloyd George
     Papers; see also Llewellyn Smith to Lloyd George, 22 May 1915, C/7/5/22,
     Lloyd George Papers.
66   [M. P. A. Hankey], 'CID Paper 214B: list of committees appointed to consider
     questions arising during the present war', 1 March 1915, CAB 42/2/2.
67   Hankey to Grant-Duff, 14 August 1914, 1/2, Grant-Duff Papers, Churchill
     College, Cambridge.
68   Earl of Oxford and Asquith, *Memories and Reflections*, 2 vols (London: Cassell
     1928), Vol. II, p. 23.
69   Diary, 4 January 1915, Emmott Papers.
70   Minutes of Evidence, Dardanelles Commission, Q. 740 (Sir E. Grey) and Q. 976
     (Hankey), CAB 19/33.
71   ibid., Q. 1110 (Churchill) and Q. 5929 (Asquith).
72   T. Wilson, *The Downfall of the Liberal Party* (London: Fontana, 1968), pp.
     23–51.

I am grateful to the editor, Dr Kathleen Burk, and to my former colleagues in the History Department of Newcastle University, Dr Martin D. Pugh and Dr David B. Saunders, for their comments on various drafts of this chapter. They are not responsible for the views I have expressed and all remaining errors of fact and judgement are my own.

I am also grateful to the following people who have kindly given me permission to quote from manuscripts to which they own the copyright: Lord Gainford (Pease MSS.); Lord Esher (Esher MSS.); Mrs Joan Simon (Emmott MSS.); Mr A Elliot and the University of Newcastle upon Tyne (Runciman MSS.); Dr R. Knight and the National Maritime Museum (Slade MSS.); Mr A. J. P. Taylor and the Trustees of the Beaverbrook Foundation and the House of Lords Record Office (Lloyd George MSS.). Crown copyright material is quoted by kind permission of Her Majesty's Stationery Office.

2

The Ministry of Munitions: an Innovatory Department

In the Second World War Lord Beaverbrook consciously modelled the way he ran the Ministry of Aircraft Production on David Lloyd George's conduct of the Ministry of Munitions in the First World War. In the public mind the Ministry of Munitions had been the administrative success story of the earlier war. The saga of an unorthodox politician and dynamic businessmen achieving the apparently impossible in output had irresistible appeal to Beaverbrook. In 1940–1, secure in Winston Churchill's favour, he commandeered resources and exhorted and harried his staff in his drive rapidly to expand production of aircraft.[1]

The Ministry of Munitions' creation in June 1915 followed a political storm over alleged shortages of munitions on the Western Front earlier in the year. Mushroom-like, the ministry rapidly grew and grew in size. It soon appropriated responsibility for large and crucial areas of the domestic economy, as well as buying supplies overseas. In so doing it encompassed, in part at least, the functions of an Ordnance Department, a Ministry of Supply, a Ministry of Labour, a Ministry of Housing, a Ministry of Science and Technology, the Board of Trade and the Home Office.

Accounts of the ministry have been friendly to say the least; some, indeed, have been eulogistic, perhaps even hyperbolic. George Dewar's *The Great Munitions Feat 1914–18*, published in 1921, set the tone for later books. He wrote of 'the munitions crusade' in a lest-we-forget spirit, and observed, 'Surveying the feat and its figures of output, I confess I cannot imagine how we accomplished it. The difficulties immediately and menacingly confronting us were Himalayan, so that we could not see beyond them.'[2] The official *History of the Ministry of Munitions* is an invaluable account — very detailed and usually careful in its judge-ments, resting on an abundance of internal documentation and first-hand knowledge; but, written by or under the eyes of leading lights of the ministry, it is very much a history of civil servants written by and for civil servants.[3]

The record of the Ministry of Munitions in its first year was to be an important part of Lloyd George's justification between the wars for his part in the December 1916 split of the Parliamentary Liberal Party. At the time the lauding of Lloyd George's role in providing munitions helped him in his rise to the premiership, just as the good publicity concerning his efficient pragmatic ways at the Board of Trade between 1905 and 1908 had helped him to succeed Asquith as Chancellor of the Exchequer. After the war his conduct at Munitions could be cited as a striking contrast to the lack of a sense of urgency displayed by those Liberal ministers who later supported Asquith. Moreover, when he wrote his *War Memoirs*, 6 vols (London: Nicholson & Watson, 1933–6) in the 1930s, in a period marked by a lack of political economic leadership, he had a considerable interest in reminding the British public of his record of improvising and getting things done. Lloyd George's picture of a ministry of bustle and achievement, in contrast with War Office lethargy and red tape, was reinforced by the publication of Christopher Addison's *Politics from Within 1911–1918*, 2 vols (London: Herbert Jenkins, 1924) and above all by the publication of his diaries, *Four and a Half Years*, 2 vols, in 1934, which record in great detail some of Addison's finest hours as an administrator (though Addison, then in the Labour Party, was careful to exclude from the printed version most of his scathing comments about Labour leaders).

The picture of the ministry thus established has not been challenged by later political or administrative historians. With the opening of Lloyd George's Papers (and other related ones) in the Beaverbrook Library in the mid–1960s and the release of the relevant Government Papers there has been an intensive revaluation of Lloyd George's career. However, the phase of his career at Munitions has not been subject to revisionism.[4] Such challenges as there have been have come from military historians who, in reappraising the reputations of Kitchener or the generals at the Western Front, have been disparaging in their assessments of the politicians at home.[5]

The Ministry of Munitions' record is such that it is unlikely ever to be subject to drastic revisionism. The problem with much of the writing about the ministry is that it tends to overstate matters, presenting the ministry almost as a revolution in government.

In this essay an attempt is made to assess how revolutionary or innovatory the Ministry of Munitions was by discussing three issues. The first is the problem of why it was felt necessary to create a new ministry in the first place. Was the War Office markedly incompetent – or did its reputation suffer unfairly from being politically outmanoeuvred on the issue of munitions supply by General French and by Lloyd George? Did the War Office lay the foundations for an adequate munitions supply and then see the Ministry of Munitions emerge at the crucial time and thereby take the credit? Did the Ministry of Munitions bring in major changes in approach to munitions supply to that of the War Office? The second issue is whether or not the Ministry of Munitions was an organisation apart from the more normal Whitehall bureaucracies. In being created from nothing the Ministry of Munitions had the chance to be administratively innovatory and to challenge the established Whitehall proprieties. Thirdly, a fundamental feature of the ministry was that it was much more of a business organisation than an ordinary administrative body. In this war of production the ministry was a major controller of scarce resources, and consequently it was faced with acute problems of economic choice. In controlling and developing industry it had great opportunities to introduce changes in large sectors of British industry. Did the ministry have a lasting effect on British industry?[6]

The War Office provided the munitions for the first year of the war — indeed, the first munitions components ordered by the Ministry of Munitions did not arrive until late October 1915. It was the first period of the war which was the particularly critical one for munitions supply as it was then that the scale of demand and the type of munitions required for trench warfare first became apparent.

Kitchener and the War Office's record in providing munitions was vigorously attacked at the time and later more publicly in memoirs by Sir John French and David Lloyd George. French conspired against Kitchener after the Battle of Festubert, using alleged munitions shortages both as a way of explaining the failure of the attack and as a handy stick with which to beat Kitchener. Later, in his memoirs, French presented himself as sacrificing his career in order to rectify the sluggish behaviour of both the War Office and the Liberal government.[7] In the war of postwar memoirs Asquith had little difficulty in rebutting French's claims concerning munitions shortages and French's supposed martyrdom on the issue. Asquith also vigorously defended Kitchener and the War Office, pointing to a nineteen-fold increase in munitions output in the first six months of the war ('Never was there a case in which the charge of apathy or lethargy was worse founded') and specifically praising Sir John Cowans, the Quartermaster-General, 'whose department with a stupendous and ever-growing burden of responsibility during the whole course of the War not only never broke down, but exhibited no sign of strain or stress'.[8] Nevertheless in 1915 it was Asquith who took the decision to create a separate Ministry of Munitions, at a time when the decision could be (and was) construed as a sign of lack of confidence in the War Office.

At the time Asquith does appear to have felt that there really was something amiss with the current arrangements for munitions supplies. It was not simply a case of bending to political or popular pressure, as in the dismissals of Prince Louis of Battenberg and Lord Haldane. Thus in March 1915 Asquith noted in his diary, 'We had our little Committee, which consisted of myself, Lloyd George, A.J.B. [Balfour], Winston

[Churchill] and Montagu, to consider the much-vexed question of putting the contracts for munitions on a proper footing. The discussion was quite a good one and we came to some rational conclusions. But we may have some difficulty with K....'[9]

In fact on many of the points at issue over munitions supply Kitchener appears to have been more flexible than the War Office as a whole.[10] The main shortcomings attributed to the War Office over munitions supply were, first, a failure to be realistic in ordering munitions – a failure to order enough and of the right type, and to ensure that deliveries were not grossly late; and, secondly, a general lack of imagination or flexibility in achieving greater production – matters ranging from a reluctance to go outside of the circle of normal suppliers to a marked ineptness in handling labour.

Kitchener himself did not lack foresight. Like Lloyd George, early on he predicted a long war. In October 1914 he was placing orders with an American firm on this presumption. According to Sir George Arthur, he informed an American industrialist, 'This war is not going to be a short one. I foresee five years of it at least. I want you to pledge that the control of the Bethlehem Steel Corporation will not be sold by you and your associates under five years from now.'[11] Kitchener also appears to have foreseen that the supplies necessary for a war of this scale would be too much for the existing War Office machinery to cope with. At the outset of the war he told Walter Runciman, 'When a war of this magnitude breaks out the President of the Board of Trade should immediately be made Joint Secretary of State for War, Supply Department', and went on to explain:

The old fashioned little British Army was such an infinitely small proportion of the world's demand that looking after its equipment was not much more difficult than buying a straw hat at Harrods. But now I am going to need greater quantities of many things than have ever been made before, and I fancy this will equally be true of the Navy and perhaps the Flying Corps. Surely we cannot allow competition to arise, as will be inevitable between the Services unless there is some central control of the distribution of supplies. Undoubtedly the public will have to go very short and the responsibility for that will become a part of the duties of a War Service Board of Trade.[12]

As well, Kitchener appears to have been fairly flexible in his approach to getting adequate supplies – at least more so than many in the War Office. Kitchener was willing to allow the War Office to put out orders to contractors other than its usual suppliers; but the War Office officials for a long time put up an effective resistance to this. Kitchener was also willing to bring in outside businessmen to help organise supplies. Both

Sir Percy Girouard and George Booth started their wartime work for the government at the War Office. Kitchener appears to have been very keen on the experiment. In late March he apparently asked Cecil Baring for 'fifty Booths and Mr. McKenna [the Home Secretary] for fifty Factory inspectors to be attached to them' and to have written to Runciman for ten Booths or 'men slightly younger but with his business capabilities and push'.[13] Lloyd George — at least in October 1914 — could praise Kitchener for his open-mindedness on new ideas, observing that 'Kitchener is a big man. He does not resent advice or criticism.'[14] After Kitchener's death, Lloyd George's verdict was that 'he had flashes of greatness. He was like one of those revolving lighthouses which radiate momentary gleams of revealing light far out into the surrounding gloom and then suddenly relapse into complete darkness.'[15]

However, in making this case for Kitchener one is led to the conclusion that his main weakness in respect to munitions may well be that he did not control his department adequately. Lloyd George, for one, was complaining that 'whatever he may have done in the past [he] pays no attention to details and does not properly control his staff'.[16] Kitchener, who was used to military command, was not so adept at controlling the Whitehall bureaucracy. Kitchener personally was very much aware that the recruitment of skilled men in essential war work was counterproductive; indeed in September 1914 he made a speech emphasising that men working in munitions production were doing their duty — and the War Office issued a poster to that effect. Yet for all Kitchener's reassurances on the matter recruiting officers persisted in recruiting skilled engineers. Moreover the War Office's arrangements — or rather lack of them — for recruits caused Kitchener embarrassment. Asquith recorded in his diary:

> Kitchener presented himself today in what he called frankly a white sheet, admitting that the recruits had been and were being badly treated in the way of clothing, boots and other necessaries. He says that his orders have not been carried out and he is furious with the War Office. We agreed to dismiss the Chief Director of Contracts, and to set on foot a better and more business-like system. I thought this had been done. It was certainly ordered at least three weeks ago.[17]

Kitchener's record at the War Office also suffered from the fact that he was not a politician. He was politically insensitive over such matters as Welsh and Irish recruiting and the treatment of nonconformist recruits. He was not used to sharing responsibility and needlessly annoyed his Cabinet colleagues by concealing information and even lying about matters which were the proper concern of the Cabinet. This is well illustrated by the outcome of a discussion in the Cabinet on the recruitment of the Welsh Army Corps. Charles Hobhouse recorded in his diary:

At length Ll.G. told K. that he forgot that he was not an autocrat but only one of a body of 20 equals, that his attitude showed his sterility of ideas and ignorance of British conditions, and that he must expect and would certainly get criticism of his doings. K. retorted that he was ready to be criticised and to retire if necessary, but he would tolerate no interference with the plans of the W.O. Everyone, even W.S.C. and Grey sided with Ll.G. and K. made us very angry by trying to laugh aside the argument. He got a great rebuff, which surprised and disgusted him, but did him good. The P.M. sat very silent.[18]

Kitchener's lack of tact, perhaps stemming from his military background, was not confined to his relations with his government colleagues. It was also revealed in his dealings with industry. Thus he showed a lack of realism in what he expected from labour. Addison, commenting on the treatment of new recruits, wrote in his diary, 'The truth is K. has forgotten what the British workman is like, if he ever knew He has been so many years dealing with Arabs and Indians that he is out of touch.' He also commented, 'He is no doubt a magnificent drill-sergeant, but he is perfectly hopeless in dealing with a big industrial community like ours.'[19] For all this Kitchener does appear more flexible on munitions than the War Office as a whole.

A complaint repeatedly made of the War Office was that it was slow to take action. The War Office officials justified their caution in introducing new designs of high explosive shells by the powerful plea of safety. However, a major complaint at the Ministry of Munitions was that the War Office was unduly slow in carrying out the necessary tests.[20] The War Office officials' lack of realism in dealing with industrialists was another cause of delay. At first they expected industry to make massive expansions of plant with no guarantees of orders beyond the first few weeks of production; thus one MP complained of a Wolverhampton firm which was expected to risk £150,000 of capital for a ten-week order from the War Office.[21] When the Ministry of Munitions was set up Addison was scandalised at the War Office's casual attitude to correspondence. He complained, 'We arranged that their correspondence about labour should be transferred to our labour department and they have sent across nearly 100,000 letters, mostly unacknowledged. This fully explains the complaints from the employers.'[22] There were also complaints by the Ministry of Munitions that the War Office was slow to pass on urgent calls for munitions from commanders in the field. In June 1915 Lloyd George was especially agitated about delays associated with Sir Stanley von Donop. Addison was remarkably severe in his comments in his diary, recording initially a discussion between Lloyd George, Reading and himself:

I rubbed in once more my own conclusion, either that Von Donop, who is Master-General of the Ordnance at the War Office, was incompetent or a traitor. I am inclined to the latter view. One of the two can be the only explanation of the fact that he has not ordered things which he himself knew, and in some cases were said, to be required, particularly machine guns and rifles, and big guns also. I suggested to L.G. that we ought to have an Information Office in France which would let us know exactly what was delivered there, so that the figures might be compared with what was delivered in this country. I feel so suspicious that Von Donop's Department will not send to France what we provide. He wrote at once to K. insisting that there should be such an organisation. He has got it at last so burnt into him that I should say the days of Von Donop are nearly over. He told me that Balfour had agreed with him when he had set out the facts, that Von Donop could not have done more even if he had been deliberately a traitor, and I agreed heartily.[23]

In addition, the War Office was criticised for being slow to realise that getting orders placed was not the same as getting supplies delivered on time. Whilst the British army did depend until April 1916 on munitions ordered by the War Office, it is also true that the proportion of War Office orders supplied on time was chronically low. Lloyd George complained, 'By the 29th May 1915, out of 5,797,274 shell bodies ordered by the War Office by or before that date, only 1,968,252 had actually been delivered — this after ten months of war.'[24] Officials were aware of this problem. Sir Frederick Donaldson, who was in charge of Woolwich Arsenal, wrote to Lloyd George deprecating the role of outside contractors, observing, 'judging by the experience of the South African War when we had to call in the assistance of a good deal of the outside trade, especially the fuzes, the reliance which can be placed on such assistance left a great deal to be desired, and I suggest that you be not very sanguine in securing very prompt results'.[25] However, the real fault of the War Office was a failure to vigorously attempt to secure labour, machinery and other scarce resources for its outside suppliers in order to ensure that they had a reasonable chance of delivering munitions punctually.

Overall then, criticism of the War Office comes down to a matter of degree. The War Office did organise the massive increase in munitions which the British army used until the spring of 1916; but, of course, it would have been scandalous if output had not increased massively in the early months of the war. It was Lloyd George, however, who was quick to realise the need for extra manufacturing capacity for high explosives, and so pressed ahead with the building of the purpose-built massive National Projectile and National Filling Factories and undertook the dilution campaign to secure the necessary labour for them. In achieving this extra output by mid-1916 Lloyd George enabled the generals to continue in their profligate policies on the Western Front; thus it was a case of radical drive being the means to enable orthodox military policies to continue.

Kitchener, in failing to control the supply functions of the War Office adequately, had some excuse in the extraordinary pressures that were placed on him in the early months of the war. With the German army advancing into France he had a great responsibility to shoulder — perhaps greater than that on any other member of the Cabinet. The rapid expansion of munitions production was just one aspect of the major task he had in the autumn of 1914. However, it seems to be the case that he made the burden on himself greater by failing sufficiently to delegate work to his colleagues. The Dardanelles Commissioners were very critical of him on this point. They commented:

All the evidence laid before us points to the conclusion that Lord Kitchener was not in the habit of consulting his subordinates, that he frequently gave orders over the heads of the Chiefs of Departments, and sometimes without the knowledge of the Chief of the General Staff...

There can, in fact, be no doubt that the principle of centralisation was pushed to an extreme point by Lord Kitchener. It proved eminently successful during the minor operations in the Soudan which he conducted with conspicuous skill. But it was unsuitable to a stronger force than that which Lord Kitchener commanded in the Soudan, or to operations on so large a scale as those in which this country has recently been engaged. The result was to throw on the hands of one man an amount of work with which no individual, however capable, could hope to cope successfully.[26]

The key point here is the massive and growing volume of work falling on the War Office in such a major European war. The rapid expansion of munitions production required all manner of specialist developments — from a greatly increased volume of experimental work to more complex labour regulation. As the munitions industry took more and more scarce resources — factory buildings, machinery, skilled labour, raw materials — its impact on the whole economy became very marked. Control of this major sector of the wartime economy became a task of too great magnitude to leave as a sub-section of the War Office's work. One does not need to find monumental bungling by the War Office in order to explain the splitting away of these functions from the War Office. However, the War Office's tardiness in taking up new ideas — certainly its reputation for this — speeded up what was surely the inevitable separation of munitions production from the War Office's other responsibilities. Lloyd George, though, was pushing his case a little too far when he wrote in his *War*

Memoirs of the Ministry of Munitions, 'Its very existence was a statutory expression of a national verdict of failure delivered by the High Court of Parliament against the War Office.'[27]

The development of the Ministry of Munitions into a massive bureaucracy in a short space of time offered great opportunities for administrative innovation. Lloyd George did have to create an administrative machine in Whitehall from very little, though his famous anecdote of starting with just 'two tables and a chair', and one of those chairs immediately being removed by the War Office,[28] has led some later commentators to forget that Lloyd George inherited much administrative machinery from the War Office.

The most striking innovation in the creation of the ministry was the extent to which non civil servant personnel, especially businessmen, were brought in. Lloyd George proclaimed in his *War Memoirs*, 'The Ministry of Munitions was from first to last a business-man organisation. Its most distinctive feature was the appointment I made of successful businessmen to the chief executive posts.'[29] Kitchener had done this on a more limited scale. Some of those who were transferred from the War Office were one legacy about which Lloyd George and Addison had their reservations. Addison repeatedly expressed strong doubts about Girouard's competence and his loyalty to the new ministry. Similarly Lloyd George acidly observed of one memorandum by George Booth, 'Had he shown himself as well polished in the facts and figures of his own Department…as he seems to be in all the arguments and views of the Treasury and War Office about the methods of the Department, he could never have committed such an elementary blunder.'[30] However, whatever Lloyd George may have felt at times about some of the businessmen he inherited, he was keen to enrol many more to his ministry. According to Lloyd George, in July 1915 there were 'at least 90 men of first class business experience' in the ministry.[31]

Many of these businessmen were to be very successful in their tasks. This was recognised in the knighthoods that were showered on them; so many were given that Lloyd George in his *War Memoirs* mistakenly credited one to George Booth.[32] Lloyd George was quick to recognise the talents of a man such as Eric Geddes and to put him in to deal with successive administrative trouble-spots, first the slow delivery of rifles and then the congestion of supplies at Woolwich. Eric Geddes was very much the type of business-man Lloyd George desired to have help him 'to create and hustle along a gigantic new enterprise'.[33]

Lloyd George's attitude to bringing in businessmen was a contrast with that of Asquith, not with that of Kitchener. Asquith had been alarmed when George Booth had spoken of widening contacts with businessmen. Asquith observed to him that he could not afford another Marconi scandal.

His attitude to businessmen's integrity clearly offended Booth.[34] Asquith's views owed much to the professional upper middle class's distaste for businessmen, an attitude reinforced by Asquith's chosen social circle. In contrast Lloyd George, from at least the time he was President of the Board of Trade, had a rosy view of business entrepreneurs. The bringing in of businessmen was a natural move in view of the commercial nature of the Ministry of Munitions' task. It also had accompanying political advantages. Committed fully to waging war, Lloyd George was again making a name for himself as a man of 'national efficiency'. He was to gain support by this move from the same groups which had admired his record at the Board of Trade – perhaps the same broad middle ground of politics he had had in mind to appeal to when framing his secret coalition proposals in 1910.

The businessmen were deemed to possess, perhaps even symbolically to represent, qualities which were the opposite of those prevalent in Whitehall. As Lloyd George intended many of these men were inclined to be impatient with Whitehall protocol. They were established figures in their own right, used to taking decisions and commanding sizeable resources in private enterprise, and not easily cowed by the Whitehall establishment. Many of the businessmen gave their services to the ministry without charge to government funds, doing this at their own or their companies' expense. So as the Treasury did not pay their salaries, it was that much harder for Whitehall to call the tune.

Whilst men such as Eric Geddes matched Lloyd George's hopes, the businessmen were by no means easily welded into a team. Some appear to have been as much concerned about status and precedence as any career civil servant. In some cases it was felt that they were not especially efficient. Addison complained in his diary of Girouard and Booth, 'After they had indulged in a good deal of "high-falutin" nonsense as to the big-businessman's methods, I brought up the fact that their registry was the most inefficient in the whole Ministry, that papers sent to them were lost and that, as a result, things were hung up and delayed.'[35] Probably this was true of several of the businessmen – but in his appraisals of them Addison appears to have been much influenced in his views by those of the very experienced civil servant operators in the ministry, in particular by Hubert Llewellyn Smith. At the time Llewellyn Smith was resisting, and resisting successfully, Girouard's attempts to place himself at the top of the ministry's administration.[36] In doing this it is highly likely that Llewellyn Smith was adroit in pointing out the businessmen's administrative deficiencies to Addison, expecting rightly that Girouard's *hubris* would soon lead to a fall, as indeed it did when Girouard repeatedly tried to treat Lloyd George as a person of little consequence.

The businessmen did not leave their pasts behind when they joined the ministry. There were fears that they would have divided loyalties –

between the ministry and the company from which they came. Thus in June 1915 Vincent Caillard of Vickers visited the ministry anxious as to his firm's good favour with it; his anxieties raised, according to Addison, by the powerful positions held in the ministry by leading figures from the rival firm of Armstrong.[37] Asquith's suspicions of businessmen in government were given some substance by the activities of a few of those in the Ministry of Munitions. In January 1916 Addison had firmly to remind Colonel Wright 'that he must try to forget that he is a businessman looking after his own interests'. Wright had been caught helping the steel interests to get better terms from the ministry. Addison wrote in his diary that Wright 'had hardly been playing the game by us and has apparently been coaching up the steel makers to demand high terms in connection with the taxation of profits, so as to induce us to allow large reductions in connection with the putting up of extensions in connection with their work... He has been apparently egging on the steel makers to demand at least an allowance of 75% on the cost of these extensions and one of them who has some notion of playing the game, has sent us his correspondence.'[38] There was also concern that businessmen in the ministry were exploiting the opportunity to advertise themselves and their firms. There was particular concern about Alfred Herbert who was appointed to be the head of the Machine Tool Department of the ministry.[39] After complaints about this Lloyd George took administrative action to see that circulars going out from the ministry went out under the name of career civil servants, not under the name of the businessmen in the ministry.[40]

Whilst the widespread introduction of businessmen was the most striking innovation in the Whitehall administration of the Ministry of Munitions, the rapid and massive growth of the bureaucracy was a most remarkable feature of its history. In this wartime scarcities of labour forced one innovation on the ministry as it did to other employers, especially those of white collar workers. As government policies 'combed out' more and more able bodied men from civilian occupations for service in the armed forces, there was an increasing proportion of women on the staff. The headquarters staff of the Ministry of Munitions grew in one year to over 12,000, and at the Armistice consisted of over 25,000 persons. At the end of the first quarter of 1916 59 per cent of this labour force was male and 41 per cent female; six months later the percentages were 50 and 50; and by the third quarter of 1918 39 per cent were men and 61 per cent were women.[41]

The recruitment of large numbers of young women to the clerical staff gave the officials of the ministry a special problem in disciplining their labour force. Apparently the new female staff at headquarters gained a bad name. A memorandum of July 1916 commented on the fact 'that a great deal of notice has been taken in the last few months in the London papers, and particularly in the illustrated dailies, of the women staff of the Ministry from the point of view which reflects on the conduct and office manners of the staff'. As a result of this Lloyd George appointed a Chief Welfare Officer who provided 'a complete scheme for the welfare supervision of the headquarters staff'. Such welfare provisions had a strong disciplinary tone to them. It was observed in the memorandum, 'It was only to be expected that a huge staff like this, collected from a great variety of sources would show itself to be a little impatient of discipline and ignorant of office ways, and it is necessary, I think, that from time to time inexperienced girls who are working here should be encouraged in the right way to adopt business-like and orderly habits.'[42] Of course the munitions factories, with their great influx of labour, had similar problems of discipline. At Woolwich Arsenal the numbers of women employed increased from under 100 in November 1916 to some 22,000 six months later, and 30,000 a year later; sometimes as many as 400 new women a day were recruited, coming from very different backgrounds.[43] This massive influx of women led not only to the usual responses in training labour to office or factory discipline but also put a new emphasis on welfare services for a large workforce.

It is clear that the running of the ministry was done in the most unorthodox manner during the time Lloyd George was at its head. At first Lloyd George's creation followed his pragmatic, untrammelled ways. Extra staff were recruited according to the urgent needs of the moment – and this was done department by department. To the Whitehall mind the most horrific bureaucratic heresies were committed in the early days of the ministry. There was little or no attempt to grade staff. There were no clear principles in fixing rates of pay. Few, if any, records of staff were kept. There was no clear-cut system of making appointments. Eventually, on 1 February 1916, Lloyd George set up an inquiry into the organisation of the ministry. At the end of the month its interim report listed all manner of unorthodoxies prevalent in the ministry and emphasised its departmental nature. The authors of the report observed: 'the staff of the Ministry is not regarded as common stock from which men and women can be drawn to meet the needs of each Department. This follows naturally perhaps from the fact that each Department is water tight in the sense that it is not subject to any central control other than that of the Minister. We know of no other public department so constituted.'[44]

During Lloyd George's last months at Munitions the ministry began to come increasingly in line with Whitehall practices. This process was continued under his successors. By the time that Lloyd George left Munitions in July 1916 the major problems in getting a sufficient volume of shells had been solved. Under Montagu and Addison consolidation was necessary. Edwin Montagu set up what he dubbed a 'General Staff' of leading administrators to overlook the problems facing the ministry and to co-ordinate departments.[45] Christopher Addison, who succeeded Montagu in December 1916, was a well-respected administrator. Lloyd George later described him as 'a man with a high order of intellectual capacity, full of ideas, resourcefulness and courage'.[46] Addison was a source of good ideas about administration, but they were not ideas that went outside the normal bounds. In his approach to administration he was in tune with the career civil servants. When Sir Percy Girouard was sacked he was replaced by Sir Frederick Black, who came from the Admiralty. Addison expressed his relief at the return to orthodoxy; he wrote in his diary, 'It is a big relief to feel that we have an experienced public servant at the head in Armaments Buildings on whom we can rely.'[47] After Lloyd George had gone unorthodox innovation in administration ended. Whitehall was back in command.

Winston Churchill, the fourth Minister of Munitions, was another strong minister likely to go against the current of civil service thinking. However, by the time he was appointed, in July 1917, munitions were no longer the top priority for national resources and he was concerned with trying to control a massive organisation, to switch production to new needs (such as gas shells and tanks) and eventually to prepare to demobilise the ministry's productive and administrative workforce. Thus there was less scope for dramatic changes. By 1917 the Ministry of Munitions' headquarters was displaying the common Whitehall tendency of empire-building, with growth becoming automatic rather than as a response to urgent war needs. This was strikingly inappropriate at a time when one of the government's foremost priorities was to 'comb out' as much manpower as possible from less essential occupations – a policy which led to serious industrial unrest. Winston Churchill clearly had to exert repeated pressure on his top administrators on the issue. In March 1918 he complained to his heads of departments, 'I have not received any marked response from the departments in regard to reduction of staff. When I arrived here I set out as the ideal, a shrinkage of 3,000 or 4,000... but so far the process has proceeded in exactly the opposite direction...' Accordingly, he informed them, 'In order to assist your labours I have decided to appoint an outside committee, which will pass in review the establishments of the different departments of the Ministry and will assist the heads of these departments in the task which really is so very necessary at the moment.'[48] The Armistice saved the ministry from the drastic reorganisation which would have ensued from this; a reorganisation which it was felt 'would not only increase efficiency but also reduce staff'.[49]

So the period when the Ministry of Munitions really earned its reputation for administrative unorthodoxy was when Lloyd George was minister and when the drive for increased munitions output was a, if not the, major national priority. With Lloyd George as dynamic and politically powerful head of the department, the *ad hoc* structure of the early days was made to work. Lloyd George was a man who focused his attention on one thing at a time — and brought to it a fresh and inquiring mind. When he set up the ministry there was one main priority — achieving a massive increase in the output of shells. Thus the needs of the situation matched his mode of working. He pursued his aim with single-minded determination — and transmitted this drive to his senior staff either by hectoring them in person or by memoranda.

Lloyd George was not cowed by his civil servants. Lord Boothby later testified that Lloyd George was the only man who ever made the Treasury do what it did not want to do.[50] He was very much in charge at Munitions. In the early days of the ministry Lloyd George was very careful to avoid having a departmental head, through whom all things would flow to him.[51] Lloyd George pressed his civil servants hard to concentrate on getting the obstacles to higher munitions output removed. Later there were complaints that his persistent memoranda harried his officials and hindered rather than helped them. Yet, if one considers the preparations for the 1916 offensive Lloyd George's concern over output appears justified. In August 1915 he was pressing Black that actual deliveries of armaments appeared likely to arrive too late for fighting in the spring and summer of 1916, and commented, 'I am anxious therefore to consider the best method of hustling the armament firms and of assisting them to deliver in contract time.'[52] In September and October he was still urging more action. On 29 September he expressed continued concern about components and complained, 'I cannot help thinking that there has been culpable negligence somewhere...'[53] The civil servants responded by producing soothing answers (thus on components, 'it is a good fault that there is at the same time a considerable excess supply of some other component') and a printed report on the issues he raised. The report appears to have been intended as something of a 'put-down' on the minister. It gave fulsome praise to the work being done ('The wonder is not so much that the system has not shown grown greater elasticity but that it has shown so much') and ended happily on the slightly defensive note, 'The impression it is desired to give in these notes is not that all difficulties have been surmounted, but that the problems of organisation involving matters of much complexity and detail are well advanced.'[54] This treatment presumably would have put most ministers in their place. However, Lloyd George returned to the issues with vigour in February 1916 complaining:

> if the estimates for the present and future months are as unreliable as that for January has turned out to be...then the whole of the summer campaign must be postponed because the anticipations of Armament Buildings have not been realised.
>
> What makes me all the more uneasy is what has occurred over components. In September and October I repeatedly called attention to

what struck me as being the unsatisfactory condition of our filling and fuse arrangements. If you will look up the minutes I forwarded to you you will see how accurately these minutes represent the actual state of things at the time. I was however assured that all was well; that the figures were very much better than the returns presented to me; and that so far from filling being short of requirements it would be well in advance...

I cannot leave things in the present state of doubt and uncertainty. The whole prospects of the Spring Campaign depend upon my informing the Army of the actual position so that they can make their plans accordingly. If I mislead them both I and my advisers deserve to be court-martialled...[55]

Lloyd George was not in the hands of his officials as to policy. He was willing to learn from any source, whether it be a businessman, the War Office, the career civil servants, or his newspaper friends. Thus he took up many of the new approaches to problems that the War Office had been tentatively trying – and accelerated their use. His approach to problems was pragmatic. If one solution did not work, then he quickly tried another. In the summer of 1915 he was much influenced by the proposals of the businessmen in the ministry for dealing with labour problems; hence his tough speeches of that June in which he almost heralded industrial conscription. However, faced with a public uproar, he retreated to the more cautious policies advocated by Llewellyn Smith, who had previously been in charge of policy at the Board of Trade.[56] Later Lloyd George found the policies of Beveridge and the Labour Department to be too rigid, and very markedly moderated them in response to serious industrial unrest, much to Beveridge's chagrin.[57]

Lloyd George's administrative innovations at Munitions may have been tempered by time, first during his own last months there and then under his successors before the ministry was renamed the Ministry of Supply in January 1919 and finally was dissolved in March 1921. However, Lloyd George himself went on to innovate in the Cabinet Office; the efficient administration there breaking away from the informal gentlemanly ways of the past. Moreover, in setting up his 'Garden Suburb', his own secretariat of five advisers (including Professor W. G. S. Adams, who had worked in the Ministry of Munitions), he again went well beyond the bounds of administrative innovation that Whitehall would accept as reasonable. As at the Ministry of Munitions, Lloyd George as Prime Minister tried to see that the civil service served him, not controlled him.

During the First World War the Ministry of Munitions was like an octopus with its tentacles reaching out into the whole economy. Control of munitions production soon led to control of essential raw materials, factory space, sources of power and labour. Throughout the war the Ministry of Munitions' controls crept steadily outwards through essential industries into the economy as a whole.[58] These controls were removed at the end of the war – but the ministry left industry a lasting legacy.

One part of this was a considerable increase in capacity in the engineering, iron and steel, and shipbuilding industries. The big armament firms began considerable expansion under the War Office. Under the Ministry of Munitions expansion of engineering capacity throughout British industry was encouraged, often with considerable financial aid. When the available capacity still proved inadequate, the ministry went in for purpose-built state munitions factories and shipyards; a considerable innovation in Britain, where the usual practice has been for the state to take over going concerns, 'controlling' them in wartime and nationalising them in peacetime. As well as larger units, another marked trend in these industries during the war was for firms to expand by buying up the smaller firms which supplied them with essential ingredients for their production.

The wartime expansion of capacity was to prove a problem for these industries in the interwar period, when world demand for their goods declined. It was to be a problem only partly mitigated by the fact that the additions of the war and postwar boom were at least modern. At the end of the First World War the state munitions factories and shipyards, unless wanted by the government or local authorities, were sold off at advantageous prices to private enterprise – advantageous given the exceptional demand in the immediate postwar period.[59] By early 1921 representatives of the machine tool trades were urging the government not to sell off surplus stock for a while 'so that such demand as may be in existence should be made available for providing employment for the people employed in the machine tool industry'.[60] Another drawback with much of the extra capacity added to private firms was that it was in the form of extensions to existing plant, a development which was less likely to lead to modern large units. In the case of steel the Ministry of Munitions staff had hoped 'to leave the firms...with modern plants... convertible to general trade after the war' but the policy of extensions undermined hopes of the creation of 'great national steel works'.[61]

The Ministry of Munitions encouraged the introduction of the latest machinery and methods in the areas it controlled. During the First World War many factories took electric power for the first time. This was very marked in those under ministry control. In the new munitions factories 95 per cent of the machinery was driven by electricity.[62] With the demand for electricity greatly increasing, the ministry was soon faced with municipal requests for financial help to expand generating capacity. In July 1915 Booth was informed that in Coventry and Sheffield 'urgent demands have been made upon the Corporation by various firms of high standing engaged upon Government contracts, and in some cases by Government owned and equipped factories for the supply of additional electric power... It is suggested that the Corporation cannot be expected to burden itself with the heavy expense involved by the provision of this additional plant unless the Government gives them an undertaking to bear at any rate a proportion, say one half, of the loss which will be incurred by the machines standing idle at the end of the war.'[63] The Treasury was informed that such additional expenditure was 'absolutely necessary to secure the output of munitions', and Coventry (which was to be the precedent) was given financial assistance by the ministry. The additional generating capacity was, of course, up to date, so it was observed of the Coventry case that 'as the new plant represents a considerable improvement in efficiency over some of that installed, it is almost certain that the Corporation will desire to take it over at the end of the war'.[64] Overall, with regard to the electricity supply industry, as the ministry's main concern was with war production, many of its policies went for short-term expedients rather than for policies which would help solve long-term problems of the industry. Nevertheless the needs of the war encouraged such development as the linking up of generating stations and gave an incentive for the setting up of more research programmes.[65]

The ministry encouraged the use of the latest techniques in engineering, iron and steel and other areas of industry that it controlled. The demands of the war were a major encouragement in the greater use of the arc furnace in the United Kingdom. The shortage of iron and steel ensured more use of scrap – and there was plenty of this from the castings of munitions.[66] The Bessemer process could not cope with a large proportion of scrap, so the ministry had to encourage the use of arc furnaces. In shipbuilding there was much wider use of pneumatic and electrical tools, whilst the spread of standardisation simplified work in many areas.[67] Similarly there was a rapid spread of standardisation in munitions manufacture, marked by the increasing use of automatic and semi-automatic machines and lathes. 'By 1917 and 1918', according to one standard work, 'the engineering industry of the Clyde had been virtually revolutionised by the introduction throughout of automatic machinery, and the adoption of mass production.'[68] During the war the Ministry of Munitions greatly encouraged the British tool industry to expand its capacity; however, this larger capacity was not maintained fully for long for the industry's output dropped heavily in the 1920s after the end of the postwar boom.[69] As well as fostering new techniques and technology the ministry encouraged greater emphasis on research and development.

It also pressed engineering firms to specialise. Insufficient specialisation before the First World War has often been deemed a major reason for the declining competitiveness of the British engineering industry. Quite probably commentators have underestimated the extent to which this was taking place before 1914 and so have exaggerated the importance of changes in the First World War.[70] Even so the ministry did leave a beneficial legacy in this respect. Overall the Ministry of Munitions was the transmitter of war-induced innovations to sizable sectors of British industry, bringing the practices of the firms under its control up towards those of the most efficient.

Management practices in industries controlled by the ministry were also subject to innovation. In financial management and labour matters, as in most other areas, the ministry's role appears to have been to accelerate the spread of the best practices already taking place in a few companies rather than to introduce something new.

One marked example of this is cost accounting. At the time inflated claims were made for the ministry's role in introducing this and these have been repeated since. Indeed exaggerated claims were made as to the nature of cost accounting. One civil servant, George Duckworth, enthusiastically wrote in a memorandum, 'For the first time in history it has been possible to subject to a similar form of scrutiny a large number of firms producing similar articles', and went on to mention warmly 'some definite proposals' which had been made by one of his colleagues 'for the institution of a Department of the State, whose whole business should be the consideration of the results shown by a common system of cost accounting'.[71] Cost accounting cannot work miracles — and the civil servants were to find that factories with different equipment and financial liabilities were not that easily compared, even when producing a common article.

Relatively sophisticated cost accounting took place in some British factories before the First World War.[72] What the Ministry of Munitions did was to spread efficient costing systems through both the national and the controlled factories. This speeded up the spread of its application in British industry, so providing managements with a much more accurate index of costs on which they could base their decisions.

Most of the dramatic changes in labour regulations that took place during the war under the Munitions of War Acts and the Defence of the Realm Acts were swept away at the end of the war.[73] However, there were areas of labour management in which innovations were longer lasting. The setting up of purpose-built factories gave opportunities for experiments other than just in cost accounting. Time and motion studies were facilitated by them. Thus at the Mossend National Factory the manager, a Mr Walton, carefully applied the results of time and motion studies to the cost of fuse inspection. George Duckworth observed in one memorandum, 'Mr. Walton had been influenced in his work by a study of Professor Gilbreth's books on Fatigue and Motion Study, and had determined to apply his theories in some branch of his own Factory. For the purpose of his experiment he chose the work of gauging fuses.' As well as speeding up the work, having changed the way it was carried out, he also 'found it possible to use maimed soldiers, possessing only one arm, in place of men or women with two arms who had previously been employed on this work.[74]

It also seems that some of the managerial talent imported into the ministry used its opportunities to press ahead with changes that it had been found difficult to introduce in peacetime. Thus when Allen Reith approached James McKechnie, general manager of Vickers at Barrow, to supply the ministry with a rate-fixer his appeal was couched very blatantly in terms of future benefit to Vickers. He wrote that this should be done 'because I think it would be very much to your advantage if the premium bonus system is spread as much as possible in other establishments, and, if it is to be spread, then it should be worked on the right lines... in these days the disadvantages which will follow such a transfer will be more than outweighed by the assistance a general adoption of the bonus system would give to you in maintaining your present practice'.[75]

The Ministry of Munitions was also notable for encouraging the spread of welfare provisions in the factories under its control. This was partly a response to the need for at least some changes given the huge influx of women into the engineering industry. It was at the same time a necessary response to one of the big problems of the war for industry – the high mobility of labour. Good pay *and* good conditions proved a winner in holding labour. This approach is the usual one when there is a scarcity of some type of labour in the labour market, and, of course, the First World War was a period marked by an extraordinary demand for labour. In the USA at this time such improvements in welfare in many sectors of industry came ahead of government intervention. Provision of such facilities was also in line with some contemporary strands of management thinking – paternalistic altruism and tough efficiency. The less attractive side of this thinking was expressed by a speaker to the American Society of Mechanical Engineers in May 1917: 'What is needed is a doctor, a combination of general repair and safety engineer, to look after the human machinery, to study stresses and strains on it, to give warning of a probable break-down, to advise easing up on the load until the human mechanism has been readjusted, to do the hundred and one things that make for comfort of mind and body.'[76] The Ministry of Munitions' Welfare and Health Section expressed its task as being 'to convince employers that it is both good business and good management, as well as a duty, to regard with sympathetic consideration the health and comfort of their employees'. It reported, of a large Lancashire munitions factory, that 'The Manager spoke most highly of the moral tone that had been infused into the place through Welfare work. There had been no trouble with the girls and that was more than could be said of any neighbouring works.'[77]

The Ministry of Munitions' managerial policies generally smack of tough efficient capitalism. It seems to have purveyed the scientific management of Taylor and his disciples, to have gone for the combination of high output and relatively high pay, sweeping aside impediments be they trade union safeguards or old management practices. The ministry pressed on those factories under its control the latest ideas in technology and management and attempted to bring the policies of the least efficient into line with those of the best.

Lloyd George, with his high regard for businessmen, was a very appropriate head of such a ministry. During the First World War he concentrated his considerable energies on defeating Germany, pragmatically adopting whichever policies would achieve this quickly; but nevertheless, he had an eye on the postwar world. In June 1915, speaking at Manchester, he observed, 'We are fighting against the best organised community in the world; the best organised whether for war or peace, and we have been employing too much the haphazard, leisurely, go-as-you-please methods, which believe me, would not have enabled us to maintain our place as a nation, even in peace, very much longer.'[78]

During the war leading trade unionists suspected that Lloyd George intended that trade union restrictive practices would not in fact be restored after the war. He had guaranteed the trade unions a return to the prewar situation — but in speeches he repeatedly put the onus on the unions to insist on the restoration of prewar practices. Lloyd George's speeches in which he contrasted peacetime methods with those of wartime were not flattering to the British trade unionist. Thus, for example, when addressing miners' representatives in July 1915 he commented:

There is too much disposition to cling to the amenities of peace. Business as usual, enjoyment as usual, fashions, lock-outs, strikes, ca'canny, sprees — all as usual. Wages must go up, profits also improve; but prices must at all costs be kept down. No man must be called upon to serve the State unless he wants to; even then he has to be called upon to do exactly what he would like to do — not what he is fit for, not what he is chosen for, but what he would like to do ... Freedom implies the right to shirk, Freedom implies the right for you to enjoy and for others to defend. Is that freedom?[79]

Such speeches as this, and especially the remarkable speech at Manchester on 3 June 1915, in which Lloyd George called for virtually unlimited powers for the war effort, created great unease among trade union leaders. At the end of the war they took great pains to press the government to fulfil Lloyd George's pledges on the restoration of prewar conditions. In December 1918 at a meeting of the Trade Union and Employers Advisory Committee Churchill was warned, 'Already the tension is very rife amongst the skilled sections of the workmen because at the present time they are walking the streets and the dilutees are being retained and doing their jobs.'[80] In the face of such pressure the government was forced to keep its pledges. So, despite Lloyd George's hopes, there were no lasting gains in productivity stemming from major relaxation of the unions' working practices.

The Ministry of Munitions was a body that was receptive to new ideas. Unlike the War Office it could focus its attention solely on the problem of achieving sufficient supplies. In organising production the ministry transmitted many of the latest ideas in technology and management practice to the firms under its control, generally trying to bring them all up to the standards of the best companies.

However, the ministry's aims were basically short term – to organise the supplies necessary for running the war. In such circumstances many changes in industry were made on short-term considerations, not on the long-term needs of the specific industry. This was also the case in training labour. Thus, for example, when formulating policy for training labour to manufacture aircraft, it was specifically decided that 'the course of training should aim at turning out work people competent of performing accurately a few given operations, and that no attempt ought to be made to turn out workmen skilled all round'.[81] Though, of course, in labour matters the short-term approach was reinforced by the promise to the unions to remove dilutees at the end of the war.

The experience of the Ministry of Munitions left a lasting impression on people's thinking, and not just on that of politicians and civil servants. After the First World War many industrialists, bankers, politicians and trade unionists became disillusioned with free market competition at home and abroad and favoured co-operation in industry, mergers and large-scale organisation.[82] The Ministry of Munitions could be eulogised as an example of what could be achieved.

Notes: Chapter 2

1   A. J. P. Taylor, *Beaverbrook* (London: Hamish Hamilton, 1972), ch. 17.
2   George Dewar, *The Great Munitions Feat 1914–18* (London: Constable, 1921), pp. v–vii. Dewar earlier had been the editor of the *Saturday Review*.
3   Work on it began in July 1916, with Professor W. G. S. Adams at first collecting and editing material. For a detailed account of its preparations see Denys Hay, 'The official history of the Ministry of Munitions 1915–19', *Economic History Review*, vol. 14 (1944), pp. 185–90. H. Wolfe's *Labour Supply and Regulation* (London: Oxford University Press, 1923) drew on material in the official history. Brigadier O. F. G. Hogg's *The Royal Arsenal*, Vol. 2 (London: Oxford University Press, 1973), ch. 22, 'The First World War', relies heavily on Volume 8 of the official history.

4 The only recent monograph devoted to this subject, R. Q. Adams's *Arms and the Wizard* (London: Cassell, 1978) does not seriously question Lloyd George's version of his record at the Ministry of Munitions.

5 For a recent example of this see H. Cassar, *Kitchener: Architect of Victory* (London: William Kimber, 1977), in which Lloyd George is severely denigrated in the process of resurrecting Kitchener's reputation.

6 I am grateful to those who discussed these issues when I presented earlier drafts of parts of this essay in February, May and October 1979 at research seminars in the Department of Economics, Loughborough University and (at the Twentieth Century British History and the Military History ones) in the Institute of Historical Research, London University.

7 Field-Marshal Viscount French of Ypres, *1914* (London: Constable, 1919), ch. 18, especially pp. 356–61.

8 The Earl of Oxford and Asquith, *Memories and Reflections*, Vol. 2 (London: Cassell, 1928), pp. 76–9 and 81–2.

9 Diary extract 22 March 1915, ibid., p. 67.

10 As well as differentiating between Kitchener's role and that of the War Office as a whole, it might be fair in the case of the slowness to increase the proportion of high explosive shells manufactured to differentiate between the War Office and certain commanders at the Front, as the War Office asked for their advice on the matter and the latter were slow to realise the importance of high explosive in such a war. See Sir George Arthur, *Life of Lord Kitchener*, Vol. 3 (London: Macmillan, 1920), pp. 273–4. Arthur had been Kitchener's personal secretary.

11 ibid., p. 271.

12 Duncan Crow, *A Man of Push and Go* (London: Hart-Davis, 1965), p. 71.

13 ibid., p. 99.

14 *Lord Riddell's War Diary* (London: Nicolson & Watson, 1933), p. 35, entry for 13 October 1914.

15 *War Memoirs of David Lloyd George*, Vol. 2 (London: Nicolson & Watson, 1933), p. 751.

16 *Lord Riddell's War Diary*, p. 36, entry for 25 October 1914.

17 The Earl of Oxford and Asquith, *Memories and Reflections*, p. 34, entry for 22 September 1914. However, Kitchener's own remarks on the allegations of overcrowded conditions for recruits were crass ('the damned fools of doctors were always insisting on ridiculous allowances of cubic space'); see Asquith's diary for 8 September 1914, ibid., p. 32.

18 Edward David (ed.), *Inside Asquith's Cabinet* (London: John Murray, 1977), p. 204, entry for 28 October 1914.

19 Christopher Addison, *Four and a Half Years*, Vol. 1 (London: Hutchinson, 1934), pp. 39 and 79, diary entries for 22 October 1914 and 17 May 1915.

20 See Addison's memorandum of 22 November 1915, reprinted in Addison, *Four and a Half Years*, Vol. 1, pp. 148–50. Lloyd George was fully aware of the dangers of premature explosion; see, for example, his letter to Von Donop, 24 September 1915, D/17/6/25, David Lloyd George Papers (hereafter LG), House of Lords Record Office, London.

21 J. F. Mason to Austen Chamberlain, 20 May 1915. Also Chamberlain to Lloyd George, 7 June 1915 and Addison to Chamberlain, 17 June 1915, Box 4, Addison Papers, Bodleian Library, Oxford.

22 Addison, *Four and a Half Years*, Vol. 1, p. 106, diary entry for 16 July 1915.

23 Addison's diary for 25 June 1915, Addison Papers, Box 97. A much expurgated version is published in *Four and a Half Years*, Vol. 1, p. 101.

24 *War Memoirs*, Vol. 1, p. 265.

25   Sir F. Donaldson to Lloyd George, 29 May 1915, LG D/2/3/1, copy in Addison Papers, Box 2.
26   *First Report*, 12 February 1917 (Cd 8490), p. 13; cited in P. Magnus, *Kitchener* (London: John Murray, 1958), p. 378. This view was challenged by Sir William Robertson and Asquith; however, it is striking that Robertson insisted on conditions before he would take the office of Chief of General Staff. See Oxford and Asquith, *Memories and Reflections*, pp. 81–2. Other sources tend to confirm the Dardanelles Commissioners' view; for example, Hobhouse, in his diary for 22 October 1914, observed, 'He is always unfair to his departmental chiefs and branches. He doesn't consult them, ridicules them to us, and throws them over perpetually.' David (ed.), *Inside Asquith's Cabinet*, p. 201.
27   *War Memoirs*, Vol. 1, p. 238.
28   ibid., pp. 242–3.
29   ibid., p. 245.
30   Lloyd George to Sir Frederick Black, n.d. (probably December 1915 or January 1916), LG D/3/4/21. Addison's diaries are filled with disparaging remarks about Girouard; for example, 'Evidently Girouard has been inclined for some time to play us off against the War Office', diary entry, 29 June 1915, Box 97, Addison Papers.
31   *War Memoirs*, Vol. 1, p. 254.
32   ibid., p. 251.
33   ibid., p. 247. On Geddes see P. Cline, 'Eric Geddes and the "experiment" with businessmen in government 1915–22', in K. D. Brown (ed.), *Essays in Anti-Labour History* (London: Macmillan, 1974), pp. 74–104.
34   Crow, *A Man of Push and Go*, p. 69.
35   Addison, *Four and a Half Years*, Vol. 1, p. 104, diary entry for 7 July 1915.
36   Roger Davidson, 'Sir Hubert Llewellyn Smith and Labour policy 1886–1916', Cambridge University PhD thesis, 1971, pp. 326–7.
37   Addison, *Four and a Half Years*, Vol. 1, pp. 98–9, diary entry for 21 June 1915.
38   Addison Papers, Box 97, diary entries for 31 and 27 January 1916 respectively. For the published variations of these see Addison, *Four and a Half Years*, Vol. 1, pp. 164 and 163.
39   See complaint passed on to Addison by W. J. Glyn-Jones, MP, 6 August 1915, and Herbert's rebuttal of such complaints in a letter to Addison of 25 August 1915, Addison Papers, Box 10. Also Addison's diary entry of 24 July 1916 on Herbert's business interests, Addison Papers, Box 97.
40   Minute by Addison to Sir Frederick Black, 29 September 1915, Addison Papers, Box 15.
41   The number of men at the end of the first quarter of 1916 was 2,823 and at the Armistice, 10,058. For further details see a memorandum of July 1919, MUN 5–24–261–30, Ministry of Munitions Papers, PRO.
42   Minute by R. H. Cann, 9 July 1916, MUN 5–24–261–32.
43   Elizabeth Gore, *The Better Fight* (London: Geoffrey Bles, 1965), ch. 6.
44   Interim report by Mr Phipps and Mr Carr, 29 February 1916, MUN 5–24–261–2.
45   Described by him in a letter to Asquith, 27 November 1916, cited in S. D. Waley, *Edwin Montagu* (Bombay: Asia Publishing House, 1964), p. 99. Montagu probably got the idea from Addison, who had urged Lloyd George to do something similar earlier; letter and memorandum, 15 October 1915, Addison Papers, Box 15.
46   *War Memoirs*, Vol. 1, p. 251.
47   Addison, *Four and a Half Years*, Vol. 1, p. 116.
48   At a meeting of 15 March 1918, MUN 5–24–261–36.
49   Post Armistice Notes by D. C. Somervale, n.d., MUN 5–24–261–35.

50 Lord Boothby, *Recollections of a Rebel* (London: Hutchinson, 1978), p. 46. See also David (ed.), *Inside Asquith's Cabinet*, p. 98.
51 See the Minutes of the conference on the structure of the ministry, 27 May 1915, Addison Papers, Box 2. Also Addison's diary, 31 May 1915, Addison, *Four and a Half Years*, Vol. 1, p. 87.
52 Lloyd George to Sir F. Black, 10 August 1915, MUN 4–526.
53 See memoranda to Sir Frederick Black and others, 22, 24, 29, 30 September and 18 October 1915, MUN 4–526 and LG D/3/2.
54 See G. H. West to Sir F. Black, 12 October 1915 and Black and his deputies' printed report of 22 October 1915, MUN 4–526.
55 Lloyd George to Sir F. Black, 7 February 1916, LG D/3/2/40.
56 Davidson, thesis, pp. 328–31.
57 José Harris, *William Beveridge* (Oxford: Clarendon Press, 1977), pp. 218–27.
58 Thus for steel and iron there were nine stages of controls, from October 1915 to January 1917; see memorandum of 19 June 1917, MUN 5–113–600–2. See also Lloyd George's summary, *War Memoirs*, Vol. 1, p. 270.
59 On Government policy for disposal of national factories, see Addison to Sir Leo Chiozza Money, 24 January 1919, Addison Papers, Box 43.
60 The Machine Tools Trade to T. Macnamara, 27 January 1921, MUN 4–6831.
61 See J. R. Hume and M. S. Moss, *Beardmore* (London: Heinemann, 1979),p. 143.
62 D. A. Wilson, 'The economic development of the electricity supply industry in Great Britain 1919–1939', University of Bristol PhD thesis, 1976, p. 191.
63 Mr Strode to G. Booth, 30 July 1915, MUN 4–2103.
64 H. Llewellyn Smith to the Secretary, HM Treasury, 31 August 1915 and W. McLelland to S. Lever, 19 November 1915, ibid.
65 Wilson, thesis, pp. 55–60.
66 The need for scrap was such that the generals at the Western Front were urged to help salvage used ammunition. Thus Addison wrote at length to Haig urging 'economy in the use of ammunition and salvage', 2 January 1917, Addison Papers, Box 54, f.10.
67 W. R. Scott and J. Cunnison, *The Industries of the Clyde Valley During the War* (Oxford: Clarendon Press, 1924), pp. 88–9.
68 ibid., p. 102.
69 A. E. Musson, *The Growth of British Industry* (London: Batsford, 1978), p. 314.
70 For a valuable revaluation of the situation before 1914 see R. Floud, *The British Machine Tool Industry 1850–1914* (Cambridge: Cambridge University Press, 1976), ch. 1.
71 Dated 26 October 1917, MUN 5–107–450–3. Attached to the memorandum are some shrewd comments on it by M. Webster Jenkinson, 28 October 1917.
72 According to Webster Jenkinson cost accounting was not imported from abroad; the fundamentals were devised in Britain, only the mechanical aids were developed initially in America or Germany. Lecture given by him at the LSE, 9 October 1918, copy, MUN 5–107–450–9.
73 For a recent account of these see my *David Lloyd George and the British Labour Movement: Peace and War* (Hassocks: Harvester Press, 1976).
74 Memorandum, 26 October 1917, MUN 5–107–450–3.
75 Letter, 2 January 1917, McKechnie Papers, 300, Vickers Historical Records, 119, Vickers Ltd, Millbank Tower, London.
76 The speaker was Dr Otto Geier of the Cincinnati Milling Machine Company. Cited in H. D. Wagoner, *The US Machine Tool Industry from 1900 to 1950* (Cambridge, Mass.: MIT Press, 1968), p. 107. For Lloyd George expressing similar sentiments in July 1915, see the collection of his speeches, *Through Terror to Triumph* (London: Hodder & Stoughton 1915), p. 176.

77   Report on the Welfare and Health Section, 23 April 1917, copy in Addison Papers, Box 2.
78   Printed in *Through Terror to Triumph*, p. 104.
79   ibid., pp. 181–2.
80   A meeting of 21 December 1918, MUN 5–100–350–23.
81   Memorandum, 24 July 1916, on a meeting of 19 July, copy, Addison Papers, Box 55.
82   On this, see L. Hannah, *The Rise of the Corporate Economy* (London: Methuen, 1976), ch. 3. George Dewar's book itself was an early product of the rationalisation movement in British industry between the wars.

I am grateful to copyright holders for allowing me to cite material in this essay, especially A. J. P. Taylor and the Beaverbrook Foundation (Lloyd George) and Major-General Eustace Tickell (Addison). Transcripts from Crown copyright records in the Public Record Office appear by permission of the Controller of HM Stationery Office.

3

Cabinets, Committees and Secretariats: the Higher Direction of War

The late John Mackintosh offered the classic description of the British Cabinet before 1914, which, he wrote, 'operated in a delightfully simple manner. Including all the chief ministers, it discussed with little pre-digestion and no secretarial assistance all the issues of any importance and only in the restricted field of defence was the need for co-ordinated action appreciated.'[1] This paper examines the wartime experience of the Cabinet as the pinnacle of the British administrative hierarchy. Between 1914 and 1919 it was transformed from a political committee into a complex administrative system. This was made possible by the establish-ment of the Cabinet secretariat and by a measure of devolution to standing committees; but the central feature of wartime Cabinets, which facilitated modernisation without itself surviving long into the peace, was the practice of reserving critical decisions for inner committees. These were the War Council (November 1914 – May 1915), the Dardanelles Committee (June – November 1915) and the War Committee (November 1915 – November 1916), each of which coexisted with the Cabinet; and the War Cabinet (December 1916 – October 1919) which subsumed the powers and func-tions of both Cabinet and War Committee. Though Lloyd George's assumption of the premiership in December 1916 occasioned the greatest discontinuity, it is a mistake to assume that his reform of Cabinet struc-ture marked as decisive a break with the past as his multiplication of departments or his split with Asquith. The Cabinet's form changed to accommodate the changing demands of war, and Lloyd George's War Cabinet system was neither so different, nor so much better, than Asquith's as he or his apologists suggest.

Immediately before 1914 the Cabinet, consisting usually of nineteen ministers and meeting about forty times a year, confined itself to the overall supervision of government business, the planning of legislation and, when the occasion presented itself, the handling of diplomatic or Irish emergencies. Its contacts with administration lay through the depart-mental ministers who were its members, and through the Committee of Imperial Defence, a body comprised of ministers, civil servants and senior officers, which attempted with little success to co-ordinate defence planning. The CID, but not the Cabinet, had a secretariat, consisting of a secretary with a number of assistant secretaries seconded from the services.[2] Largely through the initiative of the CID secretary, Colonel Maurice Hankey, elaborate attempts had been made to prepare government departments for war, but this preparation had not included the Cabinet itself. The Cabinet as a whole began to take a positive interest in the details of war because of divisions over the actual decision to send an Expeditionary Force to France. The Cabinet, assisted at first by an *ad hoc* Council of War, met daily in the first weeks of the conflict, first to decide where to send the BEF, then to fret over its dispositions, supplies, reinforcements and movements until the fall of Antwerp in October 1914 and the establishment of a continuous trench line in France and Flanders in November. The same meetings kept under review both the developing diplomatic situation and what little was known of the impact of war at home.[3]

The first institutional development was Asquith's decision in November 1914 to set up the War Council to discuss future strategy, now that it was obvious that prewar plans had all been used up without bringing victory. The War Council consisted of Asquith, Lloyd George (Exchequer), Churchill (Admiralty), Grey (Foreign Office), Balfour (a member of the CID, though not in office), Kitchener (War Office), Fisher (First Sea Lord), Wolfe-Murray (CIGS), later joined by Crewe (India Office), Haldane (Lord Chancellor and formerly War Secretary), Arthur Wilson (retired admiral), McKenna (Home Office) and Harcourt (Colonial Office). As first understood, the War Council's scope was very limited. It was given no executive authority and, like the CID sub-committee which in form it was, it first reviewed systematically the military position in all theatres and the resources of the belligerents.[4] Then, on 13 January 1915, it agreed on a statement of strategic intentions for the new year, including an attack on the Western Front, an understanding that British troops might be used elsewhere in case of stalemate in the West and the planning of a naval attack on the Dardanelles. By now Balfour, included in the War Council as a leading member of the CID despite his position on the opposition front bench, was alarmed at the Council's responsibilities: 'It must, of course, be remembered that the Defence Committee (still less Committees of the Defence Committee) has no Executive power... Still, you have only got to look at the names I have mentioned to see that if the sub-committee is agreed, it is very unlikely that the Cabinet would think of disagreeing.'[5] The War Council became the natural forum for strategic debate, while the Cabinet had to deal with everything from diplomacy to the beer tax.[6] Moreover, the French refusal to support the Western offensive led to the reconvening of the War Council on 28 January to review alternatives. It approved a naval attack on the Dardanelles. It was the Dardanelles expedition, above all, which changed the role of the War Council by giving it real, if indistinct, responsibilities for the conduct of operations. As the hapless expedition was transformed from a naval attack to an amphibious operation, then to a holding campaign, Cabinet ministers who were members of the War Council discussed the innumerable problems it raised at any convenient occasion, whether the meeting was of the full Cabinet or of the War Council alone. Thus Balfour's fears were realised. Some questions were discussed in one body, some in the other, some in both;[7] some vital issues, such as the instructions given to Sir Ian Hamilton as commander of the expedition, were settled in informal meetings between Asquith, Kitchener and Churchill; and, as Churchill himself reminded the Dardanelles Commission later, 'you must not suppose that the written records and formal meetings embody the whole of the discussion between members of the War Council. On the contrary, we were always talking over the whole situation in twos and threes.'[8]

An amiable vagueness characterised the War Council's relationship with the Cabinet. Occasionally Asquith would remind the Council that it was discussing Cabinet matters; this seems to have been absent-mindedness rather than an attempt to usurp control.[9] The War Council's original brief included questions of war finance, diplomacy and the control of industry which all bore on strategy, but after February 1915 it never addressed them except in the context of the Dardanelles. Thus it failed to realise its potential as an advisory body. In its unintended role as an executive body it was even less successful, not simply because of its indeterminate responsibilities but because naval and military incompetence and secretiveness were compounded with the strategic obsessions of some civilian ministers into a perfect recipe for failure. Towards the end of Asquith's Liberal Cabinet the War Council met less frequently than the Cabinet and seemed likely soon to disappear from view.

After the Coalition Cabinet was formed in May 1915 the mantle of the War Council fell on the initially reluctant shoulders of the Dardanelles Committee. This body was modelled not on the CID but on a type of Cabinet committee familiar before the war, which would typically be set up to resolve a conflict over details and report to the full Cabinet, whereupon it would be dissolved. On this occasion many incoming Conservative ministers opposed the Dardanelles operation, and the committee consisted of five Conservatives and six former members of the War Council, who were asked to decide whether reinforcements should be sent. Had the Conservative sceptics prevailed, the operation, and hence the committee, would probably have been abandoned; but, swayed by their colleague Selborne, they agreed to send the reinforcements required. Recognising that the committee would stay in being to supervise future developments, Asquith asked Hankey to attend its meetings.[10] The Dardanelles Committee was larger than the War Council and consisted of ministers only, without serving officers. Its intended scope was confined to warfare and diplomacy in the Eastern Mediterranean, and general strategic analysis was neglected. It shared the worst features of the War Council: it was starved of information by the War Office (despite its explicit interest in tactical matters), and it met less frequently than the Cabinet. From the moment it recommended continuing the operation it found its decisions challenged frequently in Cabinet, and its command over policy was correspondingly slight.[11] In Cabinet Grey as Foreign Secretary could ignore its pressure for a forward diplomacy in the Balkans, while at the other end of the chain of command, field commanders made and bungled their own plans for the landing at Suvla Bay in August.

In the autumn of 1915 a political crisis temporarily improved the standing of the Dardanelles Committee. Conservative demands for con-scription, supported by Lloyd George and Churchill, came to a head just as proponents of 'Eastern' and 'Western' strategies were losing patience with one another. Civilian ministers had already lost patience with Kitchener, who had in August persuaded them to authorise yet another futile Western offensive and was in any case both secretive and manifestly incompetent in running the War Office. In late September it became clear that Bulgaria was about to join the Central Powers, thus threatening Serbia, opening the land route from Germany to Turkey and marking thereby the failure of Britain's Eastern Mediterranean strategy. So many ministers were so annoyed that the imminent collapse of the Cabinet was widely rumoured, but discontent was unfocused and Asquith was able to preserve unity and his own position by astute juggling of committtees. The first step was to insist on the appointment of a stronger CIGS, Sir Archibald Murray, who began to attend Dardanelles Committee meetings.[12] With the information which he, unlike Kitchener, was willing to provide, the committee broadened its discussion and, like the War Council earlier, was briefly an alternative forum for strategic debate between Cabinet ministers. The change was emphasised when it was renamed the 'War Committee' on 5 October, and confirmed when Asquith reconstructed it with a different and smaller membership on 5 November.[13]

The new War Committee, consisting at first of Asquith, Lloyd George, Balfour, Bonar Law and McKenna, was given responsibility for military operations in all theatres. It met frequently, and the CIGS and First Sea Lord were always present to give information. Hankey took its minutes in the form of 'Conclusions' and, on Asquith's instructions, circulated them to all Cabinet members as well as affected departments.[14] During its lifetime the division of labour between War Committee and Cabinet was clearer than it had ever been with the War Council or the Dardanelles Committee. Despite these advantages the War Committee, howsoever effective in routine war matters, was unable to take firm control of the war and conduct it with success. There were three reasons. First, the Cabinet retained a final authority, albeit exercised less often than against the Dardanelles Committee, which enabled it to delay action whenever a group of the excluded Cabinet members felt strongly enough that their colleagues on the War Committee had erred. The most notorious example was the delay in evacuating the Dardanelles in December 1915, which arose because whereas evacuationists were fortuitously in a majority on the War Committee, the Cabinet was more evenly balanced.[15] On most other operational issues the War Committee majority more accurately represented the views of the Cabinet as a whole. The War Committee's second handicap was the position accorded to Sir William Robertson, who succeeded Murray as CIGS in December 1915. By the 'Kitchener-Robertson Treaty', the Army Council speaking through the CIGS became the sole source of military advice to the Cabinet and War Committee. This had the heartily desired effect of reducing Kitchener to a cipher, but it left the War Committee at the mercy of Robertson's uncompromising 'Western' opinions. Robertson bluntly declined to discuss any other strategy than an attack in France, and moreover discontinued Murray's practice of giving a full military appreciation every week until Hankey persuaded him to restore it in a limited form in June 1916.[16] Thus, though the War Committee was able to be decisive, it was given no alternatives for the most important strategic decision which had to be made.

The third and most fundamental reason for the War Committee's failure, which was the occasion of the most complete failure of Cabinet government during the war, was the division within the Cabinet over conscription. To avoid a recurring Cabinet crisis, Asquith chose, after October 1915, to fight his rearguard action against conscriptionist ministers through a thicket of *ad hoc* committees. After a Cabinet committee on a National Registration Bill, convened to bridge a gap between Conservative conscriptionists and their Liberal opponents, had reported in June that a policy on industrial compulsion was needed,[17] a War Policy Committee was set up 'to ascertain and examine the resources of this country and our allies for the prosecution of the war up to the end of the year 1916'. In September the majority reported in favour of military conscription.[18] This only aggravated the difficulty but, as Hankey observed later, 'Mr Asquith scotched [the War Policy Committee] by reorganising the ill-conceived Dardanelles Committee into a better-balanced War Committee.'[19] The War Committee was indeed balanced between conscriptionists (Lloyd George and Bonar Law) and anti-conscriptionists (McKenna and Balfour): but it was never given the chance to discuss either conscription or the related issue of the size of the army because the conscriptionists' next move was to fight the matter out in Cabinet. Asquith compromised with the 'Derby scheme', and when that failed set up, at the beginning of January 1916, a 'Military-Finance Committee' consisting of himself, McKenna and Chamberlain to decide the proper size of the army; meanwhile a preliminary measure of conscription was put into force. By the time of the committee's second report, in April 1916, conscription fever was once more running high. At Lloyd George's insistence the report, concluding that further compulsion would not solve the immediate problem, was referred to the Army Council, which took the opportunity to withdraw a previous commitment to a sixty-seven division army and now asked to recruit to an indefinite size.[20] Yet another Cabinet committee, the Committee on the Size of the Army, was convened for a single sitting on 18 April to reconcile the Army Council with the Military-Finance Committee.[21] The compromise which emerged was rejected by the Commons, and on 29 April the Cabinet accepted a policy of general conscription. This was a long-awaited victory for the conscriptionists, which pre-empted all future decisions about strategy and the organisation of industry and agriculture. The struggle had moved the *locus* of decision away from the War Committee and even from the Cabinet, first into the hands of *ad hoc* committees and then to the Army Council. Asquith, and later Lloyd George, were to regret both the decision and the manner of its taking.

Subsequent criticism of Asquith's Cabinet and its 'war' committees has followed, with little variation, Carson's analysis made in justification of his resignation in November 1915.

> The whole question is one of concentrating responsibility, and if you have three or five men, I care not which, who are to be accountable to the Cabinet, or for whom the Cabinet is taking responsibility, you will only be back in the same system...I would much prefer to see the Rt. Hon. gentleman exercise the right he has of cutting his Cabinet down even to five or six from twenty-two, placing upon those five or six the whole burden of responsibility, and then the country would know that there was no divided responsibility, or anything of the kind.[22]

The same critics who level the charge of conflict of authority are reluctant to discriminate between the different 'war' committees, and hold up Lloyd George's War Cabinet as an example of the benefits of small size and undivided responsibility.[23] This is to miss the point of what was happening under Asquith, and to exaggerate, as we shall see, the integrity of Lloyd George's system. The essential change in Cabinet practice during 1915 and 1916 was in the attitude of the Cabinet towards the supervision of departmental activity, a change brought about by military failure and an unprecedented need to co-ordinate departmental action. For a while even the Cabinet had intervened in the affairs of the BEF. The War Council and the Dardanelles Committee, beginning with the large principles of strategy, descended more or less rapidly to detailed military and diplomatic co-ordination. The War Committee, meeting more frequently than either of them, was immersed in miscellaneous business from the beginning, which it handled by acting as a court of final decision between departments. This was not the business to which the Cabinet was accustomed or well adapted; the division of responsibilities, with few exceptions, represented a fruitful division of labour.

The real casualty of Asquith's regime was not decisiveness in the conduct of operations but decision-making in matters of broad war policy: whether to concentrate on land warfare in the West or to use sea-power and amphibious operations, and whether to raise a large conscript army or to leave a strong industrial labour force at home. The multiplicity of *ad hoc* committees gave opportunities for delay and in-fighting which were exploited by both sides in these controversies, and the authority both of the Cabinet and of the War Committee was thereby reduced. But, for all the condemnation of Asquith's lack of leadership, the real trouble was not administrative but political. The only way to get a straightforward decision out of the Coalition Cabinet would have been to sack the dissentient minority: in which event, which minority (Westerners, Gallipolist Easterners, Salonica Easterners, conscriptionists, anti-conscriptionists) was to go? Lloyd George found his own solution in late 1916, which was to dress up a purge as an administrative revolution.

After a political crisis of extreme complexity, in which the structure of the Cabinet had been a vehicle for disputation but never the central issue, Lloyd George became Prime Minister of a reconstructed Coalition on 6 December 1916.[24] His final bid had been for a new War Committee under his own chairmanship, answerable to the Cabinet but omnicompetent in the day-to-day running of the war; the manifest purpose was to give Lloyd George himself a free hand, untrammelled by Asquith and other leading Liberals. The War Cabinet which he thereupon established achieved the same end in a wholly different way. Consisting of five members, it nominally combined the functions and powers of the Cabinet and the War Committee. It met almost daily with Hankey as secretary, and its minutes had the force of instructions to departments. Departmental ministers, though retaining 'Cabinet rank', were invited only to discuss their departmental business except that Bonar Law, as Chancellor of the Exchequer, was in the War Cabinet and Balfour, as Foreign Secretary, was almost always present at its meetings. The four colleagues whom Lloyd George chose for the War Cabinet reflected the new balance of power rather than any aspiration to efficient administration. Bonar Law had to be in, as Conservative leader. Curzon stood for the old guard of Conservative ministers who had sold their loyalty to Asquith at a very late stage in the proceedings, and at a high price; like Bonar Law, he had contributed mightily to the confusion of the late regime. Henderson was the token Labour member. Only Milner, a political isolate included as the safer alternative to his unreliable and histrionic ally Carson, carried administrative credibility. None of these would be expected ever to persist in thwarting Lloyd George on war matters; this fact, with the exclusion of all other ministers from the central decision-making body, justifies Hankey's description of the new arrangements as a 'dictatorship in commission'.[25]

Propaganda and subsequent historical writing have suggested that the essence of the War Cabinet system was the concentration of final decision into the hands of a single small body, meeting frequently. In practice, though, many functions were hived off during 1917 and 1918, and in the struggle for effective economic and strategic direction the undivided authority of the War Cabinet was unobtrusively redivided. The first step was to delegate decisions to individual War Cabinet members, then to give them small *ad hoc* committees of officials and departmental ministers to help. Finally, standing committees, with War Cabinet members presiding, were established to co-ordinate policy between departments whose spheres of action regularly intersected: the most effective of these, the War Priorities Committee, is examined in more detail below. The most important departure from the principle of undivided authority, though, was the creation of inner committees of the War Cabinet to determine strategy. This was a practical recognition of the need to separate strategic planning from daily administration. Thus between December 1916 and December 1918 the War Cabinet itself gradually diminished in significance, while remaining the eponymous centre of a system of administration. Responsibility for various questions was transferred to standing committees, to inner groups, or even abroad to the Supreme War Council, set up at Versailles in October 1917. Early hopes that the War Cabinet would settle everything in daily meetings collapsed under the weight of routine business piled on it with devastating efficiency by Hankey's secretariat. The outcome was that the War Cabinet came to resemble more closely Asquith's War Committee, with the difference that its scope was larger and its authority clearer. Fundamental questions, which under Asquith had been lost in the toils of Cabinet disagreement, were either decided informally by Lloyd George or in various inner groupings; and conflict between these groupings and the War Cabinet was insignificant because there was no internal opposition to Lloyd George's leadership.

If Lloyd George had a single dominant motive in attacking Asquith's regime it was to strengthen the Cabinet's influence over the departments, both military and civilian. After creating the War Cabinet his next step was to create new departments: the Ministries of Food, Shipping and Labour, a department of National Service, and a new Air Board. Some of the departments, such as Labour, consolidated functions previously shared between departments; others, such as Shipping, provided a common service which had previously been 'co-ordinated' by a Cabinet committee. The machine thus created was inexperienced and unwieldy, and suffered from awkward duplication, such as that between Labour and National Service. It took Lloyd George and the War Cabinet some months to get a grip on it.

During 1917 the First Lord of the Admiralty (Carson), the Minister of Munitions (Addison), the Director General of National Service (Neville Chamberlain) and the Food Controller (Devonport) were all replaced (respectively by Eric Geddes, Churchill, Auckland Geddes and Rhondda). Changes at the Admiralty and the Ministry of Food were preceded by visitations: Lloyd George's day spent, with Hankey's help, in forcing the Admiralty to introduce convoys is well known,[26] but it is matched by the investigation of the Ministry of Food by Milner and Henderson, with the help of members of Lloyd George's own secretariat.[27] Both exercises brought pressure on departmental ministers which had no precedent in Asquith's Cabinet. The systematic supervision of groups of departments by individual ministers was never part of the War Cabinet's system, but the practice of remitting certain interdepartmental questions to War Cabinet members either alone or as chairmen of committees of other ministers began in early 1917.[28] Milner supervised preparation of the agricultural programme for 1917, collating needs for transport and other resources and presenting them to the War Cabinet, but even he was unable to prevent the War Office recruiting skilled agricultural labour.[29] Henderson was given some labour questions to settle, arising largely from the duplication of effort between the Ministry of Labour, the Director General of National Service and the labour departments of the Admiralty and the Ministry of Munitions, and he helped to initiate the Committee of Inquiry into Industrial Unrest.[30] G. N. Barnes, who succeeded him as Labour representative in the War Cabinet in August 1917, undertook similar commissions and was also responsible for pensions questions in 1918.[31] Curzon was overseer of Middle Eastern questions.[32] These ministers adopted the role of prefects sent to prevent squabbles among recalcitrant departments, and did not take major policy decisions unilaterally; in that sense their work was pure administration. The lack of a system at this level of administration is seen in the fact that many such questions were referred to the War Cabinet without pre-digestion, or allowed to drag on without intervention.[33] Whether acting as a body, or by delegation to individual members, the War Cabinet's principal and most time-consuming role was to act as the supreme court in a system of administration by adversary process.

The disorder and frustration of early 1917 were visited on the new War Cabinet, pushing high policy into the background. Some attempt was indeed made to retain full control in the hands of the War Cabinet by means of the 'A' series of meetings, which were a front line of defence against administrative details. These meetings were never attended by more than a very few outsiders, and freedom of discussion was the greater because the minutes were not circulated.[34] The War Cabinet, usually accompanied by Balfour, used the occasions to settle important, but usually short-term, problems such as the attitude to be adopted towards Austrian peace negotiations in December 1917.[35] Problems of longer-term significance were remitted to committees, of which two acquired a central role by virtue of their subject matter. The War Policy Committee, consisting of Lloyd George, Curzon, Milner and Smuts, was established in June 1917 because 'the War Cabinet considered that the time had come for reviewing our policy as a whole and forming fresh plans'.[36] Bonar Law, whose strategic philosophy was to trust the generals, was excluded and Henderson, the only other member of the War Cabinet, was absent in Russia. The War Policy Committee was thus an inner War Cabinet, convened to intimidate Robertson and Haig into changing their plans. The attempt failed. After a series of meetings at which a succession of ministers, officials and generals were interviewed, the committee decided on 25 June 1917 to accept Haig's plan, which became the costly Passchendaele offensive.[37] It reconvened in September to contemplate the failures of the campaign.

Over the winter a series of upheavals in the strategic direction of the war radically altered the War Cabinet's position. In November the Supreme War Council was established at Versailles, the first step towards a unified Allied command. It acted as a counterbalance to the influence of the General Staff in London, to the considerable advantage of Lloyd George, who found it increasingly difficult to rely on his War Cabinet colleagues in confrontations with the Staff.[38] In February 1918, in a row about the powers of the British military representative at Versailles, Robertson was dismissed as CIGS and replaced by Sir Henry Wilson. In April 1918 Derby, who had as Secretary of State for War consistently backed the generals, was sent to the Paris Embassy and replaced by Milner. Though Haig was not replaced, for lack of a plausible substitute, the changes cumulatively altered the relationship between Lloyd George and the army to the advantage of the former. The Prime Minister's influence was now exerted on the War Office through a like-minded colleague, and Wilson, though a 'Westerner', was more forthcoming and flexible than his predecessor. Moreover, the strategic situation was altered: instead of working for a frontal offensive as they had done for the past three years, Haig and his subordinate commanders were, after 21 March 1918, kept busy defending themselves against a vigorous and initially successful German assault. This coincidence of events and personalities enabled the Prime Minister to assume control of the fighting in France through a committee consisting of himself, Milner and Wilson, who met before each War Cabinet to discuss the progress of the battle and the prospects of taking an offensive either in France or elsewhere. Auckland Geddes, the Minister of National Service, also attended some of these conversations to advise on the availability of manpower. The 'X' committee survived the emergency and continued to supervise strategy until the armistice.[39]

The War Policy Committee and the 'X' committee took essential strategic decisions without reference to the War Cabinet. They were thus an important element in the diffusion of authority which took place in 1917 and 1918, and which gained further impetus from the appointment of a Home Affairs Committee, under Sir George Cave, in July 1918.[40] The HAC took responsibility for domestic legislation, which was falling into arrears because of pressure on the War Cabinet. Its early meetings were confined to a limited range of subjects, though, and it was only after the war, while War Cabinet members were involved in the Paris peace conference, that its scope substantially increased. Other matters of postwar policy were devolved to the Economic Offensive Committee, convened under Carson in September 1917 to plan the exclusion of Germany from postwar world markets, and succeeded by the Economic Defence and Development Committee.[41] Like the Home Affairs Committee, the latter body had a special place in the structure of Cabinet government because matters within its remit were passed to it automatically without initial reference to the Cabinet: but neither had the right, nor the opportunity, to commit the government over major matters of policy, nor did their decisions pre-empt the work of other committees.

Devolved Responsibility – Committees in the Cabinet Structure

Ad hoc sub-committees, convened to resolve a temporary difficulty and dissolved once their work was done, had long been a feature of the Cabinet. A new development during the war was the establishment of standing sub-committees of the Cabinet to co-ordinate departmental functions. Asquith's committees – for shipping, food production and air matters, all set up in 1916 – have understandably received a bad press.[42] They tended to fail because their powers over departments were ill defined and their scope not comprehensive. After December 1916 they were replaced by ministries with executive functions, but the committees' failure is not wholly explained by lack of executive authority. All three were priority committees, confronting departments which had come to expect an unchallenged control over the factors of production for their particular area of responsibility. The committees of 1916 faced obstreperous departments without the weapon of a clear war policy against which to test conflicting demands. The Cabinet could not agree on a manpower policy to cover the most important scarce resource, and no manpower committee was established; the other committees had no overall economic plan to which they could refer. Circumstances, rather than structures, increased the chance of failure.[43]

Lloyd George's priority committees were more impressive, both in structure and achievement. The Tonnage Priority Committee, under Curzon, allocated shipping space according to general priorities laid down by the War Cabinet, leaving it to the Shipping Controller to find the ships.[44] The War Priorities Committee, under Smuts, established in September 1917 as the Aerial Operations Committee, allocated resources between manufacturing departments. Its organisation was a model of devolved administrative responsibility. Below the main committee of ministers − Smuts, Eric Geddes (First Lord), Derby (War), Churchill (Munitions), Rothermere (Air), Auckland Geddes (National Service), Addison (Reconstruction) and Stanley (Board of Trade) − a number of sub-committees dealt with broad groups of resources. Below this tier sixteen allocation sub-committees dealt with particular commodities. The whole was held together by a special secretariat, under Colonel F. G. Byrne from the Ministry of Munitions, separate from the War Cabinet secretariat and consisting of officers with technical and supply experience.[45] Under this system difficulties in the Allocations Sub-Committees were referred upwards to the second tier of committees, usually to the permanent (or General Services) sub-committee, which was staffed by officials. Disputes in the second tier were referred to the full committee of ministers.

The War Priorities Committee was manifestly successful, though some qualification must be made to the contented conclusion of its report 'that the result of the committee's activities has been to obtain many of the advantages which are claimed for a single supply department'. It achieved its success by 'bringing competing departments into physical contact' [sic],[46] and thus informing each department of the true state of resources and the necessity for give and take. This was not always an easy business. From his appointment as Minister of Munitions Churchill had battled against the Admiralty's claim to 'a super priority upon all supplies'.[47] The Aerial Operations Committee had been set up to allocate supplies such as oxygen which were in contention between the two departments, and the War Priorities Committee, once established, had to contain the furious row between Churchill and Eric Geddes over the Admiralty's manufacturing operations.[48] Geddes's brother Auckland, at the Ministry of National Service, fought off the attempt to include labour in the committee's remit, and won Smuts's backing.[49] In May 1918, when a permanent Labour Sub-Committee was finally established, he pressed unsuccessfully for it to be responsible to a separate committee of ministers.[50] Throughout its life the committee took a minimalist view of its responsibilities, ordaining that its Allocation Sub-Committees should not intervene if supplies of a commodity were adequate, and should ask departments to issue control orders if they were not, only intervening if departmental action was not successful.[51]

During 1918 the committee's practices changed, Byrne wrote to Smuts on 5 March 1918:

> At first the cases referred to the War Priorities Committee were important and moderately numerous. Many of its decisions were, however, appealed against and in most of these cases they were either reversed by the committee itself or by the War Cabinet on reference to them. By degrees the number of important matters referred for consideration to the War Priorities Committee has fallen off and the present situation is that the committee are not performing in any sense the duties originally assigned to them.[52]

Byrne tentatively suggested the creation of a Ministry of Priority to co-ordinate the allocation sub-committees, whose success he did not deny: but his alternative suggestion of strengthening the direction of the War Policy Committee was more confident, and in retrospect more plausible. The War Priorities Committee was successful precisely because it could refer its most contentious problems upwards, to the War Cabinet. The priority to be accorded to shipbuilding, for example, depended on war policy which was more than the departmental concern of the ministries represented on the committee. On lesser administrative matters, it steered delicately between obstacles. Should control of labour be the responsibility of the users (Munitions, the Admiralty) or of a monopoly 'supplier' (National Service)? There were compelling arguments for both sides, founded in the experience of 1915 to 1917; the solution finally reached gave control of labour to the supplier who had comprehensive information about availability, under the supervision of a committee upon which the users were equally represented. This delegation of the War Cabinet's 'supreme court' function had undeniable advantages over the creation of a new department, whose conflicts with other departments would necessarily have had to be referred to the War Cabinet itself.

The Cabinet Secretariat

The development of the secretariat of the CID into a secretariat for the Cabinet and its committees was closely related to Hankey's role as a strategic adviser to the two wartime Prime Ministers. The CID itself was redundant after the outbreak of war, and its assistant secretaries were allowed to rejoin their units. The War Council, in form a CID sub-committee, gave the secretariat new life. Hankey took minutes at the meetings, and papers were circulated according to CID practice. Subsequently Hankey was secretary of the Dardanelles and War Committees and the more important *ad hoc* Cabinet committees, as well as the Air

Board, while his assistants acted for other committees. Thus under Asquith the CID system was put at the Cabinet's disposal, though the Cabinet itself still lacked a secretary, or minutes apart from Asquith's customary letters to the King.[53] The principal departure from CID practice was in the circulation of the minutes of the 'war' committees.

The minutes of the War Council were kept in the form of compressed debates, with each speaker's contribution noted. The main record, hand-written by Hankey or an assistant, was never circulated, but 'conclusions' were extracted and sent to the departments concerned. The practice of the Dardanelles Committee was similar; the conclusions of both Council and Committee were also reported orally in Cabinet meetings. Asquith initiated a major change by having the 'conclusions' of the War Committee circulated for information to all Cabinet ministers.[54] As a method of conducting business even the War Committee practice had drawbacks: the full records, which might be needed subsequently to elucidate the reasoning behind decisions, all too frequently represented with chilling accuracy the inconsequential discussions which governed action, and were in any case not checked by participants. The 'conclusions' gave minimal information and did not cover all the subjects discussed at a meeting. Hankey subsequently made many apologies for the inadequacy of the system; but he gave no reason, except the preservation of secrecy, why the CID practice of confining the record to a fully reasoned conclusion, circulated for checking and then issued in full, was not adopted imme-diately for the War Council and its successors.

The secretarial demands of the Cabinet's burgeoning committee struc-ture, including the preparation of agenda and the circulation of memoranda as well as the handling of minutes, made a substantial burden of work for Hankey and his assistants. Nevertheless Hankey found, and quickly seized, increasing opportunities to make recommendations for policy, bringing his growing strategic experience to bear through his access to the Prime Minister. His path to influence lay through the Dardanelles. On Christmas Day 1914, after submitting much miscellaneous advice in previous months, he had 'an uncontrollable desire to put on paper an appreciation of the war situation as a whole, which took the whole day'. Remarking on the *impasse* on the Western Front he suggested a number of solutions, some depending on gadgetry, some on peripheral warfare. Though undiscrimi-nating in its strategic suggestions, the document, known by Hankey as the Boxing Day Memorandum, placed him firmly in the centre of strategic discussions preceding the Dardanelles expedition. Circulated to members of the War Council in early January, it coincided with pressure from Lloyd George and Churchill for attacks on Germany's weaker allies.[55]

When the Dardanelles expedition was approved Hankey could at last apply the accumulated expertise of the CID secretariat to the conduct of war. Between January and July he submitted ten documents to Asquith about the Dardanelles, dealing in increasing detail with the military and naval problems posed by the expedition. In the absence of appreciations from the Admiralty or the War Office, Hankey's papers came to stand by default as the only expert summaries of the campaign, though he continually pressed the Cabinet to insist on full information and advice from the service departments.[56] On 16 July 1915 Asquith sent him, in place of Churchill, to inspect the expedition. His reports, revealing to the Dardanelles Committee much that had been concealed by the Admiralty and the War Office, led ministers to give him the new responsibility of 'advising the War Office and the Admiralty respectively on the operations at the Dardanelles'.[57] Hankey thereupon reconstructed the CID secretariat so that Col. E. D. Swinton became his full-time understudy, accompanying him to Dardanelles Committee meetings to take the minutes, while each assistant secretary took an area of responsibility within which he collated information reaching the secretariat.[58] This shifting of the major clerical burden of his work marked the transformation of Hankey's status to that of a confidential adviser to the Cabinet, and especially to the Prime Minister.

Hankey's advocacy of the Dardanelles sprang from his background, first as a Marine officer and then as a protégé of Admiral Ottley in the prewar CID secretariat. He had learned to believe that the navy was Britain's ultimate weapon, to be used to preserve her economy during the war, to blockade the enemy and to support attacks on vital points on the periphery of enemy territory.[59] The same 'navalism' set him against conscription and the use of mass armies on the Western Front – a view which endeared him to Asquith when the conscription crisis intensified after October 1915. Hankey wrote papers against conscription and criticised the Kitchener-Robertson treaty, which, he claimed, 'would raise the CIGS to a position out of all proportion to the importance of our military, as compared to our naval and financial effort in this war'.[60] As secretary of the Military-Finance Committee he negotiated indefatigably to reduce the manpower demands of the War Office,[61] and in May 1916 he undertook a spirited campaign to extract more information for the War Committee from the General Staff.[62] While Hankey's views on conscription won him Asquith's confidence, his criticism of the Western Front strategy adopted by the General Staff made him equally welcome as a *confidant* and adviser when Lloyd George became Prime Minister. Unlike Lloyd George, Hankey never deviated from his 'Eastern' convictions. His Boxing Day memorandum was followed by another general review of the war in June 1915 urging postponement of the attack in the West.[63] Later in the year he argued that conscription was only necessary because of the army's incorrigible squandering of troops in France and Flanders.[64] In the summer of 1916 he reluctantly took the position that the Western offensive, once begun, should be finished, but he was never fully converted to a 'Western' view, and the failure of the 1916 offensive led him to call in November for a war for limited objectives.[65]

At the Paris conference of 16–17 November 1916, when the politicians accepted the generals' plan to repeat in 1917 the offensive which had just failed so expensively, Hankey had long conversations with Lloyd George about the machinery of government in England. Back in London on 21 November he met him again to discuss plans for a reconstructed War Committee.[66] Hankey's first loyalty was to Asquith, and he tried to conciliate between Asquith and Lloyd George, putting forward an alternative scheme of twin war and civil committees to satisfy both Lloyd George and McKenna.[67] Nevertheless his anti-Western views and his manifest loyalty to the office of Prime Minister rather than the man enabled him to move easily into Lloyd George's confidence after the change of government, and he was able thereby to add to his own influence and consolidate the position of his secretariat.

Within days of the establishment of the War Cabinet Hankey set out rules of procedure which remained in force with little amendment until October 1919, and turned the CID secretariat into a body serving the whole Cabinet, which in due course became the Cabinet Office.[68] Procedure was modelled closely on that of the CID. Minutes, cast in the form of conclusions, were distributed in full to War Cabinet members and the heads of principal departments, while other ministers received extracts relating to their own departments' work. Such extracts had the force of instructions. The agenda was determined by the Prime Minister, though subordinate ministers could raise questions by notifying the secretary, who kept a priority list of matters for discussion. The War Committee had followed Cabinet instructions or its own unguided inclinations in shaping its discussions. By contrast, the new regime ensured not only a steady flow of decisions outwards but also a steady flow of problems inwards; it thus facilitated the 'adversary process' of government which was a major defect of the new system.

With Lloyd George's approval Hankey also increased the flow of circulating information. The Admiralty, War Office and Foreign Office already circulated their more important telegrams and reports. Other departments were asked for weekly or fortnightly reports, and two weekly digests of foreign affairs were instituted, to be edited within the Cabinet secretariat.[69] The CID memoranda series was adapted for the circulation of all this material. These measures represented an enormous organisational achievement, justifying the large expansion of the staff of the secretariat which soon took place; but although the volume of information circulating was far greater than before December 1916 no attempt was made to discipline it, for example by insisting on the circulation of a document before War Cabinet discussion. Moreover, the forty or so routine reports produced to order every month (out of about 200 papers circulated) tended to give solemn attention to such matters as the Board of Agriculture's fifth class for travelling instructors in fruit and vegetable bottling.[70]

Two expedients were adopted to predigest information for War Cabinet members. Lloyd George acquired a private secretariat — his 'Garden Suburb' — at the behest of some of his junior supporters who were disappointed of office. Contrary to intention, it had little working contact with Hankey's secretariat. Its influence was considerable, especially in organising Irish policy after March 1917, in shipbuilding policy and in the genesis of the Corn Production Act, and it helped to maintain a liberal and progressive atmosphere around Lloyd George.[71] Its administrative impact during the war was much greater than that of the other attempt at predigestion, the 'ideas' branch of the War Cabinet secretariat. In taking up this suggestion, made by Thomas Jones, a Welsh academic and civil servant, it seemed at first that Hankey was hoping to create for the War Cabinet secretariat the position of expert critic to which the CID secretariat had at first aspired within its limited field.[72] The institution which resulted did not live up to these aspirations.

Hankey himself was responsible for the limits on the secretariat's achievements. Since his appointment in 1912 he had been preoccupied with the neutrality of his office, and he insisted from the first not only that the new secretariat was 'neither an Intelligence Department nor a General Staff', but also that 'Assistant Secretaries are particularly enjoined to bear in mind that it is no part of their duties to do work which pertains to the Departments'.[73] Jones himself, who had expected to be a 'fluid person' moving among ministers, was soon absorbed into the routine of War Cabinet business and the control of circulated paper which occupied the former CID secretaries whom Hankey had kept on to keep the machinery running. His emergence as a confidential adviser to Prime Ministers had to wait until after the war.[74] G. M. Young, the historian who joined the 'ideas' branch as Henderson's nominee, spent only four months at work in the secretariat before going to Russia with Henderson. He then fell sick, and did not return to the secretariat before his appointment in October 1917 as joint permanent secretary to the Ministry of Reconstruction. The other two 'ideas' men, both MPs, suffered more acutely from Hankey's denying ordinance. Leopold Amery, an ardent Milnerite, entered the secretariat as a substitute for junior office. After a brief moment of glory as Hankey's chief assistant at the Imperial War Conference, where he was able to insinuate into a sub-committee report the Milnerite notions of closer imperial union and a strategically coherent empire, he lost sympathy with the more routine aspects of the secretariat's work. He suggested to Hankey that he was 'not in any sense an official, but ... a junior member of the government in the same general position as an Under-Secretary'.[75] Hankey, who did not altogether trust him, readily agreed that Amery should be gently separated from the secretariat's main work. His papers were no longer circulated in the official series, and though he briefly held positions as secretary to the Economic Offensive Committee, liaison officer at the Supreme War Council at Versailles and minutes secretary to the 'X' committee, he was more occupied with unofficial political lobbying than in using his official positions to effect change.[76] At the end of 1918 he noted: 'I have been chafing at the collar most of the time, making work where I could, hanging about in attendance, worrying people with my ideas, but without a real definite piece of work to do.'[77] Sir Mark Sykes, equally ambitious for influence if not for office, used the secretariat as an office-desk from which to advance his project of British hegemony in the Middle East. In April 1917 he encompassed his own appointment as 'Chief Political Officer' to the Middle East expeditionary force and had a limited success in renegotiating the Sykes-Picot agreement for which he had been responsible when on the War Office staff.[78] On his return to England he condemned the insensitivity of the 'gnome imperialists' – he meant Milner and Curzon – whose ultimate policy was acceptable but who trampled on Allied and anti-imperialist feelings.[79] Finding no opportunity in the War Cabinet secretariat to cut back the 'crop of weeds' of suspicion and rivalry in the Middle East, he successfully applied for a transfer to the Foreign Office in January 1918.[80]

Hankey did not extend to himself the restrictions he placed on his subordinates. He continued to write general appreciations of the war situation and to give them first to Lloyd George, then to other War Cabinet members. But this was no more than his subordinates could do if they wished; the key to Hankey's position as a confidential adviser was that he accompanied Lloyd George to every meeting at home and abroad, saw him more frequently than any of the Prime Minister's War Cabinet colleagues and kept the minutes of all the most secret meetings. His knowledge of the problems of the war was consequently vast, and his opinions on them, at least during 1917, were extremely attractive to Lloyd George. His first contribution to the policy of the new government was a summary for the War Cabinet of the strategic problems facing it in 1917. Insisting that 'the maintenance of seapower is the first consideration' and that it was essential to reduce dependence on imports, he concluded that the mainly military effort would have to be made in the Western Front: 'I think that an offensive is absolutely unavoidable, although I have still the gravest doubts whether we can smash the German army by means of it.'[81] Lloyd George's respect for his advice had been evident before the change of government: the similarity of this memorandum to Lloyd George's own preferences, together with the antagonism Lloyd George felt for Robertson, left Hankey as the leading official with strategic expertise to whom the Prime Minister could readily turn. Hankey thus acquired an influence over the direction of strategic thought in 1917 which even his biographer understates.

Hankey was always present to sustain Lloyd George's awareness of the country's economic needs, while moderating any tendency to launch an onslaught on Robertson and Haig. He mediated at the Calais Conference on 27 February 1917, when Lloyd George sought to subordinate Haig to the French Commander-in-Chief, General Nivelle.[82] He persuaded Lloyd George against Haig's dismissal when Nivelle requested it in March, arguing that Haig's plan of an offensive in Flanders to attack the German submarine bases was fundamentally sound, and better than Nivelle's schemes.[83] His affection for the Flanders offensive was long-lived, and may seem perverse in an avowed 'Easterner'; but Hankey was convinced that since a Western Front attack was Robertson's policy 'it is better to have a second-best plan, which the army have their hearts in, and conform all your policy and strategy thereto, than a more perfect plan which those who have to carry it out don't believe in'.[84] He also believed that it was possible to conduct a Western attack in a way which would limit casualties. In retrospect the latter belief seems the weak point in his position, and significantly it was over this matter that the decisive split between Hankey's thinking and that of Lloyd George occurred in late 1917. During the difficult month when Lloyd George feared the loss of Cabinet support in his struggle to control the generals, he discussed at length with Hankey his expectations for 1918. Hankey argued that 1918 would be the decisive year, when Britain's economic effort would weaken Germany to the point that a vigorous attack in the west would bring victory. Lloyd George, more pessimistic and looking further into the future, insisted that Germany was not yet defeated by economic means and probably could not be, that an attack in 1918 would destroy the British army, and that the likely outcome would be that Britain would emerge at the end of the war without the military force to impose her will at the peace conference. He therefore proposed to conserve British forces for the 1919 campaign.[85]

After this conversation there was no break in confidence between Lloyd George and Hankey, but Hankey, in essence, subordinated his strategic views to those of Lloyd George, and contributed no further independent policy recommendations.[86] He was not for that reason any the less useful to the Prime Minister as a *confidant* and mediator, and his supreme organisational talents were brought to bear on the secretariat of the Supreme War Council and later at the Paris Peace Conference, but his contribution of independent expertise was less and less important.[87] In Paris he played a smaller part in the substance of diplomacy than Philip Kerr, Lloyd George's private secretary; and in peacetime his interests and knowledge were to be of less use to Lloyd George and succeeding Prime Ministers than the more civilian talents of Tom Jones, who had no scope at all during the war.[88]

During the war the secretariat brought to a high pitch of efficiency the circulation, preservation and indexing of minutes and papers; and as secretary Hankey won a position of influence through his close personal relationship with Lloyd George. The essential routine of the Cabinet Office has since continued to be that laid down in the last weeks of 1916. Hankey is to be credited with the creation of the Cabinet Office and its spirited and successful defence against Warren Fisher and the Treasury in 1922.[89] Yet the body he set up during the war was but a weak and clumsy instrument, particularly in its advisory function, compared with the Cabinet Office of later years. This is partly to be explained by Hankey's service background and the secretariat's inheritance from the CID. It was a body of soldiers, sailors and irregular civilians, without civil servants to link it with bonds of sympathy to official Whitehall: Amery, for example, once described the officials with whom he worked on committees as 'these old departmental golliwogs'.[90] Very few civil servants were to enter the Cabinet Office before the 1930s.[91] Independence itself might have been useful, but Hankey's restrictive attitude to the advisory work of his subordinates turned independence into isolation. The influence of the Cabinet secretary was inevitably a subtle matter, dependent as it was on the personal relationship between the secretary and the Prime Minister; but the institutional isolation of the Cabinet Office from Whitehall, born of wartime conditions, aggravated the degree to which Hankey was a floating kidney in the body of government, giving advice based on his own experience and prejudice rather than on a broad understanding of government or a systematic access to departmental knowledge. This analysis would probably not have worried Hankey if he had been confronted with it in 1918, but it is a serious qualification to the conventionally favourable view of his contribution to the development of Cabinet machinery.

Epilogue

Peace and a General Election raised expectations that some familiar form of Cabinet would return. Many departmental ministers had regretted during the war that they had little opportunity to comment on the general line of policy, and in response Lloyd George had made a practice of seeing his Liberal and Conservative ministerial colleagues in alternate weeks to explain the war situation and the War Cabinet's intentions.[92] In the event the War Cabinet remained in being until October 1919, meeting less frequently than before and occasionally meeting in Paris when Lloyd George was at the Peace Conference. Lloyd George's fear that the Coalition was losing political coherence seems to have prompted the return of a larger Cabinet in October, with a membership of twenty to accommodate the personal ambitions of important figures. Hankey and his secretariat continued to serve; but he attended the Cabinet without assistants and the conclusions, kept in a more abbreviated form than during the war, were given a more limited circulation. Full dress Cabinets were interspersed with conferences of ministers, selected according to the subject matter under discussion.[93] These conferences, besides enabling Lloyd George to exclude awkward colleagues, served to maintain the Cabinet's control over the detailed execution of policy. Thus the extension of Cabinet activity initiated haltingly by the War Council in 1915 was sustained, albeit in a very different form, during the peace.

The new system, exploiting the opportunities presented by the Cabinet secretariat and reflecting new ambitions for the Cabinet inspired by wartime experience, offered new scope for the exercise of power by the Prime Minister, who controlled the personnel and agenda of both Cabinet and conferences. Moreover, the survival of the Home Affairs Committee, which worked up legislation on domestic matters, perceptibly reduced the access of those ministers who were not members to decision-making on the committee's subjects. This potential imbalance of power was exploited fully by Lloyd George, less so by his immediate successors, who substituted more formal Cabinet committees for the conferences and were in any case less anxious than Lloyd George to pursue an active policy in all directions. Nonetheless, it pointed the way for developments in the more distant future, when serious doubts could be entertained in the 1970s that the Cabinet, as a single supreme executive body, any longer existed.[94] In this respect, as in his reliance during the war period on an organised personal staff, Lloyd George was in advance of his time. The war showed, to those who were prepared to see, that increasing state intervention demanded increasing administrative participation by the Cabinet, which in turn could only be achieved by dividing responsibility among subordinate Cabinet committees. The Cabinet itself necessarily remained in being as a political committee, more important in peace than in war because the will to victory was no longer there to impart coherence and discipline to the government. But the Cabinet's unity as an executive body was destroyed by the First World War which, by foreshadowing the demands of an interventionist government, stimulated the development of alternative means of executive control.

In the conventional historiography of the First World War, the undue generosity shown to Asquith in political matters has been matched by an unduly high opinion of Lloyd George's administrative achievements.[95] Lloyd George's government, indeed, guided the nation to victory, but most of the hard decisions, as on conscription and the direction of industry, had been taken before December 1916, and the two major decisions of principle taken by the War Cabinet system – on the 1917 offensive and on Irish conscription – were both bungled. Economic choices were starker as the war went on, and decisions easier to take; nevertheless the efficacy of the new departmental apparatus of early 1917, subject to duplication and personal rivalry, must be treated as doubtful. Most important, the system of Cabinet government adopted by Lloyd George was, as is argued above, not a monolithic dictatorship despite its imposing structure of authority and the bureaucratic trappings of the War Cabinet secretariat. The argument for dividing the war sharply at December 1916 and comparing the two periods to Asquith's detriment is therefore weakened. Both Asquith and Lloyd George grappled with the problem of combining long-term planning and short-term administration within a single structure. Their solutions tended to converge, as became obvious when the War Cabinet succumbed to the pressure of routine business and the War Policy Committee was set up. The essential difference between Lloyd Georgian and Asquithian Cabinet government was political, not administrative: Lloyd George, unlike Asquith, was able to rid himself of significant internal opposition.

The co-ordination of departmental action, which the First World War made into a Cabinet responsibility, has in modern times become an essential function of government. The wartime solutions, though, did not provide an adequate pattern for future developments because they were developed at too high a level. The appointment of a small team of senior ministers to sit *de die in diem* adjudicating departmental conflicts, as seen in the War Committee and the War Cabinet, placed a huge burden on the ministers concerned which was aggravated by the standing committees and *ad hoc* investigations of the War Cabinet period. The War Cabinet with its efficient secretariat and comprehensive scope positively attracted work upwards, to such an extent that even in 1917 Hankey began to press departments to settle more matters between themselves.[96] Direct communication between departments is now an established Whitehall practice; but it depends on recent institutions and conventions, such as standing interdepartmental official committees, official committees to 'shadow' Cabinet committees, the 'open structure' of senior appointments which now gives senior officials experience of more than one area of government, the common view imposed (arguably at an unacceptable cost) by the Treasury, and above all the assumption that a civil servant's duty is to smooth the path of his minister's wishes by resolving difficulties early with his counterparts in other departments. Since none of these was present except in the most rudimentary form in the Great War, not least because so many departmental officials were 'men of push and go' without official experience, the Cabinet and the Cabinet secretariat undertook the huge task of remedying the imperfections in the civil service. It is a tribute to the industry of those involved that the attempt was sustained so long, but it could never have been a lasting solution. The concluding judgement on the Great War period in Cabinet development must be that it broke down resistance to system and positive action, but offered only an uncertain guide to the future.

Notes: Chapter 3

1 John P. Mackintosh, *The British Cabinet*, 3rd edn (London: Stevens, 1977), p. 4.

2 Nicholas D'Ombrain, *War Machinery and High Policy, Defence Administration in Peacetime Britain* (London: Oxford University Press, 1973); cf. F. A. Johnson, *Defence by Committee* (London: Oxford University Press, 1960) reviewed by John P. Mackintosh in *English Historical Review*, vol. CCIV (1962).

3 Records of Cabinet meetings are in Asquith's letters to the King, CAB 41/35, Cabinet Papers, Public Record Office, London. Council of War, 5 and 6 August 1914, CAB 22/1; cf. John Gooch, *The Plans of War* (London: Routledge & Kegan Paul, 1974), p. 301.

4 Minutes in CAB 22/1.

5 Balfour to Lansdowne, 9 January 1915, cited in Cameron Hazlehurst, *Politicians at War* (London: Cape, 1971), pp. 160–1.

6 The War Council, for example, was the object of Lloyd George's 'Suggestions as to the military position', 1 January 1915, CAB 24/1. For the subjects of Cabinet discussions see Asquith's letters to the King in CAB 41/36.

7 The double discussion included both Dardanelles issues (in Cabinet, 20 January, 9 March and 27 March 1915, CAB 41/36; and in War Council on 9, 16, 19, 24, 26 February and 3, 10 March 1915, CAB 22/1) and others such as drink control at munitions factories (in Cabinet, 24 February 1915, CAB 41/36; in War Council, 19 March 1915, CAB 22/1).

8 Hankey, *The Supreme Command*, 2 vols (London: Allen & Unwin, 1961), Vol. I, p. 291; Churchill's evidence to the Dardanelles Commission, 25 September 1916, CAB 19/28, p. 39.

9 e.g. in a discussion of war material on 3 March 1915 Asquith remarked that the 'Chancellor of the Exchequer's Bill ... was rather a question for the Cabinet'. CAB 22/1.

10 Hankey, *Supreme Command*, Vol. I, pp. 336–40. In the Minutes, printed for the Dardanelles Commission in 1916, Hankey tendentiously added that 'The War Council was continued as the Dardanelles Committee of the Cabinet.' CAB 22/2. The Committee consisted of Asquith, Grey, Crewe, Lloyd George, Churchill, Kitchener, Bonar Law, Balfour, Lansdowne, Curzon and Selborne. Carson joined in August 1915.

11 e.g. on 18 June 1915 over reinforcements, Asquith to the King, 19 June 1915, CAB 41/36/27, and again on 30 June over negotiations with the Balkan States, Asquith to the King, 1 July 1915, CAB 41/36/30.

12 Called for by the Cabinet on 22 September 1915, CAB 41/36/45. cf. Gooch, *Plans of War*, pp. 317–18.

13 Asquith tried on 22 September to set up a structure of two committees – a 'War Committee' and a committee on domestic questions – but this was resisted by his colleagues and then ignored. See CAB 41/36/45; Roy Jenkins, *Asquith* (London: Fontana, 1964), pp. 420–1; Mackintosh, *The British Cabinet*, p. 355. A month later, in different political circumstances, a strengthened War Committee emerged after a unanimous demand from the Cabinet. Mackintosh, p. 355.

14 War Committee Minutes, with relevant documents attached to the record of each meeting, are in CAB 42/5–26. Extracts, known as *Acta*, are reprinted in CAB 22/3.

15 See Asquith to the King, 24 November 1915, CAB 41/36/52; 7 December 1915, CAB 41/36/54.

16   Minutes of War Committee, 28 December 1915, CAB 42/6/14. The appreciation was cut down to a 'summary'. Hankey to Robertson, 23 May 1916, CAB 17/150.

17   Asquith to the King, 5 June 1915, CAB 41/36/24, 9 June 1915, CAB 41/36/25, 19 June 1915, CAB 41/36/27, 24 June 1915, CAB 41/36/29.

18   'Report of the War Policy Committee', 7 September 1915, CAB 27/2.

19   Memorandum by Hankey, 23 November 1948, cited in Stephen Roskill, *Hankey: Man of Secrets*, 3 vols (London: Collins, 1970–4), Vol. I, p. 233.

20   Asquith to the King, 1 January 1916, CAB 41/37/1; 'Second Report of the Committee on the Co-ordination of Military and Financial Effort', 13 April 1916, CAB 27/4; Roskill, *Hankey*, Vol. I, p. 264; Trevor Wilson (ed.), *The Political Diaries of C. P. Scott, 1911–1928.* (London: Collins, 1970), pp. 197–200; A. J. P. Taylor (ed.), *Lloyd George: A Diary by Frances Stevenson* (London: Hutchinson, 1971), pp. 105–6; Army Council document in Hankey to Asquith, 17 April 1916, CAB 17/159.

21   'Report of the Committee on the Size of the Army', 18 April 1916, CAB 27/3.

22   75 *H.C. Deb.* 5 s., 2 November 1915, cols 532–5.

23   e.g. John Ehrman, *Cabinet Government in War* (Cambridge: Cambridge University Press, 1958), p. 60 and *passim.*

24   See Lord Beaverbrook, *Politicians and the War*, 2nd edn (London: Collins, 1960), pp. 328–545; J. McEwen, 'The struggle for mastery in Britain: Lloyd George versus Asquith, December 1916', *Journal of British Studies* vol. XX, no. 1 (1980), pp. 131–56; Cameron Hazlehurst, 'The conspiracy myth', in Martin Gilbert (ed.), *Lloyd George* (London: Prentice-Hall, 1967); P. A. Lockwood, 'Milner's entry into the War Cabinet, December 1916', *Historical Journal*, vol. VII (1964), pp. 120–34; K. O. Morgan, 'Lloyd George's premiership', ibid., vol. XIII (1970), pp. 130–57.

25   As a chapter heading in *Supreme Command*, Vol. II.

26   David Lloyd George, *War Memoirs*, 2 vols (London: Odhams Press, 1938), Vol. I, pp. 684–93; Roskill, *Hankey*, Vol. I, pp. 381–5.

27   John Turner, *Lloyd George's Secretariat* (Cambridge: Cambridge University Press, 1980), pp. 48, 54–7.

28   This began with a scheme condescendingly designed by Hankey and G. M. Young to keep Henderson 'amused'. Roskill, *Hankey*, Vol. I, p. 352; cf. Henderson to Lloyd George, 13 January 1917, F/27/3/6, Lloyd George Papers, House of Lords Record Office, London.

29   In despair, he asked Derby 'to meet me over this, which I ask under the authority given to me by the War Cabinet'. Milner to Derby, 12 June 1917, Box 45, Milner Papers, Bodleian Library, Oxford.

30   See C. Addison to Lloyd George, 26 May 1917, Box 54, Addison Papers, Bodleian Library; memoranda by Henderson, 22 May 1917, CAB 24/13.

31   See e.g. G. N. Barnes, 'Government departments dealing with labour', 12 April 1918, ADM 116/1608, Admiralty Papers, PRO. cf. Hankey to Beveridge, 13 February 1940, CAB 63/159.

32   This responsibility was essentially subsumed in his chairmanship of the Eastern Committee (records in CAB 27/22–39) which was descended from an earlier Mesopotamia Administration Committee via the Middle Eastern Committee.

33   e.g. the dispute over guaranteed prices for food between the Board of Agriculture and the Food Ministry. Memorandum by the President of the Board of Agriculture, 14 May 1918, CAB 24/51.

34   There were fifteen meetings in this series, to be found in CAB 23/16. To prevent inquiries from ministers who had not received War Cabinet Minutes, Hankey gave each special meeting the number of the previous ordinary meeting, distinguished by the suffix 'A'.

35   e.g. War Cabinet 311A, 2 January 1918, CAB 23/16.
36   Report and Minutes of the War Policy Committee, 1917, CAB 27/6. The committee was set up in WC 159A, 8 June 1917.
37   11th meeting of the War Policy Committee, 25 June 1917, CAB 27/6.
38   Lloyd George, *War Memoirs*, Vol. II, p. 1371; Hankey, *Supreme Command*, Vol. II, pp. 703–7.
39   Thirty-two meetings were held between 15 May and 25 October 1918. Minutes in CAB 23/17.
40   Minutes and papers in CAB 26/1.
41   Minutes and papers of EDDC in CAB 27/44; Minutes and papers of EOC in CAB 27/15.
42   e.g. Ehrman, *Cabinet Government*, p. 70.
43   See the discussions of the administrative problem generated by intervention in W. K. Hancock and M. M. Gowing, *British War Economy* (Cambridge: Cambridge University Press, 1949), pp. 3–40; E. M. H. Lloyd, *Experiments in State Control* (Oxford: Clarendon Press, 1924), *passim*; S. J. Hurwitz, *State Intervention in Great Britain* (New York: Columbia University Press, 1949), *passim*; and Turner, *Lloyd George's Secretariat*, pp. 27–45.
44   Minutes and papers in CAB 27/20.
45   Minutes and papers in CAB 21/118/1–3. Ormsby-Gore, the War Cabinet Assistant Secretary at first appointed to the committee, was withdrawn on the grounds that the work was too specialised.
46   Report of the War Priorities Committee, n.d. (late 1918), CAB 40/117.
47   Martin Gilbert, *Winston S. Churchill, 1917–1922* (London: Heinemann, 1975), p. 42.
48   e.g. 7th and 9th meetings of the War Priorities Committee, 7 December 1917 and 4 January 1918, CAB 40–2.
49   10th meeting of WPC, 14 January 1918, CAB 40/2.
50   16th meeting of WPC, 14 June 1918, CAB 40/3.
51   8th meeting of WPC, 28 December 1917, CAB 40/2.
52   F. G. Byrne to Smuts, 5 November 1918, CAB 21/118/3.
53   Hankey, *Supreme Command*, Vol. I, pp. 226–7, 231–3.
54   ibid., Vol. I, p. 443.
55   Text in CAB 63/3.
56   Gooch, *Plans of War*, pp. 309–16, attacks Hankey for usurping the function of the General Staff and thus preventing its development. In view of Hankey's subsequent efforts to goad the Staff into life, while resisting its pretensions to the monopoly of strategic wisdom, this appears misguided as well as ungracious. See 'Proposed questionnaire to the War Office', Hankey to Asquith, 16 March 1915, CAB 63/3; 'The need for a joint naval and military committee on the Dardanelles', 20 March 1915, ibid.
57   Roskill, *Hankey*, Vol. I, pp. 211, 189–205; Hankey, *Supreme Command*, Vol. I, pp. 376–412; Hankey's letters to Asquith in CAB 63/7.
58   Hankey, *Supreme Command*, Vol. I, p. 409; Roskill, *Hankey*, Vol. I, pp. 211–12.
59   cf. D'Ombrain, *War Machinery*, pp. 170–201.
60   Hankey to Asquith, 9 December 1915, CAB 17/150.
61   Hankey, *Supreme Command*, Vol. II, pp. 471–4.
62   Correspondence in CAB 17/150; cf. Roskill, *Hankey*, Vol. I, pp. 273–4.
63   Hankey, *Supreme Command*, Vol. I, pp. 346–7; text in CAB 63/3.
64   Hankey to Asquith, 17 April 1916, CAB 17/159.
65   Hankey to Asquith, 6 November 1916, CAB 63/15.
66   Roskill, *Hankey*, Vol. I, pp. 319–21.
67   M. P. A. Hankey, 'The War Committee', 2 December 1916, CAB 63/15.

68 M. P. A. Hankey, 'The War Cabinet: rules of procedure', 24 January 1917, CAB 21/102.
69 Sykes edited the Eastern Report, Amery the Western and General Report. See draft memorandum on 'Political-War-Contacts' branch of the Secretariat, by Sykes amended by Hankey, 23 December 1916, Sykes Papers, Hull University Library.
70 'Report of the Food Production Department of the Board of Agriculture for the week ending 27 June 1917', GT 1219, CAB 24/18.
71 See Turner, *Lloyd George's Secretariat.*
72 See J. F. Naylor, 'The establishment of the War Cabinet secretariat', *Historical Journal*, vol. XIV (1971), pp. 783–803. Naylor illustrates well the in-fighting attending the formation of the secretariat, but exaggerates the 'Milnerite' influence on the outcome. cf. Turner, 'The formation of Lloyd George's Garden Suburb', ibid., vol. XX (1977), pp. 165–84.
73 M. P. A. Hankey, 'Memorandum on the organisation of the War Cabinet secretariat', n.d., B/1/4, Thomas Jones Papers, National Library of Wales, Aberystwyth.
74 Amery diary, 11 May 1917.
75 He drafted the initial definition of purposes, which appeared over Carson's name. CAB 27/15; Amery diary, 18 October 1917.
76 Amery diary, 20 June 1918.
77 ibid., 31 December 1918.
78 Roger Adelson, *Mark Sykes* (London: Cape, 1975), pp. 199–201, 220–30; 'Notes of a conference held at 10 Downing Street ... on April 3, 1917', GT 372, CAB 24/9; M. Sykes, 'Status and functions of Chief Political Officer and French Commissioner', 3 April 1917, ibid.
79 Adelson, *Mark Sykes*, pp. 236–7.
80 M. Sykes, 'The Palestine and West Arabian situation', 1 January 1918, CAB 24/37.
81 Hankey to Cecil, 2 January 1918, FO 800/198, Foreign Office Papers, PRO.
82 Hankey to Lloyd George, 8 December 1916, CAB 42/19/2.
83 Roskill, *Hankey*, Vol. I, pp. 362–5.
84 Hankey to Lloyd George, 8 March 1917, CAB 63/19.
85 Hankey papers, diary, 18 October 1916; cf. 'The Allies would not have been justified in not making their main effort on the Western front this year'. Untitled MSS. by Hankey, 18 April 1917, CAB 63/20.
86 Hankey, *Supreme Command*, Vol. II, pp. 703–7.
87 M. P. A. Hankey, 'Future military policy', 24 November 1917, CAB 63/23, was written as an aide memoire for Lloyd George, Hankey diary, 24 November 1917, Hankey Papers, Churchill College, Cambridge.
88 Roskill, *Hankey*, Vol. II, pp. 344, 387–8; R. K. Middlemas (ed.), *Thomas Jones Whitehall Diary*, 3 vols (London: Oxford University Press, 1969), *passim.*
89 Roskill, *Hankey*, Vol. II, pp. 304–20 has a full account.
90 Amery diary, 9 February 1917.
91 See list in Roskill, *Hankey*, Vol. I, pp. 637–9.
92 A good account of this is in the MS. diary of Christopher Addison, Box 98.
93 Roskill, *Hankey*, Vol. II, p. 127.
94 cf. C. Seymour-Ure, 'The disintegration of the Cabinet and the neglected question of Cabinet reform', *Parliamentary Affairs*, vol. XXV (1970–1), pp. 196–207.
95 Largely because the War Cabinet reports, on which early scholarship rested, were produced for propaganda purposes in Lloyd George's Garden Suburb. See Turner, *Lloyd George's Secretariat*, pp. 168–72.

96 Memorandum by Hankey, 28 May 1917, GT 807, CAB 24/14; cf. Robert
    Cecil, 'The work of the War Cabinet', 1 June 1917, GT 926, CAB 24/25, recom-
    mending the establishment of standing sub-committees overseeing groups of
    departments.

4

The Treasury:
from Impotence to Power

I

In time of war, the financial department of any government must accustom
itself to a position of both lesser and greater importance than during
peacetime. Military necessity rules, and lesser considerations such as
financial good housekeeping fade away; but at the same time, if the
belligerent is at all dependent on resources outside the country, finance
becomes of central concern. During the First World War the Treasury
was pulled both ways. The war was unimagined in its scope, duration
and devastation, and it transformed beyond all expectation the responsibilities and powers of the British government. No department could
remain untouched, and most certainly not the department which had,
since the time of Gladstone, played a pivotal role in the government.
The Treasury was unprepared to administer a great war, and it was up-
ended. Duties which had accrued to it for decades, that is, Treasury
control of spending and of civil service staffing, were held to be of commanding importance by few outside the Treasury itself. At the same
time, the Treasury for the first time imposed controls on the domestic
money market and involved itself with overseas finance; and in a battle
of wills with the Bank of England it emerged victorious.

The Treasury recognised very early on in the war that it had entered
a brave new world. The Treasury itself, in characteristic prose, set out
the theme in a Minute of 14 September 1914:

> The disturbance of the complex machinery of international trade and
> commerce by a war in which all the principal industrial communities
> of Europe are engaged has raised difficulties in connection with cur-
> rency, banking, international exchange and credit generally which
> are unlikely, whatever may be the course of the conflict, to exhaust
> their effects for many years to come.
>
> The result has been that the intervention of the Treasury has been
> invoked in regard to a great variety of matters which have hitherto
> been regarded as outside the province of Government, while at the

same time the ordinary finance business of the Treasury has increased in importance and responsibility by reason of the necessity for providing money for the expenses of the war and for the relief of distress and for the assistance of our less wealthy allies.[1]

The administrative class of the Treasury, whose duty it was to deal with the difficulties, was small, cohesive and consciously superior to the rest of the Civil Service. It had taken all those who had passed top in the Civil Service examination between 1906 and 1913, and 'Treasury manners' were something the rest of the Civil Service had to endure. The atmosphere was that of a gentleman's club; top hats and tails were mandatory and were worn until after 1918. Because there was no point in coming to the office until the post had been sorted and messages filed, principal, first-class and second-class clerks habitually appeared late in the morning; war, however, dented this habit. One major problem with the Treasury at the outbreak of war was that it was seriously understaffed. In 1914 the thirty-three men of the administrative class were divided into six divisions, of which the First Division, also known as the Finance Division or 1D, was the most important and prestigious. This division dealt with the raising of revenue, public expenditure and relations with the Bank of England.[2] The head of 1D was Sir John Bradbury, at the age of 41 one of the two Joint Permanent Secretaries to the Treasury in 1914 (by 1916 there were three). According to Sir Frederick Leith-Ross, one of five officials who worked under him in 1D, Bradbury had an inventive and creative mind, a sound knowledge of economics (itself unusual in the Treasury) and powers of intense application. He was remembered with affection by his staff, and known for certain oddities: one was that he smoked a hundred cigarettes a day (upon his retirement from government work he became a director of Imperial Tobacco), and another was his inability to cope with simple arithmetic.[3]

The other Joint Permanent Secretary in 1914 was Sir Thomas Heath, whose continuing hobby was Greek mathematics. During the war the duties concerned with finance fell on Bradbury, and Heath concerned himself with the adjustment of the Civil Service to war conditions. He was a civil servant of the old school, who worked best by written minute and with all deliberate speed. He did not survive the postwar reorganisation of the Treasury as Joint Permanent Secretary, but was shunted off to the post of Comptroller-General and Secretary to the Commissioners for the Reduction of the National Debt. In 1916, due to the press of war work, a third Joint Permanent Secretary was appointed, Sir Robert Chalmers. A Sanskrit scholar, he had been Permanent Secretary to the Treasury from 1911 to 1913, but had then gone out to Ceylon as Governor-General, where he was apparently something of a failure. He returned to the Treasury in March 1916. Chalmers had a mordant wit and a superior manner, and was accused of being brutal; it took a strong man to stand up to him. He retired from the Treasury in 1919.[4]

The Treasury then was a small, tightly knit élite: perhaps that was why the department was able to react so quickly and decisively to the problems stemming from the outbreak of hostilities. The activities of the Treasury during the war were complex and many-faceted; this essay will confine itself to four major areas of activity. First, there was its control of certain aspects of the domestic money market. At the very beginning of the war the Treasury established control over the currency and the Stock Exchange, and as the war progressed it came to control interest rates. Both the Treasury and the Bank of England, however, felt that these controls were specific to wartime, and by and large they were shuffled off by the end of 1919. Secondly, the Treasury became involved in overseas finance. In 1914 the Treasury had neither the machinery for, nor experience in, overseas finance; the war forced both. Thirdly, the Treasury fought with the Bank of England for control over the policy to be followed with regard to the exchange rate. This had historically been the preserve of the Bank, but the exigencies of war, and especially the amount of money being spent abroad, which the Treasury had to raise, meant that the Treasury wanted to control the policy to be followed. This conflict was one of personalities as much as of policy. The final area of change was that of Treasury control. During the war the Treasury lost control both over public spending and over the staffing of the new 'mushroom ministries', such as the Ministry of Munitions. The result was frightening, both to the Treasury and to the informed public generally. In 1917 and 1918 various committees called for strong Treasury control over spending and over the Civil Service. The result was that in 1919 and 1920 the Treasury was reorganised and given new powers of control over both.

II

The extension of controls over the domestic economy began immediately upon the outbreak of war, since a financial crisis had threatened London even before war was declared. An emergency currency was composed of Treasury, rather than Bank of England, notes; the Stock Exchange operated under rules promulgated by the Treasury; and the rate for tap Treasury bills rather than Bank Rate determined domestic interest rates.

The financial crisis of late July and early August 1914 was triggered off by panic-stricken continental bankers and investors and the closing of the stock exchanges in Europe. Since London was the centre of the international money market it could not remain unaffected. The English joint-stock banks panicked as well and refused to pay out gold to their customers in the quantities requested; the combination of the freezing of the bankers' assets and the desire of the public for cash made it clear by early August that an emergency note issue was necessary. The original intention was that the Bank of England should distribute the notes as loans to the banks in proportion to their deposit liabilities.

As it happened, the notes issued were Treasury notes (called 'Bradburys', since his signature was on them), not Bank of England notes. There were two – or possibly three – reasons for this. First of all, Scottish and Irish banks resisted the idea of Bank of England notes. Their argument was that while the authority of the British government was recognised in their countries, that of the Bank of England was not, and the notes simply would not circulate. (Indeed, until 1928 Bank of England notes were not legal tender outside England and Wales.) Secondly, Lord Cunliffe, the Governor of the Bank of England, knew that it was physically not possible for the Bank, which had its own printing works in its headquarters in Threadneedle Street, to produce the quantity of notes needed in time; instead they were printed by a commercial firm on postage-stamp paper. And thirdly, as Sir John Clapham later surmised, 'perhaps a desire at the Treasury... for "financial self-assertion" in dealing with the Bank, may have had some influence'.[5] Whatever the reasons, Lord Cunliffe for one made no secret of his regret at having to accept a Treasury note issue, and the Bank never wavered in its policy that if such notes became permanent, they should be issued by the Bank. (This was in fact achieved with the passing of the Currency and Bank Notes Act of 1928.) The Treasury accepted that the Bank should be consulted on all action taken in relation to the Treasury note issue.[6]

The Stock Exchange had been closed on 31 July 1914, not reopening until 4 January 1915. A fortnight after the closing the Treasury issued a notice that 'they wish it to be understood that until further notice, they feel it imperative in the national interest, that fresh issues of capital shall be approved by the Treasury before they are made'. The criterion for domestic stock issues was that they should be 'advisable in the national interest'; Empire issues required 'urgent necessity and special circumstances'; foreign issues would not normally be allowed at all. Shortly afterwards a Capital Issues Committee was set up to advise on applications.[7]

The rules were at first applied with some laxity; most domestic issues were allowed along with a few colonial and foreign ones. By the summer of 1915, however, a combination of the financial demands made by the second War Loan in June and the strain on resources occasioned by industrial mobilisation caused control to become much tighter. As the pressure on the exchange rate became stronger and stronger in 1916 and 1917 the control over foreign issues was strengthened by a series of defence regulations prohibiting the export of capital in any form, and by December 1917 it was illegal to send remittances out of the United Kingdom.

The end of the war, however, brought a rapid relaxation of the controls over capital issues. From December 1918 local authorities could apply for loans for public utility schemes, and on 1 April 1919 purely domestic issues were freed from any control. Because of the threat to the exchange rate and the need to devote available capital to projects within the United Kingdom, controls on foreign issues remained for some months longer. In August 1919 the ban on subscriptions to foreign loans and on the purchase of foreign securities and property abroad was ended, and in November 1919 all restrictions on the issue of foreign loans in London were brought to an end.[8]

The third area of control by the Treasury in the domestic money market was its manipulation, with the consent and co-operation of the Bank of England, of domestic interest rates. Before the war Treasury bills, which were short-term paper (payment falling due in three, six or twelve months), were issued by weekly tender; from April 1915, however, the bills were offered 'on tap' at the Bank (which carried out the clerical work involved on behalf of the Treasury), and this continued (with short breaks) until 1921. The result was that because Treasury bills were always obtainable at the tap rate, investments with lower rates of interest would not be taken up. Further, if the Bank tried to make effective a Bank Rate higher than the Treasury bill tap rate, banks would let their Treasury bills run off (that is, the bills would not be renewed), and the government would have to borrow from the Bank on Ways and Means advances (short-term loans in advance of revenue receipts). The Bank disliked the government's borrowings on Ways and Means, because it defeated the Bank's attempts at credit restriction. Thus the rate set by the government for its Treasury bills dominated the discount market. This rate had historically been set by the Bank of England by means of Bank Rate, but it would have been impossible (and self-defeating) for it to compete with the Treasury bill tap rate. The Treasury used the tap rate to keep interest rates up in order to attract foreign funds to London and thereby help maintain the exchange rate of the pound. In late 1917 the system of differential interest rates was initiated whereby foreign money received a higher rate of interest than domestic bank deposits; by January 1918 domestic deposits received 3½ per cent whilst foreign deposits received 4½ per cent interest.[9]

The Bank disliked its loss of control over interest rates — the Chancellor of the Exchequer hardly went through the motions of consultation with the Bank during 1918–19[10] — but it took some months after the end of the war to convince the government to allow Bank Rate again to be the effective rate of interest. The first step was taken in October 1919 when Treasury bill rates were brought into line with Bank Rate, and a fortnight later the discrimination between domestic and foreign deposit rates was ended. When in April 1921 the Treasury discontinued offering Treasury bills on tap, Bank Rate no longer had a serious rival.[11] It should be noted that in the interwar period, both the Treasury and the Bank argued that Bank Rate changes were the sole responsibility of the Bank and that (by implication) it was not the duty of the Treasury to interfere with the setting of the Rate.[12] The war years were seen as an anomaly.

III

The development of the Treasury's interest in overseas finance, its second major new area of activity, was a direct result of the war. Both the scope and duration of the war were unexpected. Prewar planning had been predicated on Britain's sending, at most, six divisions to the Continent, with her main war effort being concentrated on supplying her Allies and blockading Germany and the other Central Powers. However, Lord Kitchener, the Secretary of State for War, convinced the Cabinet that Britain should raise a mass army. In order to supply this army, the War Office would have to go beyond its usual circle of domestic suppliers. With the other major European countries at war, the War Office turned to the United States and sent out purchasing agents to place orders. Other belligerents had had this idea as well, and the bidding and counterbidding in the United States made for confusion and profiteering. Various British officials were witness to all this, and it was decided that British purchasing had to be systematised.

Basil Blackett, a first-class clerk in 1D, was in the United States in October and November 1914, and when he returned to London he urged strongly that something be done. It was clear to the Treasury that money would be wasted if the purchasing by the War Office and the Admiralty and others were not co-ordinated, and he wrote strong memoranda to this effect as well as actively lobbying for the change. It was not difficult to convince the Chancellor, David Lloyd George, who helped to convince the War Office. In January 1915 a purchasing contract was signed with J. P. Morgan & Co. of New York, who were to act as the sole Purchasing Agent in the United States for the War Office and Admiralty. As well, they acted as the Treasury's financial agent for paying for the goods.[13]

This was a noteworthy appointment. Morgan's after all were a foreign firm, the largest investment (merchant) bank in the United States; there were bound to be questions in Parliament about the appointment, and about the rate of commission to be paid.[14] But the government needed an organisation staffed with people familiar with industry in the United States, and it had no time to waste while it built up one of its own. Morgan's in fact had several advantages. In the first place, there were related Morgan firms in New York, London and Paris, thereby linking the major Allies with what became their major supplier.[15] Secondly, the firms had no link with German firms, a matter of some importance in the United States: the United States was neutral in 1915, and German-Americans might feel perfectly free to try and sabotage Allied transactions. Thirdly, because Morgan's were the leading bank, were in fact the banker's bank and the leader of Wall Street, they could command the information and the contracts that others could not. Finally, Morgan's were fanatically pro-British. J. P. Morgan, Jr, in fact, spent six months of every year in England, and at the outbreak of war he had turned his English residence over to the British government for use as a hospital.

The London firm of Morgan Grenfell & Co. acted as the link between the New York firm and the Treasury and British spending departments. E. C. Grenfell, the senior partner in the firm, was a director of the Bank of England as well as head of the Grenfell firm, and he personally acted as the intermediary between the Treasury and Morgan's. This may seem strange, since the normal course would be to use the British Embassy in Washington as the liaison. But the Treasury disliked going through Washington, both because of the time it took and because there was no one there, the Treasury felt, with the necessary financial expertise.[16] Thus every morning Grenfell called at the Treasury, carrying the latest exchange quotation from New York; here he would discuss with Bradbury or Chalmers the instructions to be sent to New York; then he would walk back to his office and with the help of trusted subordinates he would encode the Treasury's messages to be sent out to New York. Early in the war, Lloyd George, in a 'fit of broadmindedness', as Grenfell described it, had given permission for a secret and secure cable to run from London Grenfell to New York Morgan, the messages over which would not be subject to censorship.[17] Thus Treasury messages sent over the Morgan–Grenfell route not only reached their destination days faster than if sent over official government lines, but they were more secure.

The duties of Morgan's as financial agent for the Treasury in the beginning were mostly those relating to the disbursement of funds to American firms which were providing munitions and supplies to the British government. This included the buying and selling of exchange. However, as the amounts expended in the United States grew, the duties of Morgan's broadened. By late 1916 40 per cent of all British war purchases were made in North America,[18] and the British were experiencing great difficulty in raising enough dollars to pay for them. Gold was shipped and American securities sold for dollars, but it soon became necessary for Britain to issue collateral loans in the United States, and Morgan's handled these issues.[19] They also became direct lenders to the British government themselves, both the firm itself and the partners in their private capacities, and this activity was crucial for the Treasury's ability to pay for American goods. By 6 April 1917, when the United States entered the war, Morgan's were carrying what was essentially an overdraft of $345m. for the British government.[20]

A major reason for Britain's financial problems in the United States was that she was financing the purchases of her Allies there. It had been assumed when planning for war that Britain would help to support the activities of her Allies — this was, in fact, her historic role — but again, the scope and duration of the war threw everything out of joint. Loans to what the Treasury called 'our less wealthy allies'[21] dated from the early days of the war and grew rapidly in volume, and this made the Treasury determined to control the purchases. J. M. Keynes, having joined the Treasury in January 1915 as a member of 1D, rapidly assumed responsibility for Allied finance.

The problem was twofold: the Treasury had to decide how much to lend to each Ally, and how closely to supervise what the Ally did with the money. France presented the least problem, in that she tried to maintain herself in a position of equality with Britain for as long as possible by paying for her own supplies and helping Britain to pay for those of the other Allies. Keynes, in fact, commented in March 1916 that Britain had only one Ally, France, and that the rest were mercenaries.[22] Nevertheless, by the middle of 1916 Britain had to take over the financing of French purchases in the United States, and by April 1917 Britain was also paying for French purchases in Britain and the Empire, as well as supporting the French exchange against the dollar. As for the other Allies, British financial support began, more or less, with the war, and by April 1917 totalled about £950m. Over £400m. of this went to support Russia,[23] the most troublesome of the Allies as far as Keynes was concerned. For the other Allies as for Britain, the United States was the main source of supply. Keynes elaborated a system of Treasury control over Allied purchases much tighter than that which the Treasury exercised over British purchases, and the closest attention was paid to purchases in the United States,[24] since lack of sterling was not as much of a problem as the scarcity of dollars and the constant threat to the pound/dollar exchange.

The Treasury were, by 1916, acutely worried about the British position in the United States, since by October of that year, as noted earlier, 40 per cent of all British purchases relating to the war, for herself and her Allies, were made in North America. The major problem was the loss of Treasury control over the spending of the War Office and the Ministry of Munitions. During wartime, the War Office had traditionally had more or less a free hand as regards war expenditure, and Lloyd George, as Chancellor of the Exchequer, had told the War Office in October 1914 not to bother to come to the Treasury for approval for its purchases while the war was on.[25] Treasury officials had tried to exercise some overview, but the War Office declared its independence of the Treasury, pointing out that it was nearer the 'grim realities' than the Treasury.[26]

The new Ministry of Munitions which was set up in May 1915 under Lloyd George likewise acted independently of the Treasury. Since he had given *carte blanche* to the War Office when Chancellor, Lloyd George was hardly likely to hold back his own spending when Minister of Munitions — a post which he had taken on for the specific purpose of increasing the supply of shells and other munitions. He also specifically proposed to exploit American industry for Allied needs.[27] Thus by September 1916 the Treasury was expected to come up with payments aggregating over $200m. a month for American purchases alone.[28] Lloyd George's successor as Chancellor, Reginald McKenna, had tried on 19 May 1916 to enlist the support of the Cabinet for the Treasury's argument that Britain was heading for bankruptcy if some control was not exercised over war spending, but the Cabinet supported Lloyd George rather than the Chancellor.[29] Thus Britain was extremely vulnerable financially when the Federal Reserve Board in December 1916 warned American investors to be careful about buying Allied bonds.

The result of this warning was the temporary destruction of British credit in the United States. This crisis was the trigger for a Treasury reorganisation important for the future. The Federal Reserve Board warning had been prompted by some maladroit manoeuvres by a partner in J. P. Morgan & Co., and the Foreign Office in consequence moved to convince the Treasury that British financial interests could not go on being represented in the United States by a private American firm. The Treasury, and especially Chalmers, were equally upset by the Morgan action, and therefore decided that they would send out their own resident Treasury mission, headed by Hardman Lever, the Financial Secretary to the Treasury. The mission took up residence in the New York offices of J. P. Morgan & Co. in February 1917.[30] Lever took over the responsibility for making decisions about finance in North America from Morgan's, but Morgan's continued to act as Purchasing Agent for the British government. At the same time in London, a new division, called the 'A' Division, was carved out of 1D, the Finance Division. A Division was to be wholly responsible for overseas finance, especially for the raising of funds in the United States and the loaning of money to the Allies, and Keynes was appointed its head. Two months later the United States entered the war, and a month after that the American Treasury made its first loan to the British government. This was the genesis of the war debts, and their existence ensured that overseas finance would continue to be of importance to the Treasury. Thus although A Division was originally intended to be a temporary wartime section of the Treasury, and was in fact largely staffed with temporary civil servants, its functions outlived the war, and in the Treasury reorganisation of 1919 one of the twelve new divisions, 2D in the Finance Department, was devoted to overseas finance.[31]

From the entry of the United States into the war in April 1917 the Treasury mission under Lever negotiated directly with the American Treasury, rather than going through Morgan's. Lever's major duty was to convince the American Treasury to lend enough money to the British government to enable it to pay for its purchases in the United States. All of the other Allies were also asking the American Treasury to finance all of their American purchases, and the American Treasury took fright. By threats to withhold funds, the American Treasury forced the Allies in August 1917 to agree to co-ordinate their requests through an Inter-Allied Council for War Purchases and Finance.[32] In order to co-ordinate British submissions to this council, an interdepartmental committee, called the American Committee, was set up in Whitehall.[33] The Treasury was represented by Keynes, and all of the spending departments who wanted to make purchases in the United States had to submit their requests to this committee, which arranged them in order of priority. Then Keynes, representing the British government, would go to Paris for meetings of the Inter-Allied Council, which included representatives of all the Allies, plus, as chairman, the Under Secretary of the American Treasury, Oscar P. Crosby. This council then decided which of the requests of the Allies were to be submitted to the American government. The American government dealt with these requests through its own body, the Allied Purchasing Commission, which decided which of the Allied requests were to be met, having regard to the amount of money the American Treasury would lend. The irony of the situation was that the American Treasury, with threats of financial deprivation, was by the end of 1917 enforcing some measure of control over the British spending departments, control which the British Treasury had itself been powerless to impose.

IV

The third section of this essay is concerned with the conflict between the Treasury and the Bank of England over which institution was to control exchange rate policy. The Governor of the Bank of England since April 1913 was Lord Cunliffe, tough, aggressive and autocratic in his control of the Bank. Because he and Lloyd George had met the situation in August 1914 'like lions',[34] the comparison drawn between their courage and the timidity of the joint-stock bankers had strengthened Cunliffe's position in the financial world. These chance circumstances merely encouraged his natural temperament. As Sayers notes, 'Already before the war Cunliffe had been recognised as an exceptionally assertive browbeating type: "bully" is the word that springs to the lips of almost all who recall him nowadays...'[35] Curiously, Cunliffe got on very well with Lloyd

George when he was Chancellor. Sayers further notes that 'The roots of this friendship are not obvious. It was not that they worked well together, for there is little evidence of any real teamwork. Rather it seems to have been that Lloyd George was well content to watch vigorous and apparently successful action in affairs which...he himself neither understood nor cared about.'[36] By contrast, relations with Reginald McKenna, Chancellor from May 1915 to December 1916, were uneasy,[37] and relations between Cunliffe and Andrew Bonar Law, Chancellor from December 1916 to the end of the war, were bad, with open warfare breaking out in July 1917. Cunliffe treated the Treasury officials, with the possible exception of Bradbury, as mere minions of the Chancellor.[38] His conduct worsened over the four years of war and became so bad – many thought him mad – that the Bank eased him out of the Governorship in April 1918. It should be noted, however, that Grenfell offered a physical explanation for Cunliffe's conduct: in addition to the strains of the war, he attributed it to 'the neglect of his teeth which had poisoned his system through inability to spare a few hours in time with the Dentist.'[39] Whatever the cause of Cunliffe's deterioration, it did not prevent the War Cabinet from naming him chairman of the Committee on Currency and Foreign Exchanges.

Historically the Treasury had had little to do with exchange rate policy, that being the province of the Bank, but the corollary of the Treasury's increased spending overseas was an increasing concern to maintain the exchange rate of the pound against the dollar and thereby its purchasing power. This agreed with the policy of the Bank, and there would have been few problems if the Bank and the Treasury had been able to work together. But Cunliffe became suspicious about the means by which the Treasury was financing its overseas purchases. Cunliffe intended to maintain, to the last ounce of gold, the external value of the pound, and he was extremely concerned in the summer of 1915 by the Cabinet's lack of concern when the pound fell against the dollar.[40] In this he was joined by the Treasury officials, who were equally concerned to maintain the rate, but his distrust of McKenna and his contempt for the Treasury officials prevented him from co-ordinating action with the Treasury. Besides, Cunliffe's suspicions were correct in so far as McKenna was not really in command of his material as Chancellor, and was not as concerned about the falling rate of exchange as he might have been. Cunliffe's suspicions were in fact shared by E. C. Grenfell, who during the summer of 1915 himself repeatedly tried to make clear to McKenna the implications for British purchases in the United States of the pressure on the exchange. After one meeting between Grenfell, Cunliffe and McKenna, Grenfell wrote to one of the New York partners that 'We left the Chancellor somewhat chastened, but he has a lot to learn, and we none of us can afford the time to teach him...Still, we have got to make the best of our material.'[41]

The overdraft which Morgan's was supplying for British purchases was in the name of the Bank rather than the Treasury, and the country's external reserves of gold in Ottawa were also held in the name of the Bank. Cunliffe was angered that the Cabinet appeared to be leaving the Bank to carry the burden of worrying about the exchange, when it was government purchases which were causing the difficulty. In August 1915, without consulting the Treasury, he gave instructions to Morgan's to cease supporting the exchange, and instructions to Ottawa to ship gold to Morgan's to pay off the overdraft. In the absence of official intervention the markets became erratic and disorderly.[42] Cunliffe got away with his actions, but it was a sign of the lengths to which he was willing to go to enforce his will.

The result for the regulation of exchange rate policy was that the authorities set up in November 1915 the American Exchange Committee, later called the London Exchange Committee. This was made up of the Governor and Deputy-Governor of the Bank (Brian Cokayne) plus two City bankers (Sir Felix Schuster and Sir Edward Holden), since the committee was meant to oversee private exchange business as well as that of the Bank and the Treasury. The duty of the committee was to regulate the foreign exchanges, and it had at its disposal all the gold the authorities could muster plus all the foreign currency raised by borrowing and by the sale of securities. These were amazingly wide powers to be given to an organisation of private bankers,[43] and Bonar Law, when he became Chancellor a year later, could hardly believe their breadth. Nevertheless, because the powers conferred were so wide, it was quite impossible for such a committee to exercise them, and the committee became in essence an advisory body dominated by Cunliffe, who kept the actual giving of advice securely and aggressively in his own hands. Detailed operations fell to Treasury officials, and especially to Keynes and Chalmers.[44] Tension grew after Bonar Law became Chancellor, and the summer of 1917 saw open conflict between the two men, ending with the defeat of Cunliffe and with his defeat the ending of the Bank's pretensions to sole control of exchange rate policy.

From 18 April to 11 June 1917 Cunliffe was in the United States as a member of a political mission headed by A. J. Balfour, the Secretary of State for Foreign Affairs. While in the United States Cunliffe carried on his warfare with the Treasury by making statements which had the effect of undermining Lever, the Treasury's representative, in his negotiations with the American Treasury.[45] Upon his return to London, he found that Keynes and Chalmers were so deeply entrenched in deciding external policy that they did not always bother to give the Bank information. Cunliffe was incensed. His opportunity to strike back came owing to the confusion between the Treasury and the Bank of formal powers with regard to assets and liabilities in North America. Morgan's on 3 July 1917 warned the American Treasury that certain loans from Morgan's to the British government would not be renewed, the intention being to force the American government to repay them on behalf of the British government. One of these loans stood in the name of the Bank of England, and when Cunliffe found out, without consultation he ordered Ottawa to place enough gold at the disposal of Morgan's to liquidate the loan held in the name of the Bank. On the next two days he saw cables which indicated that Lever was having more gold shipped from Ottawa to New York in order to pay off more of the loan; this would reduce the amount that the Bank could show in its published reserves. Without reference to the Committee of Treasury in the Bank, ministers or Treasury officials, Cunliffe cabled to Ottawa in effect to ignore any further instructions from Lever, the Treasury's representative. To cap it all he also, at some point, demanded that the Chancellor sack Keynes and Chalmers.[46]

The Chancellor had had enough. Cunliffe had apparently counted on his private friendship with Lloyd George, who was now the Prime Minister, but Lloyd George was, if anything, more angry even than Bonar Law. He called Cunliffe to 10 Downing Street for some sharp words, and he even threatened, at one point, to 'take over the Bank'.[47] Eventually Cunliffe had to apologise, and in effect to place his resignation in the Chancellor's hands to be used if necessary. The Chancellor strengthened the Treasury's control over exchange policy by putting Stanley Baldwin, Joint Financial Secretary to the Treasury, on the London Exchange Committee, and by changing the formal arrangements for borrowing in New York and for the control of the gold in Ottawa. And in November 1917 the power of the Treasury over external financial policy was underlined when the British government, under the Defence of the Realm Act, took powers for a rudimentary foreign exchange control.[48]

V

The fourth major development in the activities of the Treasury was the increase in its powers to impose Treasury control over government spending and the Civil Service. Unlike its new involvement in overseas finance, Treasury scrutiny of spending proposals and of the Civil Service predated the war. The taproot extends back to Gladstone; more recently a 1910 Order-in-Council had directed that the Treasury should investigate pay and numbers of staff employed by any government department. But the Fourth Report of the Royal Commission on the Civil Service, published in 1914, revealed that the influence exercised by the Treasury fell far short of real control; for example, the Report quoted the evidence of Sir George Murray, Permanent Secretary to the Treasury 1903–11, to the effect that the Treasury could not force a given form of organisation on a department against its will. The Report recommended the creation of a special section within the Treasury for the supervision and control of the Civil Service, but the onset of war meant that no decision on the recommendation was taken.[49]

Nevertheless administrative developments during the war lent a certain urgency to the problem of Treasury control. Many of the 'mushroom ministries' thrown up by the war, such as the Ministries of Labour, Food, Shipping and the Air Board, were not subject to Treasury control over their numbers or organisation; rather, the Acts establishing these organisations left to their ministers the power to determine the size of their staffs. As a result the staffs multiplied according to the whims of their ministers. But even more horrifying to the Parliamentary Select Committee on National Expenditure, which reported in 1917 and 1918, was the total lack of Treasury control over the domestic spending of the War Office and the Ministry of Munitions.[50] The complaints of both the 1914 Royal Commission on the Civil Service and the 1917 Select Committee were repeated and amplified by the Haldane Committee on the Machinery of Government, which reported in January 1919. The Haldane Committee echoed the call of the Royal Commission for the setting-up in the Treasury of a section to oversee the Civil Service, and it underlined the urgent need, as demonstrated by the Select Committee, for the imposition of stricter control over departmental spending, although it did not call so much for the elevation of the Treasury as for ways to strengthen the internal finance branches of individual departments themselves. The Haldane recommendations coincided with those being developed by a departmental Committee of Inquiry into the Organisation and Staffing of Government Offices, which was chaired by Bradbury. Not surprisingly, Bradbury's committee called for the full restoration of Treasury control over staffing, and it explicitly aligned itself with the recently published Haldane Report in calling for the setting-up of a special section in the Treasury to carry it out.[51]

As the war came to an end, therefore, there was no shortage of recommendations as to how the Treasury could re-establish its position. In 1919 and 1920 these recommendations were by and large implemented. The three major themes are, first, the reorganisation of the Treasury itself, in order to fit it for carrying out its duties; secondly, the reimposition of Treasury control over the Civil Service; and finally, the strengthening of Treasury control over public spending.

In September 1919 the Treasury was wholly reorganised. The written evidence is sparse, but fortunately Lord Geddes, the former Sir Auckland Geddes, who had been a member of the Finance Committee in question, described how the reorganisation had come about during a debate in the House of Lords in 1942. The occasion for the reorganisation was the nearly simultaneous retirement of a 'rich crop' of civil servants. The Prime

Minister decided that a committee should consider how to replace them, and the Finance Committee of the Cabinet, which included Lloyd George, Bonar Law, Austen Chamberlain, Lord Milner and Geddes, set to the task. Lord Milner had long been interested in matters of organisation and control of the government machine, and he took the opportunity to draw up a plan of comprehensive reorganisation.[52]

As noted earlier, the Treasury in 1914 was composed of six separate divisions, of which only the Finance Division was organised at all by function. The other five divisions each covered several departments of state, the arrangement being determined by the most rudimentary organising principle — for example, the Foreign Office and the Colonial Office were handled by the same division, and one division concentrated on the work of the Parliamentary Clerk — and during the war, in fact, duties were transferred from one division to another according to which was the most overworked. The war also required the setting up of two new temporary divisions, 'A' division to handle foreign exchange and financial security questions, and 'B' division to deal with the new departments, such as the Ministries of Munitions and Shipping. Now, instead of being arranged according to client, the Treasury was to be organised functionally into three separate departments: (1) Finance, to be concerned with domestic and overseas finance; (2) Supply, to be concerned with public spending; and (3) Establishments, to be concerned with the whole range of Civil Service pay and organisation. At the head of each of the three departments was placed a 'Controller', each of whom ranked in status as a permanent secretary. During the war there had been no less than three Joint Permanent Secretaries to the Treasury, which could lead to a certain lack of cohesion in Treasury initiative and response; now there would be one Permanent Secretary to the Treasury, who would control the Controllers. The new Permanent Secretary, Sir Warren Fisher, replaced the wartime triumvirate. Chalmers had retired in March 1919; Bradbury became the British Representative on the Reparations Commission; and Heath became Comptroller-General and Secretary to the Commissioners for the Reduction of the National Debt. The government's decisions were incorporated in a Treasury Minute of 4 September 1919, and communicated to other departments by a Circular dated 15 September 1919.

Fisher in 1936 disclaimed all responsibility for this reorganisation, since he only took up his post as Permanent Secretary on 1 October 1919. He claimed that he had told ministers that the three-headed scheme would not work. He added that he had done his best to make it work, but that 'it was an extremely unwieldy and top-hampered and unsatisfactory arrangement'.[53] The scheme was modified in 1927 by the amalgamation of the Finance and Supply Departments. Finally in 1932 the Treasury reverted to the divisional form of organisation with a Permanent Secretary, a Second Secretary and three Under Secretaries in charge of the work of the Divisions. The three departments disappeared, and there remained only one department, the Treasury as a whole.[54]

The setting-up of the Establishments Department in 1919 was the most important element in the reorganisation of the Treasury, and the first step in the reimposition of strict Treasury control over the Civil Service. As Lord Geddes noted in 1942, 'The idea in Lord Milner's mind was that we should get a powerful, strong, central Department to be the Department of the Civil Service, and that is the Establishments Division of the Treasury as it was created.'[55] (Lord Milner's mind had clearly moved in accord with those of the Haldane Committee, which had also recommended the setting-up of an 'establishments' branch in the Treasury.[56]) The second step was the designation of the Permanent Secretary to the Treasury as Head of the Civil Service, as well as Permanent Secretary to the First Lord of the Treasury, the Prime Minister. The major reason for this seems to have been a desire to make manifest the intention to unify the departments of government into a Civil Service, with staff loyalty flowing towards the Service as a whole. Lord Geddes explained that the purpose was 'to provide a definite figure who would impersonate the Government as the employer in the vast extents of the Civil Service...'[57] The Head was also to be a symbol of a Service which would work together, rather than as a group of independent departments and permanent secretaries who would act only to defend their own fiefs. Fisher himself wrote later that 'Departments did not really think of themselves as merely units of a complete and correlated whole; and in the recognition by each Department of the existence of others there was, from time to time, an attitude of superiority, of condescension, of resentment, or even of suspicion.'[58] To encourage this desired sense of unity, Fisher habitually promoted interdepartmental transfers, especially for promotion. This was made easier to effect by the promulgation of another Treasury Circular on 12 March 1920 which announced that the consent of the Prime Minister, who would, of course, be advised by his Permanent Secretary, would be required for all appointments at upper and senior level in the departments. Finally, on 22 July 1920 an Order-in-Council consolidated the Treasury's legal authority over the Civil Service with the stipulation that the Treasury could make regulations for controlling the conduct of departments.

These legal controls might well be onerous to other departments of the Civil Service — and especially to those departments which had sprung up during the war and had thus never before really felt the heavy hand of the Treasury — since they were bound to restrict their freedom of manoeuvre. This was, indeed, part of the intention. But the major consideration was the need to give the Treasury the means by which it could limit public spending, which seemed to be wholly out of control. This perception of runaway expenditure as a fundamental threat to society and the state was one shared by the Treasury, the House of Commons and a wide section of the informed public.

During the war, exact schedules of Estimates, approved by the Treasury, and by the House of Commons after days of debate, had been replaced by the granting of huge Votes of Credit. The Comptroller and Auditor-General and the Public Accounts Committee of the House of Commons by 1917 were calling for a return to stricter control by the Treasury, arguing that the departments had abused their wartime freedom in disposing of their financial resources.[59] The Parliamentary Select Committee on National Expenditure reacted with great concern to the lack of control by the Treasury over the spending on contracts and capital expenditure by the War Office and Ministry of Munitions. The Committee was also disturbed by evidence that the Cabinet had not supported the Chancellor of the Exchequer when he had tried to establish some limit to the spending of the purchasing departments.[60] Control of spending by the Treasury was not wholly in abeyance during the war, since it controlled all spending abroad. The Treasury as well had some control over salaries, and continued to exercise its usual control over non-war departments. But it was the spending of the war-related departments which caught the public eye.

Once the war was over those who sought to limit public spending had the support of most of the vocal public. Throughout the debates on the Finance Bill in the House of Commons during the summer session of 1919 the recurrent theme was one of decrying the levels which government expenditure had reached, despite the fact that the war was over. On 4 June 1919, for example, one MP moved 'That the present state of Public Expenditure causes anxiety in regard to the financial stability of the country, and that all possible means for the reduction of expenditure should receive the immediate attention of the Government'.[61] Public opinion supported MPs on this, with, for example, the *Economist* running a series of pro-economy leaders during 1919.[62]

One theme of the 4 June debates was that the Chancellor, now Austen Chamberlain, was doing his best to control expenditure, but that his colleagues in the Cabinet were not co-operating. (One point which clearly disturbed Thomas Davis, MP, was the number of motor cars in St James's bringing officials to lunch; Capt. Wedgwood Benn, MP, further noted that the Ministry of Reconstruction possessed no fewer than fifty-nine motor cars for the use of its officials.[63]) The Chancellor was in fact haranguing his colleagues in Cabinet about their extravagant habits, and more to the point, their extravagant policies.[64] This supported Fisher's point to Lloyd George that Treasury control was not just about the control of waste in government departments; in addition, and more importantly, 'The big money is in policy. The margin of difference between a government machine which is perfectly adjusted for the execution of that policy and a machine which is too large ... is − in terms of cash − insignificant relatively to the huge figure of a modern Budget.'[65] Thus there had to be some control over ministers as well as over departments.

By the middle of July 1919 the Prime Minister was just as worried as the Chancellor about the financial situation, and Lloyd George asked the Chancellor to prepare a statement for the Cabinet. This Chamberlain did, circulating on 18 July a short statement, marked secret and urgent and for the eyes of ministers only, prophesying ruin for the country if expenditure were not cut back drastically. The major problem, as the Treasury saw it, was that of funding the huge amount of floating (short-term) debt: if the money raised by the Victory Loan of June 1919 was devoted to budget expenditure, it would not be available to fund the debt, which amounted to over £1,000m.[66] As Morgan notes, the 'liquidity which is the attraction of the floating debt for its holders, is a potential source of trouble for the authorities; a large floating debt, like a large volume of legal tender money or of bank deposits, represents spending power which can be very little influenced by the normal methods of central banking policy'.[67] The large holdings of Treasury bills by banks meant that if the Bank of England tried to be restrictive (and reduce the cash holdings of the banks), the banks could get cash by running off Treasury bills (as they in fact did in 1920). The policy of the Bank and of the Treasury was directed towards an eventual return to the gold standard (support of the exchange rate of the pound had ceased in March 1919), but to achieve this would require the reduction of prices by means of deflation. The existence of the floating debt, however, was an inflationary element, and thus an alarming threat to Treasury plans.[68] On 5 August 1919 the new Cabinet Committee on Finance met in order to consider the Chancellor's request for some measure of Treasury control over proposals for spending which ministers might wish to bring before the Cabinet.[69] Finally, on 13 August 1919 the Cabinet agreed 'That no Bill involving a charge shall come up to the War Cabinet or Home Affairs Committee until the Treasury have approved the charge, or, in the event of the Treasury having withheld sanction, until the Minister responsible has expressed a desire to appeal'.[70]

This now gave the Chancellor some accepted measure of control over his colleagues, but the Prime Minister still felt it necessary to respond to the political attacks on his government by urging that waste in the departments be cut. He made a two-pronged attack. First, he wrote to the members of the Cabinet a circular letter on 20 August 1919, pointing out that 'The time has come when each Minister ought to make it clear to those under his control that if they cannot reduce expenditure, they must make room for somebody who can.'[71] He made it clear the same day in the Cabinet Finance Committee that he intended to prod the Treasury to home in on items of waste and extravagance which should be eliminated. Thus he sent J. T. Davies, a member of his secretariat, to see Fisher and insist on a memorandum from him setting out what the Treasury was going to do about cutting down expenditure.[72]

Fisher responded on 3 September 1919 with several suggestions. He noted, as had others,[73] that the Treasury was absurdly understaffed — there were, at the end of the war, only thirty-eight members of the administrative class, as compared to thirty-three in 1914 — and he proposed to increase their numbers. He suggested that 'War time Departments should ... be wound up as rapidly as possible and *not continued* ...' Finally, after noting, as quoted above, that policies, not waste, were the major causes of expenditure, he suggested that the permanent civilian head of a department, that is the Permanent Secretary or Under Secretary, should be responsible for finance and office organisation in that department and that his appointment should be subject to the approval of the Board of Treasury.[74] To underline the last point, the Treasury in 1920 firmly restated the principle of 1872 that the permanent head of each department was responsible for the economical running and financial propriety of his own department.[75] And finally, in 1924, the Cabinet rule was formulated that 'no memorandum is to be circulated to the Cabinet or its Committees in which any financial issue is involved, until its contents have been discussed with the Treasury'.[76]

VI

The First World War, therefore, acted as a catalyst for the administrative development of the Treasury. It permanently enhanced its duties and status in unfamiliar areas such as external finance and the control of exchange policy,[77] and, despite a temporary setback, in the Treasury's traditional areas of interest, namely, control of public spending and of the Civil Service. It was perhaps a mark of the importance of these tasks which the Treasury had traditionally performed that the absence of Treasury responsibility was perceived so quickly as a matter of grave concern. This concern, manifested in the final years of the war by a whole phalanx of committees, made it relatively easy for the Treasury to re-establish itself, but with greatly increased powers, in those traditional areas of responsibility. The upshot was that the Treasury faced the difficult interwar years reorganised, enlarged and reinforced in power. How well the Treasury then exercised these powers is, of course, another question.

THE TREASURY 103

Notes: Chapter 4

I am very grateful to Dr David French, Professor Susan Howson, Dr M. Jewess, Dr. H. C. G. Matthew and Dr G. C. Peden for commenting on various drafts of this chapter. I am also greatly indebted to Morgan Grenfell & Co. Ltd, London, who not only gave me full access to their papers, but also generously provided space for me to work.

1 Treasury Minute 19304/14, f. 157, T.197/7, Treasury Papers, Public Record Office (PRO), London. At least one observer apparently believed that the reactions of the Treasury to the possibility of war, and its onset, fell far below what was necessary. Sir Maurice Hankey wrote in 1922: 'In this great work of preparation for war there was only one of the main Departments whose chapter in the War Book was belated and unsatisfactory, and that was the Treasury... Their War Book... is jejune and inadequate. Even on the financial side there was practically no preparation... If their record on the financial side was bad, as a Central Department of Government it was worse. They made no preparations at all.' It should be noted that when Hankey wrote this memorandum, he was fighting to prevent the Cabinet and Committee of Imperial Defence Secretariat from being absorbed into the body of the Treasury. Stephen Roskill, *Hankey: Man of Secrets*, 3 vols (London: Collins, 1970–4), Vol. I, pp. 137–8. For information on the unsympathetic response by the Treasury to the prewar CID's attempts to prepare for a possible war, see David French's essay in this volume.

2 For an outline of the six divisions of the Treasury in 1914, giving the duties of and number of personnel in each, see Henry Roseveare, *The Treasury: The Evolution of a British Institution* (London: Allen Lane, 1969), p. 230. Sir Andrew McFadyean, *Recollected in Tranquillity* (London: Pall Mall Press, 1964), p. 45. In the Civil Service examination in 1906, J. M. Keynes passed second, with Otto Niemeyer, Controller of Finance in the Treasury 1922–7, first.

3 Sir Frederick Leith-Ross, *Money Talks. Fifty Years of International Finance* (London: Hutchinson, 1968), p. 22. McFadyean, *Recollected in Tranquillity*, p. 45.

4 M. F. Headlam, 'Sir Thomas Little Heath', *Proceedings of the British Academy*, vol. XXVI (1940), pp. 425–38. McFadyean, *Recollected in Tranquillity*, p. 46. Leith-Ross, *Money Talks*, p. 21. Sir Thomas Heath and P. E. Matheson, 'Lord Chalmers 1858–1938', *Proceedings of the British Academy*, vol. XXV (1939), pp. 321–32.

5 'Sir John Clapham's account of the financial crisis in August 1914', Appendix 3 in R. S. Sayers, *The Bank of England 1891–1944*, 3 vols (Cambridge: Cambridge University Press, 1976), Vol. III, p. 36. Sayers's account of the crisis as it affected the Bank is in Vol. I, pp. 66–78. For details of Treasury activities during the same period see E. V. Morgan, *Studies in British Financial Policy, 1914–25* (London: Macmillan, 1952), ch. 1.

6 Sayers, *Bank of England*, Vol. I, p. 76.

7 Excerpts from the Treasury notice printed in Morgan, *British Financial Policy*, p. 263. The members of the committee were Viscount St Aldwyn (the former Chancellor, Sir Michael Hicks-Beach), chairman, Lord Cunliffe, Sir F. G. Banbury, MP, Sir T. P. Whittaker, MP and Mr G. Stapylton Barnes.

8 Morgan, *British Financial Policy*, pp. 263–5.

9 ibid., pp. 143, 177. Sayers, *Bank of England*, Vol. I, pp. 95–8. Immediately after the war, the Treasury bill tap rate was used to keep interest rates down. See Susan Howson, *Domestic Monetary Management in Britain 1919–38* (Cambridge: Cambridge University Press, 1975), pp. 10–11, 23.

10 Sayers, *Bank of England*, Vol. I, p. 112.

11 ibid., Vol. I, pp. 117–18. Morgan, *British Financial Policy*, pp. 177, 211. But see Howson, *Domestic Monetary Management*, p. 25.

12 Nona Newman, 'The role of the Treasury in the formation of British economic policy 1918–1925', Durham University PhD thesis, 1972, p. 37. Dr Newman cites T.176/13, pt 1, but the PRO was unable, when requested, to produce the file. Howson, *Domestic Monetary Management*, ch. 3, n. 44, also cites T.176/13. See also the letter from Niemeyer to Leith-Ross dated March 1925, printed in *Money Talks*, pp. 95–6.

13 For information on British purchasing in the US, including details on the Morgan firms, see the author's *Britain, America and the Sinews of War* (forthcoming), chs 1–3.

14 Two per cent of net price of all goods purchased up to £10m. and then 1 per cent upon excess of that. 'Commercial agreement', 15 January 1915, D/12/2/1, David Lloyd George Papers, House of Lords Record Office, London. The commission was later varied for different duties. United States Senate, *Munitions Industry: Supplemental Report... of the Special Committee on Investigation of the Munitions Industry* (74th Cong., 2nd sess., 1936), Hearings, exhibit no. 2161, part 26, 8094, 8096. In the end, the British government paid the Morgan firms $30m. in purchasing commissions, and an additional unknown sum in banking commissions. ibid., Senate Report 944, v. 75.

15 J. P. Morgan & Co., New York; Morgan Grenfell & Co., London: Morgan Harjes et Cie, Paris.

16 Bradbury to A. J. Balfour (Secretary of State for Foreign Affairs), 13 January 1917, no. 11101, FO 371/3070, Foreign Office Papers, PRO.

17 E. C. Grenfell to Thomas Lamont (a partner in J. P. Morgan & Co.), 14 October 1915, file 12, Box Hist. 11 – Letters, Morgan Grenfell Papers, Morgan Grenfell & Co., London.

18 'The financial dependence of the United Kingdom on the United States of America', 6 November 1916, CAB 42/23/7, Cabinet Papers, PRO.

19 Between the beginning of the war and mid-July 1917 Britain sent £305m. (somewhat less than $1,500m.) in gold to the US; this included gold borrowed or purchased from France and Russia. Elizabeth Johnson (ed.), *The Collected Writings of J. M. Keynes*, Vol. XVI (Cambridge: Cambridge University Press, 1971), p. 249. Between August 1914 and 14 July 1917 the Treasury sold $750m. worth of securities in New York; large amounts were also disposed of through private sales and sales by the Bank of England. ibid., pp. 249–50. For a list of the collateral loans see Kathleen Burk, 'J. M. Keynes and the exchange rate crisis of July 1917', *Economic History Review*, Second Series, vol. XXXII, no. 3 (August 1979), p. 407, n. 4.

20 US Senate, *Munitions Industry*, Senate Report 944, vii, p. 149.

21 Treasury Minute 19304/14, 14 September 1914, f. 157, T.197/7.

22 Johnson (ed.), *Keynes*, Vol. XVI, p. 187.

23 ibid., pp. 238, 230.

24 For details see Burk, *Sinews of War*, ch. 3.

25 David Lloyd George, *War Memoirs*, 2 vols (London: Odhams, 1938), Vol. I, p. 80.

26 C. Harris, War Office, to Bradbury, 8 October 1914, T.1/11662/17287.

27 Lloyd George to D. A. Thomas, 14 June 1915, D/12/1/3, Lloyd George Papers.

28   'Our financial position in America', 18 October 1916, CAB 37/157/40.
29   CAB 37/148/6.
30   Foreign Office to the Treasury, 3 January 1917, no. 255636/45/A, FO 371/ 2800. Bradbury to the FO, 13 January 1917, no. 11101, FO 371/3070. For details of the December 1916 crisis and its consequences see Burk, *Sinews of War*, ch. 5. Lever's duties as Financial Secretary to the Treasury in London were carried out by Stanley Baldwin from 26 July 1917. Treasury Minute 21426/17, 26 July 1917, T.197/7.
31   The temporary civil servants in A Division included Dudley Ward, Rupert Trouton and Oswald Falk. McFadyean, *Recollected in Tranquillity*, p. 65. Newman, thesis, p. 22. After Sir Hardman Lever returned to Britain in July 1919, J. P. Morgan & Co. were named the British Financial Agent in the US.
32   For details see Kathleen Burk, 'Great Britain in the United States, 1917–1918: the turning point', *International History Review*, vol. I, no. 2 (April 1979), pp. 228–45.
33   ibid. Lord Buckmaster was the first chairman and Austen Chamberlain was the second. Andrew McFadyean was the secretary. McFadyean, *Recollected in Tranquillity*, p. 66.
34   Cunliffe's words, quoted by Sayers, *Bank of England*, Vol. I, p. 74.
35   ibid., Vol. I, p. 101.
36   ibid.
37   Lord Beaverbrook thought the core of the problem was that Cunliffe insisted that matters of foreign exchange were his exclusive province and McKenna thought otherwise. Lord Beaverbrook, *Men and Power 1917–1918* (London: Hutchinson, 1956), p. 93.
38   Sayers, *Bank of England*, Vol. I, p. 68.
39   Grenfell to J. P. Morgan, 14 January 1916, ECG's Letter Book, 1897–1930, Morgan Grenfell Papers. Grenfell had some sympathy for Cunliffe, noting that 'I am still the only person to whom Walter [Cunliffe] will talk on the very rare occasions on which he lets go.' Grenfell to J. P. Morgan, 24 August 1915, f. 277, file 13, Box Hist. 11 – Letters, Morgan Grenfell Papers. Sayers remarks that Montagu Norman called Cunliffe's behaviour 'dangerous and insane'. *Bank of England*, Vol. I, p. 109.
40   ibid., Vol. I, pp. 101, 89. It should be remembered that Britain was effec-tively (although not legally) off the gold standard during the war. See Howson, *Domestic Monetary Management*, ch. 2, n. 19.
41   Grenfell to H. P. Davison (a partner in J. P. Morgan & Co.), 5 August 1915, f. 736, file 13, Box Hist. 11 – Letters, Morgan Grenfell Papers. His view had hardened a few weeks later and he wrote that 'As regards Finance, undoubtedly McKenna is a very ignorant man... [who is] inclined to try to appear wise.' Grenfell to J. P. Morgan, 24 August 1915, f. 277, ibid.
42   Sayers, *Bank of England*, Vol. I, p. 89. The members of the Nye Committee of the US Senate, during the hearings held in 1936 on the munitions industry, closely questioned J. P. Morgan and Thomas W. Lamont on the failure to support the exchange in August 1915. From the direction of the questioning it is clear that the committee suspected that the British government and J. P. Morgan & Co. had somehow connived to let the exchange fall in order to force the American government to change their loan policy in order to permit loans to belligerents. *Munitions Industry*, Senate Report 944, vi, pp. 39–42.
43   Sayers reports that the powers were said to have been accepted in haste under pressure from Holden. He suggests that Holden possibly saw this as a source of power for himself and other commercial banks (he was chairman of the

London City and Midland Bank), relative to that of the government and the Bank of England. *Bank of England*, Vol. I, p. 90.

44 ibid.

45 For details see Burk, *Sinews of War*, ch. 6.

46 Sayers, *Bank of England*, Vol. I, pp. 103–5. Burk, *Sinews of War*, ch. 9.

47 Sayers, *Bank of England*, Vol. I, p. 105.

48 ibid., pp. 105–7. Robert Blake, *The Unknown Prime Minister* (London: Eyre & Spottiswoode, 1955), pp. 351–4. Beaverbrook, *Men and Power*, pp. 102–10.

49 *Parl. Papers 1914*, Vol. xvi (Cmd 7338), *Fourth Report of the Royal Commission on the Civil Service*, p. 86. For Treasury control under Gladstone see Maurice Wright, *Treasury Control of the Civil Service, 1854–1874* (London: Oxford University Press, 1969).

50 *Parl. Papers 1917–18*, Vol. iii, *First Report from the Select Committee on National Expenditure*, pp. 6–10. ibid., *Second Report from the Select Committee on National Expenditure*, p. 15.

51 *Parl. Papers 1918*, Vol. xii (Cmd 9230), *Ministry of Reconstruction: Report of the Machinery of Government Committee* [Haldane Committee], Vol. 20, p. 10. Roseveare, *The Treasury*, pp. 245–6.

52 125 *House of Lords Debates* 5 s., 26 November 1942, cols 285–8. The author looked through the relevant Milner Papers in the Bodleian Library and found no mention of the scheme.

53 *Parl. Papers 1935–36*, Vol. v, *Public Accounts Committee*, p. 431 (evidence given on 30 April 1936, no. 4443). For the Chancellor of the Exchequer's explanation of the reorganisation see 120 *House of Commons Debates* 5 s., 29 October 1919, cols 743–5.

54 For the structure and role of the Treasury during the interwar period see G. C. Peden, *British Rearmament and the Treasury 1932–1939* (Edinburgh: Scottish Academic Press, 1979), ch. 2.

55 125 *H.L. Deb.* 5 s., 26 November 1942, col. 286.

56 *Parl. Papers 1918*, Vol. xii, p. 20.

57 125 *H.L. Deb.* 5 s., 26 November 1942, col. 286.

58 Evidence given to the Tomlin Commission on the Civil Service, 1930, quoted in Sir H. P. Hamilton, 'Sir Warren Fisher and the public service', *Public Administration*, vol. XXIX (Spring 1951), p. 14. For the final Report see *Parl. Papers 1930–31*, Vol. x (Cmd 3909), *Report of the Royal Commission (1929–31) on the Civil Service*, pp. 517ff.

59 Roseveare, *The Treasury*, p. 243.

60 See above, n. 29. *Parl. Papers 1917–18*, Vol. III, pp. 9, 15.

61 The MP was Mr J. A. Grant. 116 *H.C. Deb.* 5 s., 4 June 1919, col. 2133.

62 See, for example, *The Economist*, vol. LXXXVIII, 17 May 1919. Newman, thesis, pp. 182–3.

63 116 *H.C. Deb.* 5 s., 4 June 1919, col. 2147.

64 See, for example, War Cab 589, 8 July 1919, and War Cab 594, 16 July 1919, both CAB 23/11.

65 Fisher to Lloyd George, 3 September 1919, T.171/170.

66 'The financial situation', 18 July 1919, T.171/170; circulated as GT 7729, CAB 24/84.

67 For details on the floating debt and Treasury fears as to its effects see Morgan, *British Financial Policy*, pp. 142–6.

68 I am grateful to Susan Howson for elucidating this point. For an analysis of postwar financial problems see Howson, *Domestic Monetary Management*, ch. 2; D. E. Moggridge, *British Monetary Policy 1924–31: The Norman Conquest of $4.86* (Cambridge: Cambridge University Press, 1972), pp. 16–28.

69 War Cab 606A, 5 August 1919, CAB 23/11.
70 War Cab 613, Minute 3, 13 August 1919, CAB 23/11.
71 T.171/170.
72 Finance Committee 3, 20 August 1919, CAB 27/71. Lloyd George to J. T. Davies, 28 August 1919, T.171/170.
73 *Parl. Papers 1917–18*, Vol. iii, p. 14.
74 Fisher to Lloyd George, 3 September 1919, T.171/170. For details on Fisher's attempts to get this accepted by the Public Accounts Committee see Hamilton, 'Sir Warren Fisher ...', pp. 18–22.
75 Roseveare, *The Treasury*, p. 247.
76 ibid., p. 243, n. 2.
77 It should be noted that during the period of Britain's return to the gold standard, 1925–31, the Bank of England resumed responsibility for external finance.

Addendum to Section V, pp. 97–8, and note 52:
Since this essay went to press Mr Eunan O'Halpin of Churchill College, Cambridge has informed me of contemporary evidence which suggests that Lord Geddes may have been mistaken in attributing to Lord Milner the plan for the re-organisation of the Treasury in 1919. A memorandum by Sir John Bradbury to Austen Chamberlain in the *Chamberlain Papers*, Birmingham University apparently makes it clear that Bradbury drew up the scheme, even to selecting the Controllers, and gave it to Chamberlain the night before the Finance Committee meeting; the Finance Committee then approved the scheme more or less on the nod. I am grateful to Mr O'Halpin for providing me with this information.

5

The Ministry of Labour, 1916-19: a Still, Small Voice?

The creation of a Ministry of Labour was one of Lloyd George's first acts on becoming Prime Minister in December 1916. It was essentially a political gesture, designed to win the parliamentary support of the Labour Party; but it also had some administrative logic. Before 1916 ministries of labour had been established in many industrial countries and since the 1890s there had been intermittent demands for one in Britain. In particular, the expansion of social administration after 1909 had led to calls for the separation of the commercial and labour responsibilities of the Board of Trade; and during the war itself there had been demands for the better co-ordination of labour policy under a single department which − unlike the Ministry of Munitions − had the confidence of organised labour. All these arguments Lloyd George deployed, with his usual guile, to win the support of Labour Party leaders at their crucial meeting on 7 December. He argued:

> Up to the present we have had only one Labour head of a Department. I won't suggest that there should be two... but I suggest an absolutely new Department − a Ministry of Labour... which could incorporate the Labour section of the Board of Trade and the Ministry of Munitions under one head. That Department would certainly be one of the most important Departments in the Government because, however important a Labour Ministry would be in time of peace − and it would essentially be a Department whose decisions would very naturally affect the lives of millions of people in this country − in times of war it is almost doubly important... I propose that that Department should have at its head a Labour representative.[1]

For reasons that will be discussed below, Lloyd George's wartime plans for the ministry were never realized. There was no amalgamation of the labour departments of the Ministry of Munitions and the Board of Trade and in both the formulation and execution of industrial relations and manpower policy, confusion continued to reign. Throughout the war, the ministry's prestige at both a political and administrative level remained negligible. As one of its senior officials was later to confess, few of those 'responsible for the vast complex business of war production were disposed to listen much to the still small voice of our infant Ministry'.[2]

The peacetime record of the ministry also did not accord fully with Lloyd George's predictions, for throughout the interwar period the ministry remained politically 'one of the least important home departments'.[3] Admittedly, its political sensitivity, as the government's main channel of communication with the trade unions and as the ministry primarily responsible for industrial relations and unemployment relief, ensured its continuous representation in Cabinet — an achievement unmatched by any other department created during the war. However, no interwar government was prepared to confer on the ministry the ambitious political role which its prewar advocates had sought.[4] The Labour Party, once established as the alternative party of government, no longer saw the need to build up its own 'embassy' in Whitehall and quickly abandoned its concept of the ministry as a 'national authority for unemployment' or a 'Ministry of Industry'. Similarly Lloyd George and Baldwin, despite their declared intentions, failed to expand the ministry. They deferred instead to their backbenchers, whose hostility towards the ministry (in the 1920s at least) was best expressed in the 1922 Geddes Committee recommendation that it should be abolished and its responsibilities either abandoned or returned to the Board of Trade.[5] The ministry consequently lacked political muscle, a fact underlined by a succession of ineffectual ministers.[6] Ministerial appointments fully conformed to the mystifying interwar convention that, in spite of the enhanced importance of social policy after the trebling of the electorate in 1918, social services departments should be regarded still as second-rate departments — 'a transitional step to higher office or a graveyard where a dying career could be quietly buried'.[7]

The administrative history of the ministry, however, was different; indeed, in this respect the ministry did fulfil Lloyd George's prediction that it would be 'one of the most important Departments in the Government'. Initially it was desperately weak. Before its official recognition as a permanent department of state in December 1923, its very existence had been challenged politically by the Geddes Committee and administratively by the Treasury.[8] Resources were consequently so scarce that in 1920, for instance, 77 per cent of the staff were temporary and 80 per cent were working in posts above their official grading. Thereafter, however, the ministry's administrative strength and influence developed rapidly. By the late 1930s its officials — having both mastered the details of the most pressing political problem (unemployment) and experienced the practical difficulties of policy-implementation at first hand (through its unique regional organisation) — were beginning to dominate the formulation of domestic policy. They not only ran the new semi-autonomous bodies, such as the Unemployment Assistance Board and the Special Areas Commission, but had also been promoted to key posts within the Treasury.[9] During the Second World War, they were as much in demand to improvise wartime administration as had been the 'young turks' in the National Health Commission during the First.

The contrast between the political and administrative fortunes of the interwar ministry raises a major problem for an assessment of its contribution to the permanent transformation of British government after the First World War: to what extent is it proper — either constitutionally or historically — to judge a ministry separately as a political and as an administrative entity? Can a ministry be said to enjoy an administrative life 'independent' of its political development? Any assessment of a ministry, moreover, must take account of the political and industrial environment within which it works. Ministries do not function in a vacuum. The immediate postwar years, in particular, were a time of rapid change in which the idealism of wartime reconstruction became rapidly engulfed in the pessimism of economic depression. Any judgement of the interwar ministry, therefore, must be made in the light of rapidly changing administrative and political priorities.

With these considerations in mind, two major questions can be asked of the ministry's peacetime contribution to the evolution of modern British government. First, the ministry's establishment helped to dismember the prewar Board of Trade with its proven record of statistical research and administrative achievement. How then did it improve the quality of the decision-making and the overall efficiency of government? Did the separation of labour from industrial administration enhance the policy-making process? Did not the ministry's creation dissipate the administrative and political resources needed to defend the new interventionist services against increased economic conservatism in both Westminster and Whitehall? What were the full consequences of the loss to domestic policy formulation of such pre-eminent Edwardian administrators as Sir Hubert Llewellyn Smith, William Beveridge and George Askwith? Secondly, how well did the new ministry rise to the new, and somewhat contradictory, political and administrative challenges posed by the growing democratisation of British government? On the one hand, the extension of the franchise in 1918 anticipated the greater provision by central government of social services. Increased bureaucratic initiative became inevitable once there was the need for delegated legislation in Whitehall (to frame the regulations by which Acts of Parliament could be implemented) and discretion in the locality (to adapt these regulations to the real needs of individual clients); a new breed of civil servant with increased specialist expertise and 'political' imagination was also needed once government moved away from purely regulative administration. On the other hand, the growing influence of vested interest groups (in particular the trade unions) forced central government to work within a more pluralistic framework, where the onus was on civil servants not to dictate but to debate or explain policy. The ministry's success depended on its resolution of this potential contradiction in its role.

The Ministry at War

The ministry was formed by the simple transfer from the Board of Trade of its semi-autonomous labour departments. First, there was the predominant Employment Department with some 6,000 staff, the majority in the 356 employment exchanges and 949 branch offices throughout the country and the rest at headquarters checking the records of approximately 3 million workers insured against unemployment. Secondly, there was the Chief Industrial Commissioner's Department, presided over by Sir George (later Lord) Askwith, which had permanent responsibility for the government's conciliation and arbitration service but which, even by the end of the war, employed a staff of only thirty. Thirdly, there was a Trade Boards Department responsible for overseeing the regulation of minimum wages in nine trades. Lastly, there was a small Labour Statistics Department.

The two ministers appointed during the war were trade unionists, John Hodge (December 1916 – August 1917), the steelworkers' leader and acting chairman of the Labour Party, and George Roberts (August 1917 – December 1918), a former Labour Party whip. Both had as their parliamentary secretary a Conservative, W. C. Bridgeman. At an official level only two senior appointments were initially made. D. J. (Sir David) Shackleton, a former Labour MP and chairman of the TUC, was made Permanent Secretary with H. B. Butler, the former controller of the Home Office's Industrial Department, as his deputy. As Shackleton came to concentrate on his role as the government's chief labour adviser, so Butler began effectively to run the ministry and to determine long-term policy. During 1917 he created two small divisions: a Labour Intelligence Division to prepare a weekly report on the labour situation for the War Cabinet and a Joint Industrial Councils Division to promote the establishment of Whitley Councils throughout the industry. The latter division was headed by the economist Henry Clay, and staffed by labour intellectuals such as J. L. Hammond and J. J. Mallon.

The ministry from its inception was administratively weak. Not only did it find it hard (in a period of acute manpower shortage) to recruit officials of the requisite standard, but it was also rent by personal animosities which led, for instance, to Beveridge's dismissal as head of the Employment Department by Hodge in December 1916 and to the reluctance of Askwith to report through his Permanent Secretary (a former trade unionist) or to abide by ministerial decisions.[10] Moreover, fundamental differences of policy arose between the old Board of Trade departments, jealous of their previous autonomy, the radical enthusiasm of Butler and his new headquarters divisions and the cautious conservatism of Shackleton.

The main administrative weakness of the ministry, however, was not internal but external. Logically (as some contemporaries argued and as the Second World War was to show) a wartime Ministry of Labour should have responsibility for three areas of policy, manpower, industrial relations and the planning of demobilisation and industrial reconstruction; but in each of these areas, rival authorities were erected during the course of 1917. A Department of National Service was created, simultaneously with the ministry, to supervise the distribution of manpower. Concordats were speedily signed between the ministry and all production departments, confirming the initial responsibility of the latter to resolve industrial disputes within their controlled industries. In August 1917 a new Ministry of Reconstruction was established. Finally, the appointment of a labour representative to the War Cabinet deprived the ministry of the prestige it might otherwise have derived from 'representing labour' within government. With some justice, MacDonald could warn Lloyd George on the ministry's creation: 'You are not adding to the efficiency of your organization of state, but you are simply presenting new points of friction, misunderstanding and trouble.'[11]

To chronicle the 'friction, misunderstanding and trouble' which characterised labour policy during the First World War would be a thankless task, especially as its smooth administration during the Second World War showed that the correct lessons were duly learned. However, it is necessary to examine some of the major controversies to illustrate the deleterious, as well as invigorating, effect that Lloyd George could have on the machinery of government and to help to explain the depth of hostility to bureaucracy which existed in the interwar period.

Manpower policy has been described as 'the worst administrative failure of the First World War'.[12] For its success, there were two overriding prerequisites: the regular drafting of a manpower budget, to estimate the size of the potential workforce and to apportion it among competing demands, and the restriction of production unrelated to the war effort. In addition skilled labour had to be husbanded, in particular by 'dilution'; the unskilled labour force had to be enlarged, mainly by the 'substitution' of potential conscripts by ineligible male or female labour; labour had to be directed, and then restricted, to essential industries (without raising fears of 'industrial conscription'); and, finally, welfare services and good industrial relations had to be maintained to prevent loss of production. Between 1914 and 1918, as was perhaps inevitable in a war that was initially expected to be neither prolonged nor 'total', these objectives were only slowly, and even then imperfectly, attained. No manpower budget, for instance, was drafted until late 1915 and no real attempt at allocation was made until August 1917.

By late 1917, it has been claimed, the new Ministry of National Service had at last instituted an effective manpower policy.[13] Such a claim, however, is ill founded for the ministry's achievements were confined largely to paper. The legacy of earlier policies, which had created so many vested interests and so much industrial ill-will, continued to impede the efficient distribution of manpower. Notorious amongst these impediments was the state of incipient warfare between the body responsible for formulating policy (the Ministry of National Service) and the agency for its execution (the employment exchange service). The Ministry of National Service naturally sought direct control over the exchanges, but its advances were fiercely, and successfully, resisted by the Ministry of Labour which, had it been deprived of the exchanges, would have been on its own admission a 'mutilated fragment with no very obvious reason for further existence'.[14]

The employment exchanges were clearly the only national organisation capable of implementing manpower policy. They alone had the trained officials and the network of local offices that could survey the industrial capacity and manpower resources of the country, enrol volunteers under the various recruitment schemes and register, place and transfer labour. It was from their files that candidates for dilution and especially substitution were suggested; and throughout the war, they placed daily an average of 4,000 people, including many of the 1½ million women recruited into the labour force who needed special help to move and settle down in the new munitions centres. From the discharge of these functions, the exchanges acquired an expertise which made them resent detailed instructions from Whitehall, especially those issued by a new and separate ministry, set up in the middle of the war and staffed by untried and purely temporary civil servants. Their willing co-operation with the Ministry of National Service was therefore minimal.

The consequent friction between the Ministries of National Service and Labour was at its most intense during the first eight months of 1917 and included an attempt by the former to develop local 'substitution' offices to bypass the exchanges. It did not abate until both ministers, Neville Chamberlain and Hodge, were dismissed. A concordat was then drawn up to define clearly the respective roles of the ministries but its achievements were limited. By March 1918 the new Minister of National Service (Auckland Geddes) was complaining to Lloyd George:

lines of demarcation, easy to establish on paper, have been found impractical in action. There has been delay, there has been friction, there has been inefficiency ... Whoever is responsible for labour supply, must be in a position to control the machinery which distributes the labour. Daily employers and trade unions press upon me the need of improving the working of the employment exchanges. When I explain to them that this is none of my business they simply do not understand it. They say 'Are you or are you not responsible for Manpower?'. Involved distinctions as to the responsibility for policy divorced from executive action merely make them regard the whole Government machine as absurd.[15]

The situation did not improve. In September 1918, at the climax of yet another interdepartmental battle, the Permanent Secretary to the Ministry of National Service was dismissed.

The fundamental cause of the friction between the two manpower departments can be easily explained. There simply was no need for two ministries; and the government, having once established them, did little to define or regulate their respective roles. The initial confusion was best summarised by Auckland Geddes when he wrote of Chamberlain that he was 'asked to use a department which did not exist to solve a problem which had never been stated'.[16] As early as April 1917 a parliamentary Committee of Inquiry recommended that the two departments should be merged but the War Cabinet ignored its report.[17] No record exists of the reasons why an independent Ministry of National Service was erected; it can only be surmised that the War Cabinet, three of whose five members were Conservatives, was apprehensive about assigning such an important responsibility to a ministry widely regarded as a 'sop for labour men'.[18] The consequences were nevertheless serious. State intervention and state machinery were brought into disrepute. The creation of local advisory committees, through which the Ministry of Labour hoped to popularise the exchanges, was disrupted by the conflict over substitution and the Ministry of National Service assembled a powerful labour advisory committee headed ironically by J. H. Thomas (Lloyd George's original choice as Minister of Labour) which poured scorn on the exchanges.[19] The Ministry of Labour was consequently deprived of both the managerial experience and the public esteem which attended its successful direction of manpower policy during the Second World War.

Industrial relations were as badly administered as manpower policy. Again there was a confusion of departmental responsibilities and again government prevarication. The personal opinion of Askwith was that 'the government had no policy, never gave signs of having a policy and could not be induced to have a policy'.[20] He was no unbiased witness but his conclusions were supported by a disinterested member of the Cabinet who protested in September 1918 that owing to 'the exigencies of war... new Departments have been created and new duties assigned as the need arose without any precise definitions of the scope of their authority'. As a result the Cabinet's time was occupied in listening to discussions between Departments on questions which would have been much better thrashed out between them before the subject was brought to the Cabinet, or in giving decisions on questions of which we have no direct personal knowledge and on which our information is insufficient to give us confidence in the soundness of our decisions. Such a state of things must be detrimental to all concerned. Labour questions are settled piecemeal without any general policy ... Now that we have a Labour Ministry, labour questions should be more and more concentrated in the hands of a Minister of Labour.[21]

No such concentration, however, was achieved during the last years of the war. Instead, responsibility for industrial relations was dispersed among four other departments – the Ministry of Munitions, the Admiralty, the War Office and the Board of Trade. It was they who effectively determined day-to-day policy and controlled conciliation and other labour officials in the provinces.

Industrial relations was admittedly an extremely difficult area of policy to administer. Before the war, there had hardly been industrial harmony. Many employers were still reluctant to recognise trade unions and consequently the unions were suspicious of the permanent use to which wartime concessions might be put. There was also a bitter rivalry between skilled and unskilled unions which could only be intensified by the increased use of automatic machinery (and dilution) which inevitably upset long-established wage differentials. Centralised influence was hard to exert over an industrial structure which boasted 1,100 trade unions and 1,300 employers' associations; and it was made more difficult by the absence of any effective excess-profits or anti-inflation policy, without which sectional demands for wage increases could not be resisted. With the full employment of the war, moreover, labour was enjoying a moment of rare economic strength and understandably was tempted to seek permanent increases in rates of pay. Even if the official leaders had bound themselves to accept compulsory arbitration, the rank and file could still press their claims through the unofficial shop steward movement. Faced with all these difficulties, government policy – to be successful – had to be well planned, firm and consistent. At no time during the war was this the case.

To impose its authority the ministry had, from its establishment, to act decisively. Instead it became bitterly divided over two possible courses of action.[22] On the one hand Askwith wanted to concentrate all conciliation work in his department, subject to the overview of the arbitration court, the Committee on Production (of which he himself was chairman). He was scornful of the ability of the inexperienced officers in the production departments to master the complexities of the industrial situation, especially when their sponsoring departments had an overriding interest to maximise production and hence to avoid disputes. On the other hand, official departmental policy was to maintain the *status quo*. In the uncontrolled industries the ministry, as in peacetime, was to provide conciliation and arbitration services when required. In the controlled industries, however, the conciliation officers of the production departments were to have primary responsibility for the resolving of disputes (subject to procedural guidelines laid down by the ministry and broad financial criteria pronounced by the Committee on Production). Should they be unsuccessful, the dispute was to be referred to the ministry's conciliation officers and if they, in their turn, were unable to resolve it within twenty-one days, the dispute was to be passed to the Committee on Production. That committee was in all cases to be the sole authority for making awards covering more than one group of workers. The ministry advanced three reasons for clinging to the *status quo*. First, any change would cause too great a hiatus in wartime administration (including legislation to remove statutory obligations placed on the Ministry of Munitions). Secondly, it doubted whether the Chief Industrial Commissioner's Department had the resources or Askwith the temperament to co-ordinate all conciliation work. Thirdly, production departments, as contractors, were held to have the necessary economic sanctions to bring both sides of industry to the negotiating table.

The weakness of the official policy, which ultimately prevailed, was that it deprived the ministry of real executive authority and that by divorcing the formulation of policy from its execution (as in manpower policy) it confused rather than clarified responsibility. The ministry, through shortage of staff, had to drop all pretence of conciliation work and referred disputes either back to the production departments or on to the Committee on Production. Deputations became frustrated with the ministry's inability to resolve disputes and Shackleton's patiently reiterated apology that 'the Department does not adjudicate, it only sees fair play'.[23] At the same time, the intransigence of the production departments and the prevarication of the Cabinet prevented the ministry from co-ordinating policy effectively. Two major disputes, with the Coal Controller in May and with the Ministry of Munitions (over Churchill's award of a 12½ per cent rise to skilled workers on time rates) in July 1917, particularly exposed its inability to control pay settlements which had serious repercussions for grades of workers outside the awarding department's competence. After both disputes the War Cabinet emphatically endorsed the ministry's policy but it was nevertheless continually thwarted. The War Cabinet's reaction to repeated breaches of its guidelines was epitomised by the instructions given to its negotiators in the autumn: 'If an imminent strike appeared to be inevitable all the concessions asked for should be granted.'[24] Neither the ineffectuality of the ministry nor the anarchy of government intervention commended to industry the future peacetime use of the ministry's conciliation and arbitration service.

The third area of the ministry's wartime responsibility was the planning of industrial reconstruction and demobilisation. In the field of reconstruction, the ministry recorded its most solid achievements, the passage of the Trade Union (Amalgamation) Act and the Trade Boards (Amendment) Act. Together they realised two of the TUC's long-standing demands, the easing of the conditions under which, respectively, trade unions could combine and minimum wages could be established in individual industries. Its administrative overlap with the Ministry of Reconstruction did lead to some clashes of principle and policy implementation especially over the speed of industrial reform. The planning of reconstruction, however, had none of the urgency of manpower or industrial relations policy and its weaknesses could be obscured by the evasion of decisions. Its real significance, for the history of the ministry, lay in the differences of attitude and policy which it revealed between the new ministry and the Board of Trade. For this reason it will be discussed more fully in the succeeding section.

Demobilisation policy, on the other hand, if it were to be successful, required prompt decisions; and the widespread confusion after the Armistice over the discharge and maintenance of soldiers and munition workers shows that they were not taken. For this neglect, the War Cabinet rather than individual departments was primarily responsible. For example, a scheme of demobilisation to minimise economic and social dislocation after the war had been devised by the Board of Trade as early as the autumn of 1916. As late as August 1918, however, the Cabinet was still refusing to endorse it for fear of encouraging a 'peace atmosphere'.[25] Similar delay in Cabinet over the choice between rival schemes of unemployment insurance disrupted plans for the maintenance of the demobilised. At the Armistice, consequently, the planned ideals of economic demobilisation and contributory insurance had to be abandoned, to be replaced hastily by the expedients of 'first in, first out' and a free 'dole'.

The formulation and execution of wartime labour policy reflected badly on the Lloyd George government in general and the Ministry of Labour in particular. To some extent, both were victims of circumstance. As the Ministry of Munitions (of all departments) advised the United States government on its entry into war: 'the one clear piece of machinery necessary for the effective control of labour during the war is a single, powerful and wide Labour Department';[26] but by the time such a ministry was actually created in Britain, so much industrial ill-will and departmental vested interest had been generated by previous policies that the freedom of action of both the new government and the ministry was severely constrained. There was little evidence, however, of either's determination to master these constraints. As an administrator, Lloyd George suffered from serious defects which have been well summarised by Lord Riddell:

> (1) lack of appreciation of existing institutions, organization and stolid dull people, who often achieve good results by persistency, experience and slow, but sound judgment...(2) Fondness for a grandiose scheme in preference to an attempt to improve existing machinery. (3) Disregard of difficulties in carrying out big projects. This is due to the fact that he is not a man of detail.[27]

These defects fully manifested themselves after December 1916 in the proliferation of ministries with ill-defined responsibilities and in the War Cabinet's continuing inability to determine and enforce policy. Largely absorbed in military strategy, Lloyd George — unlike Churchill in the Second World War — showed little readiness to ensure that either the Cabinet or individual departments could function smoothly in his absence.

On the other hand, the ministry lacked both political leadership and administrative drive. Neither minister was a success. Hodge was a 'rampaging and most patriotic working-man' who at a convivial 18 stone 'looked the part to perfection';[28] but he had neither the administrative ability nor the political imagination properly to establish the ministry or to develop its policies. His successor, Roberts, did hold sincere views on industrial reconstruction but lacked political presence and was dismissed by the public as 'a good music-hall turn rather than as a preacher of a new social gospel'.[29] Neither minister should be pilloried, however, for their individual weakness was a reflection of the political immaturity of the whole labour movement. Between 1916 and 1918 there simply was unavailable to Lloyd George a labour leader who could bridge the gap between government and the shop floor, as could Ernest Bevin in 1940.

Administratively the ministry lacked drive. The self-confident assertiveness of the old Board of Trade departments was either destroyed by the dismissal of key men in December 1916 or submerged beneath Shackleton's conservatism and the intellectual commitment of Butler and his closest advisers to the principle of decentralisation. As a result the ministry's officials, in the last resort, were willing to collude in that division of policy formulation and implementation which so impeded good wartime administration. For example, when the opportunity arose, they shunned any assumption of the Ministry of National Service's powers (for fear that the employment exchanges might be further associated with fears of 'industrial conscription') and declined to take over the conciliation functions of the production departments (for fear that the reputation of the conciliation service would be tarnished by involvement with compulsory arbitration).[30] Serious unresolved flaws also existed in their plans for reconstruction.

The tragedy of the war years was that, by their actions, both Lloyd George and the ministry hastened the very developments they hoped to prevent. The multiplicity of government ministries, with the consequent waste of public money, led directly to calls for retrenchment and the strengthening of Treasury control, which in their turn restricted departmental initiative. On the other hand, the confusion of labour administration provoked demands for decentralisation and 'home rule for industry' and thus the rejection by both sides of industry of the peacetime services provided by the ministry.

The Ministry in Peace

With the coming of peace, the real test of the ministry's contribution to the permanent transformation of British government commenced. Responsibility for demobilisation and resettlement gave it the executive authority it had previously lacked and the implementation of reconstruction programmes assayed the viability of its wartime philosophy and policies. The economic and political climate, however, was far from propitious. After June 1919 the deterioration of the economy intensified the industrial, political and administrative suspicion of central government generated by the war. As the economy declined, so the parliamentary anti-waste campaign strengthened, providing the political context within which the major administrative development of the war, the formal extension of Treasury control, could flourish. These developments seriously threatened the ministry's future.

The ministry's initial postwar responsibilities were formidable. In the short term they included the resettlement of 5½ million demobilised men and women, the hastily improvised payment of the out-of-work donation (which amounted eventually to £62·5m), the development of training and re-training programmes (through which over 180,000 people had passed by 1925) and the supervision of industrial relations (by January 1919, half a million workers were already on strike). In addition the ministry had to plan – in conjunction with the National Industrial Conference – long-term policy including the permanent improvement of industrial relations machinery (the 1919 Industrial Courts Act), the establishment of minimum wages, the regulation of hours of work and the extension of unemployment insurance.

All these responsibilities had to be discharged in a state of administrative confusion as great as, if not even greater than, that prevailing during the war. To the prevarication of the Cabinet (intensified by the Coupon election and then Lloyd George's regular absences in Paris) was added the obstruction of the Treasury which, even before the deterioration of the economy, was determined to reassert its detailed control over the whole Civil Service. The ministry itself was inundated by 4,000 officials from disbanded war departments and had hastily to recruit a further 16,000 to meet the immediate demobilisation crisis. Dislocation was considerable in Whitehall, where responsibility for the greatly increased staff was mainly concentrated in a new temporary department – the Civil Demobilisation and Resettlement Department – headed not by ministry officials but by personnel transferred from the Ministry of Munitions. It was no less serious in the provinces, where nine-tenths of the staff were temporary and had usually to work in inadequate premises.[31] The intense irritation felt during these months was most aptly summarised by the general manager of the employment exchanges who, in welcoming the appointment of a 'permanent boss' to the Civil Demobilisation and Resettlement Department in April 1919, expressed the hope that 'we shall soon have a permanent policy, permanent buildings and a permanent staff'.[32]

Despite the confusion, however, the ministry rose to its immediate challenge as successfully as had the Board of Trade to the introduction of the prewar system of employment exchanges and unemployment insurance. Departmental reorganisation was completed so successfully that by 1920 a sub-committee of the Cabinet's powerful Finance Committee could report that, to the department's 'great credit', there was little 'excessive or uneconomical administration'.[33] Each of the inquiries appointed to examine the discharge of policy also vindicated the ministry. The Aberconway Committee on out-of-work donation, for example, reported that 'there were no grounds for supposing there had been extensive fraudulent abuse' and that 'on the whole the work of the staff had been exceedingly good'; the Permanent Secretary appointed by the Treasury to cast a 'fresh official eye' over the ministry similarly concluded that few economies could be made 'without either ignoring statutory obligations or repudiating pledges given by the Government'.[34] The ministry also helped to secure several administrative developments of more wide-ranging significance. By championing the establishment of Whitley Councils and the adoption of the principle of arbitration and conciliation, it helped to drag industrial relations within the Civil Service into the twentieth century. It also successfully led the resistance to the Treasury's plan to permanently downgrade social service departments by restricting the appointment of administrative class (university-trained) officials to small secretariats advising the minister, leaving the main policy departments to be run by executive class officials (composed largely of school-leavers).[35] Despite being preoccupied with its own reorganisation, the ministry was able to exert more influence than most other departments on the development of the postwar Civil Service.

In the immediate postwar years, however, the ministry did slowly suffer a series of reverses at the hands of the Treasury and the anti-waste campaign; and, in the medium term at least, its ability to act with the vigour and conviction of the prewar Board of Trade was thereby diminished. These reverses have been described elsewhere and need not be repeated in detail.[36] Briefly, the quality of service the ministry could provide for its clients (through, for instance, trained counter-staff at exchanges) was severely restricted by lack of finance. The means by which the Board of Trade had established its reputation for the planning and promotion of policy were destroyed by the Treasury's restriction on statistical research and its veto on the appointment of mature outside experts to senior posts. Policy initiative was further discouraged by the appointment within the ministry of finance and establishment officers who not only inhibited policy-making but also, by monopolising departmental negotiations with the Treasury, insulated Treasury officials from the committed policy-maker and thus from the real problems with which policy was concerned. Finally, the implementation of policy was curtailed by the administrative actions of the Treasury (sometimes in open defiance of 'accepted government policy') where, as in the case of industrial relations or trade boards, it was considered contrary to economic orthodoxy.[37] Politically, the ministry lacked the weight to defend itself successfully both in Whitehall and in Cabinet. After 1920 successive ministers were overwhelmed by the complexities of social administration, as had been all but the presidents of the Board of Trade before the war.

The administrative and political erosion of the ministry greatly influenced the formulation of interwar policy and must therefore be at the heart of any assessment of the long-term significance of the ministry's supercession of the Board of Trade. Two contrasting interpretations can be offered. On the one hand, the ministry's erosion can simply be taken as confirmation of prewar fears, expressed in particular by Llewellyn Smith, that good government would inevitably be impaired by the separation of the Board's responsibilities for commercial and labour policy.[38] The formulation of commercial (and hence industrial) policy lost its vital contact with the problems of social policy and the development of social policy was stunted by the new ministry's lack of administrative capacity and political strength. In other words administrative reorganisation, rather than Treasury control or the anti-waste campaign, destroyed the prewar momentum of reform. On the other hand, it can be argued that in the changed postwar world, the influence of even an undivided Board of Trade would have been undermined. First, the structural weaknesses of the economy (and hence mass unemployment) would have proved unamenable to its traditional policy of economic *laissez-faire*. Secondly, an increasingly hostile economic and industrial climate would have challenged its programme of social reform. New liberalism's equation of social with productive expenditure, for example, had been replaced by a general acceptance of the Treasury view that all public expenditure was to be deprecated as lost investment. Moreover leading employers, who before the war had been prepared to accept selective social investment, were being dragooned by new bodies such as the National Confederation of Employers' Organisations into relating the cost of social expenditure to their lack of international competitiveness. Most important of all, however, it should be remembered that by 1916 — if not by 1914 — the Board had reached an administrative and political impasse. In the vigour of its assault on the irrationality of the labour market, it had failed to carry public opinion with it and had antagonised vested-interest groups. The future of its reform programme was thus already jeopardised.

The significance of the Board's dismemberment depends on the choice between those two rival interpretations. In particular, it depends on the answer to two specific questions. Could the Board's public standing and policies have been adapted after the war to meet changed economic and political priorities? Was the new ministry able to provide viable alternative solutions to Britain's economic and social problems?

Popular hostility towards the Board of Trade was given its most notorious expression by Ernest Bevin at the 1916 TUC conference when he launched his attack on that 'sinister crowd of civil servants — the Labour exchange crowd — Mr Beveridge, Llewellyn Smith and the rest'.[39] This outburst, admittedly, came after the Board's officials had become identified with the Ministry of Munitions and after both sides of industry had been antagonised by the Board's suspension of long-standing customs and restrictive practices in its attempt to expedite war production. It coincided also with the successful revolt by trade unions against the Board's attempt to anticipate the problems of civil demobilisation by obliging all munition workers to insure themselves against unemployment. Resistance to the Board's policy, however, had been widespread before the war. Individual employers had remained uncommitted to new services such as the employment exchanges. Workers had resented the way in which (for instance) de-casualisation threatened to upset traditional work patterns. Trade unions had expressed apprehension that the new social services would rival their own and thus discourage recruitment. Finally, socialists had railed against both the inequity of financing selective social services by insurance rather than by national taxation and the insidious way in which the 'impartial' conciliation services compromised the bargaining strength of trade unions. During the war, indeed, it was asserted that all the Ministry of Munitions' labour policy had done was to expose prewar Board of Trade policy for what it really was, a bureaucratic attempt to erect a 'servile state'.[40]

Postwar abatement in public hostility towards the Board depended on whether its fundamental cause was genuine differences over policy or merely the conservative reaction of vested-interest groups to major changes in government policy tactlessly introduced. On the trade union side it was often forgotten that, even during the war, the Board antagonised employers as much as the unions and secured for labour important gains which would not necessarily have been won by the exercise of naked economic power. The Board strove to be 'impartial', defending the 'national interest' in industrial disputes (according to Askwith) and preventing the exploitation of whichever side of industry was temporarily at an economic disadvantage (according to Beveridge).[41] However, what the labour movement disputed with some justification was the true impartiality of officials trained in universities and not in 'the workshops, the factories and the mines of the country'.[42] As a TUC deputation argued in 1917 when seeking the dilution of civil servants on the Committee on Production (the 'impartial' court of arbitration chaired by Askwith): 'It may be said in reply to our request for labour representation on this committee that those who compose it do not represent Capital. Well, we say that they do. We say that a stipendiary Magistrate, who is supposed to be impartial... belongs to the middle classes. The fairest stipendiaries can have prejudices without knowing it.'[43]

To allay its suspicions the labour movement demanded representation in government, or at least on government bodies which enjoyed real power. In the Board's defence, it could again be argued that it had shared power with labour to an unprecedented extent. For instance, between 1908 and 1913 at least 117 trade unionists had been appointed to the Board at an annual cost of £25,240;[44] a TUC delegation had been invited to study social legislation in Germany and its chairman (none other than Shackleton) had helped to select the initial intake of employment exchange staff; and, during the war, a whole range of advisory and judicial bodies from the Ministry of Munitions' National Labour Advisory Committee to its munitions tribunals had been established with labour representation. However, the manner in which labour was consulted and the degree of power that had been conceded left much to be desired. In the words of one critic, the Board was motivated by 'the spirit in which you govern labour for the good of labour on behalf of labour, but keep labour at a distance'.[45] Frequent consultation tended only to intensify suspicion.

The creation of the Ministry of Labour was consequently a positive step forward for at least it gave the labour movement what it demanded, direct representation in government. Although the bulk of the ministry's officials were ironically the 'sinister' Employment Department officials, Beveridge and Llewellyn Smith had been removed and the first two ministers, together with the new Permanent Secretary, were trade unionists. The ministry's new attitude towards labour was immediately revealed by Hodge when he assured the first deputation he received: 'When a representative body like the Parliamentary Committee of the T.U.C. comes on behalf of the workmen and makes representations that certain things are unsatisfactory, some solution must be found.'[46] Later, Roberts and Shackleton were even more explicit about their commitment. Roberts informed another TUC deputation: 'I may tell you that I am animated here with the same spirit as a member of the T.U.C. and the ordinary trade union movement, and as far as possible and with due regard for Ministerial responsibility I will seek to carry out that old policy, because I see that that policy is not only proper for the people we represent but also good for the State.' Shackleton likewise confided: 'I have no interest except the State, but if I have any bias it leans towards those with whom I have always worked.'

These statements might be interpreted as attempts to win easy approbation but such cynicism would be unjustified. Words were turned into action. The first full TUC deputation to Hodge in January 1917 demanded five main reforms. Within a few months all had been conceded, Hodge acting with a singlemindedness which appalled traditional defenders of 'impartiality' such as Askwith.[47] Thereafter trade union views were regularly and sympathetically expounded to the Cabinet, even by the first non-trade unionist minister (Sir Robert Horne), whom one historian has described in the first months of peace as having 'tirelessly and brilliantly expounded to his colleagues the factual basis of the workers' unrest'.[48] Advisory committees were established (such as the employment exchanges' local advisory committees) with far greater freedom to initiate discussion than the Board's committees. A restoration of prewar practices bill (one of the touchstones by which the trade unions judged the government's good faith) was enacted in the teeth of Conservative opposition. Finally, draft legislation (such as the 1919 industrial courts bill and the International Labour Organisation's charter) was submitted to the TUC for its early consideration.

The International Labour Organisation's charter epitomised the new approach to industry which, in its earliest years, the ministry strove to adopt. In contrast to the Board's policy, real power in the drafting of legislation was conceded to both sides of industry. Employers and trade unions were to be directly represented on the Organisation's Governing Body and were permitted to vote in opposition to their own government. At home, a similar revolution was to be attempted in the government's relationship with industry. As Butler declared in January 1918:

It is the strong belief of the Department that the great problems of industrial reorganization which were looming ahead before the war and which have now been brought definitely to the front by war conditions, can only be successfully solved by a policy of decentralization. It is clear that no system of bureaucratic control of industry is ever likely to succeed in this country. There are two reasons for this (a) that State interference is foreign to the whole temper and outlook

of the English people, who have always been bred in the belief that
they are competent to manage their own affairs and (b) that no system
of centralized administration is likely to produce such good results as
a system by which the people concerned are themselves interested in
the working out of their problems and the success of the scheme
adopted to solve them.[49]

Greater state intervention, in the shape of trade boards, was planned in
those industries where workers were insufficiently organised to bargain
with their employers but otherwise the overriding principle was to be
'home rule for industry'. Joint industrial (Whitley) councils were to be
established in all industries with three main objectives: to create a forum
in which both sides of industry could express their common interests, to
give workers 'a recognized share in the determination of their conditions
of work' and to provide government with authoritative advice on industrial
policy. In 1919 this policy of decentralisation was taken to its logical
conclusion when, during the experiment with the National Industrial
Conference, the ministry encouraged the Cabinet to permanently devolve
responsibility for industrial policy to a new industrial parliament.[50]

The new ministry, therefore, consciously strove to develop a new
industrial strategy. Its actual achievements, however, were negligible. The
political honeymoon between the ministry and the labour movement
was short-lived. Hodge (the president of the right-wing British Workers'
National League) and Roberts (disowned on his re-election as minister by
his local trades council for opposing British attendance at the Stockholm
Peace Conference) were never regarded by organised labour let alone the
unofficial shop-stewards as their true representatives. The ministry per-
severed with its defence of trade unions especially during the shop-stewards'
unrest in 1917. Shackleton, for example, impressed upon a delegation of
Scottish iron and steel shop-stewards:

> Any transaction regarding wage disputes, the Ministry of Labour ever
> since its inception has conducted through the accredited officials...
> That is the policy of the Ministry and unless we maintain that policy
> we will very quickly get into chaos... Obviously the Society would
> resent anything in the nature of the Ministry settling matters with
> people other than themselves. I want you to understand that this is
> the position and this position must remain so long as Trade Unions and
> the Ministry of Labour exist. The two will have to recognize one
> another.[51]

The trade unions, however, remained ambivalent in their attitude to the
ministry. An underlying hostility continued to exist towards anyone who
collaborated with government. As Shackleton lamented in 1919:

It is the experience of all ex-officials of Trade Unions who enter Government Service or act as Arbitrators that they are soon told that they have lost touch with the aspirations of the 'workers'. It has gone even further now; any leader who as a result of the additional education which close contact with employers and with economic facts afford him, has the courage to advise his members in the light of this further information, is looked upon as a 'lost soul' and told he is no longer in touch with workshop life.[52]

In such an industrial atmosphere, the mere appointment of working-class ministers and officials could do little to dispel the inherent state of suspicion that had earlier existed between the labour movement and the Board of Trade.

Political and administrative necessity also undermined the working-class credentials of the ministry. When the Labour Party withdrew from Lloyd George's coalition in 1918 a Conservative barrister, Sir Robert Horne, became the new minister. Despite his affability and initial sympathy for trade union aspirations, he gradually identified himself with conventional business wisdom (for instance, leading the attack in Cabinet against the proposed nationalization of coal) and grew increasingly hostile to the unions (as a result of their unwillingness to respond 'constructively' to his consensus policies).[53] At the same time, there was a significant change in the ministry's official recruitment policy. Before the war, trade unionists had been regularly recruited to the expanding social and conciliation services but doubts had developed about their suitability. After the replacement of Askwith by Horace Wilson as the head of the industrial relations departments in 1919, the Treasury's ban on outside recruitment and the inauguration of an Establishment Department which sought for senior appointments university graduates (though specifically not 'long-haired intellectuals of the Bolshevik type'),[54] all such exceptional appointments ceased. This restriction on recruitment coinciding with Butler's transfer to the International Labour Organisation, helped to draw official policy back into the establishment's embrace.

Even before these changes of personnel, the ministry's excessive sympathy for the trade unions had been qualified. In 1917 Hodge (in the best sporting phraseology of a 'rampaging and most patriotic Tory working-man') proclaimed: 'If one is going to make the Ministry of Labour a success it can only be done, if I may say so ... by playing cricket, that is we have got to be fair to both sides.'[55] This attitude was soon adopted by his officials, Shackleton repeating in 1919: 'I think we can be as neutral as any other Department. Our whole atmosphere is one of neutrality and if it were otherwise we could not exist for a day.'[56] The ministry's 'neutrality' smacked very much of the Board's 'impartiality' and when the postwar economic climate turned in favour of the employers, it was open to similar objections from the trade unions. In the 1920s the labour movement could even, with some justification, accuse the ministry of having (like the Board of Trade) compromised it during its brief period of economic ascendancy. In the interests of its policy of 'home rule for industry', the ministry had actively encouraged the employers to organise nationally so that they could meet the TUC on equal terms. It therefore helped to create the National Confederation of Employers' Organisations which was throughout the interwar period to represent all that was most reactionary in employers' attitudes, smothering each suggestion of reform with 'obstructive inertia'.[57]

The ministry's own reform programme also sought to incorporate the trade union movement, as indeed all consensus industrial policies must, into the conventional political framework. Organisational changes such as trade union amalgamation and Whitley Councils were championed partly because the erection of 'recognised' machinery would make administration easier. Their main objective, however, was to place greater responsibility on both sides of industry, in particular the trade unions. As the radical Intelligence Department of the ministry wrote in one of its Cabinet reports in 1919: 'Organized industrial power is a thing which cannot be abolished any more than physical force can be abolished, but can only be dealt with by being turned in the right direction and harnessed through the superposition of a corresponding responsibility.'[58] Trade union amalgamation, therefore, was welcomed because 'the greater the area over which the union is spread, the more difficult it is in the long run to have spasmodic strikes'; and, in a phrase that would delight the modern sociologist, demarcation problems were swept aside as a valid objection to the Whitley report because such problems always provided 'an obstacle to a precise and logical application of any form of social control'.[59]

In reality, therefore, the ministry's new approach to industry represented little positive advance on the prewar position of the Board of Trade. In the formulation of policy, and in particular the development of a new economic policy to combat the mass unemployment, the story was just the same. In the ministry's defence, it might be argued that the policies of the Board were themselves incapable of resolving the major economic and social problems of the interwar period. Apart from their unpopularity, administrative schemes to rationalise the labour market combined with limited programmes of public works were simply inadequate to correct the structural weaknesses of the economy. After the war many of the Board's adherents admitted the inadequacy of their prewar thinking;[60] and the Board's own interwar record revealed that it was ill equipped to administer the policies of industrial rationalisation and economic management which governments came slowly to recognise as the only remedy for the problems of the interwar economy.

The creation of the ministry, however, did nothing positive to improve the situation and indeed, by causing the Board's fragmentation, could be said to have made the situation worse. First, by divorcing the formulation of industrial and social policy, it helped to consign employment policy to a departmental limbo in which it could not satisfactorily be considered. The ministry itself, submerged in the practical details of social administration, was unable to assist the development of an alternative economic strategy and thus aspire to the role of a 'national authority for unemployment' envisaged by its prewar advocates. Rather, the concerted reappraisal of employment policy had to await the reintegration of economic and social planning under new administrative machinery.[61] Secondly, the ministry failed to bring to the formulation of policy the rigorous powers of analysis that had characterised the work of the prewar Board. Its reconstruction programme, for example, was made vulnerable to the logic of economic orthodoxy by the failure to think through its full financial implications. This failing, as has been noted, was not entirely the fault of the ministry's officials. Treasury retrenchment eroded their ability to plan policy initiatives, and even when such initiatives were developed they were pursued with insufficient conviction in Cabinet.[62] It did reveal, however, that ministry officials lacked the exceptional expertise and intellectual commitment of their Edwardian predecessors.

These shortcomings of the ministry were particularly exposed in the policy which dominated all its actions, that of decentralisation or 'home rule for industry'. In essence, this policy was an instinctive reaction to industry's hostility towards bureaucracy; it was not a positive policy capable of solving the fundamental economic and social problems facing interwar Britain. To be successful, decentralisation required genuine industrial consensus and a commitment by government to devolve power. In the 1920s neither existed. Events after the Armistice rapidly disabused those committed wartime reformers who had professed to see after 1914 the gradual growth of industrial consensus. The number of working days lost through strikes escalated, the trade union movement remained disunited over crucial issues such as nationalisation and the leadership of the employers devolved to a man (Sir Allan Smith) who had the unfortunate habit of referring to the unions as 'the enemy'. Joint industrial bodies were consequently incapable of making far-reaching agreements and even when the germs of such agreements were committed to paper (as during the first months of the National Industrial Conference) there remained so many 'mental reservations' on both sides that their translation into specific laws proved impossible. Such difficulties had been anticipated by the more realistic wartime administrators. In 1918, for example, Butler had written: 'Everybody — employers and workers alike — are saying they don't want the State to act, they want the State to keep out and let them handle their own problems; but they are *not* handling their own problems. They are doing nothing — except abuse the State ... If no-one acts, the State will,

not because it wants to, but because someone must!'[63] His advice, however, went unheeded. No fall-back position was prepared.

Even had industrial consensus been attainable, it is doubtful whether
successive Cabinets would have honoured it. As their later reaction to the
resolutions of the National Industrial Conference and the conventions of
the International Labour Organisation showed, interwar governments
resented dictation from outside bodies and were unwilling to be bound by
joint agreements.[64] Moreover, the ministry itself was often less than
sincere in its endorsement of devolved responsibility. For instance, during
the appointment of the employment exchanges' local advisory committees
Hodge sought to prevent 'the nomination of people we do not want'; and
for a long time the ministry opposed the principle of individual industries'
'contracting out' of the national scheme of unemployment insurance
so that the financial risks of unemployment could be spread over all
industries.[65] The fundamental constitutional issue of how to reconcile
ministerial responsibility to parliament with devolved administration was
never resolved and it remained to excite political controversy in the 1930s
in relation to such semi-autonomous bodies as the Unemployment Assistance Board. In truth, the ministry's policy of decentralisation soon
proved as empty as the rest of its new industrial strategy. After the brief
euphoria of wartime planning, it lost all pretence of being a positive
policy to resolve Britain's problems and degenerated into a pretext for
government inaction, a means by which the new specialist ministries could
evade their major responsibilities.

Conclusion

In the short term, therefore, the creation of the ministry did little to
improve the efficiency of government. During the war, its presence further
confused manpower and industrial relations policy and its officials added
to the contradictions inherent in the government's vague programmes of
reconstruction. In the immediate postwar years, it failed to develop either
an effective new industrial strategy or a long-term programme to resolve
the economic, social and political problems that had emerged during the
war. Fundamental issues such as the break-up of the poor law, the defence
of the 'national interest' during industrial disputes and the need to increase
social expenditure during a depression remained unresolved and largely
ignored. The ministry's achievements, such as the exclusion of politicians
from daily involvement in industrial relations, were largely negative. Any
positive achievement − for example, the extension of contributory unemployment insurance and the continuing representation of trade union views
in Cabinet − were due not so much to its own efforts but to parliamentary
concern for the unemployed and the industrial strength of the unions.

The ministry's early ineffectuality was not entirely the fault of its officials but reflected the political and administrative constraints within which they were obliged to operate. After 1920 decisive political leadership was lacking. Minority Labour governments shrank from implementing the reforms which Labour's prewar advocacy of the ministry had demanded, and, between the publication of the Geddes and May reports on public expenditure (1922–31), Conservative administrations lacked the boldness of vision to seek anything other than a return to 'prewar normalcy'. Lack of industrial consensus also fettered the ministry. In its early years, however, the ministry did pioneer one major political advance. It acknowledged – as the prewar Board of Trade failed to do – the very real limitations placed on bureaucracy by a pluralistic, democratic constitution. As one of its officials had argued in 1917, 'the success of a scheme ... is dependent in the long run on the cordial assent of the employers' associations and the unions and this can only be secured by meeting their wishes, however unreasonable they may seem'.[66] This was to be the philosophy of the ministry throughout the interwar period. Such 'stoical realism' perhaps discouraged the ministry from mounting a rational attack on fundamental economic and social problems but at least, in a time of very real distress, it helped to preserve social and industrial harmony. After the turmoil of the immediate postwar years, consensus had come to be valued as an end in itself as much as for any positive reform it might achieve.[67]

The administrative constraints on the ministry resulted from the most important single change to the machinery of government effected by the war – the formal strengthening of Treasury control. Greater homogeneity was undoubtedly needed in the Civil Service if it was to discharge the increased responsibilities which postwar society demanded of it, but ironically greater centralisation led to the standardisation of economic and social values which undermined the very departmental expertise which policy initiative required. Consequently the new specialist ministries, which the war had spawned, stifled rather than promoted new ideas. In the early 1920s the ministry was no exception, its Permanent Secretary (Sir Horace Wilson) being particularly keen to toe the Treasury line in the 'interests of the service'. The spirit of 'positive voluntarism' which had characterised the prewar Board of Trade was thereby lost.[68]

As the 1920s progressed, however, the ministry acquired greater confidence and started to challenge the administrative and economic assumptions of the Treasury. For example, the pre-eminence of generalist administrators was challenged when their doyen – Sir Francis Floud – was appointed as Wilson's successor but was able to make little impression on the ministry and had to be replaced by a departmental specialist, Sir Thomas Phillips. The orthodoxy of the 'Treasury view' also came to be seriously questioned by ministry officials after their first-hand experience of social distress in the regions. As a result, by the 1930s (when the attempt to return to 'prewar normalcy' had at last been abandoned) it was the ministry's officials in the new semi-autonomous bodies who – within the strict limits set by the conservatism of public opinion – led the way forward. In this respect it was the ministry, rather than such formal schemes for rational reform as the Haldane Report on the Machinery of Government, which emerged from the war as the 'still small voice' pointing the way to the future.

Notes: Chapter 5

This essay is part of a longer study of the Ministry between 1916 and 1945 for which I have received financial assistance from the Nuffield Foundation and the SSRC and invaluable help from many former civil servants and fellow academics. In particular I should like to acknowledge the personal help of Dr Roger Davidson and Dr Noelle Whiteside on whose research several parts of this essay are based.

1   G 245, Lloyd George Papers, House of Lords Record Office, London.
2   H. B. Butler, *Confident Morning* (London: Faber, 1950), p. 121.
3   A. Bullock, *The Life and Times of Ernest Bevin*, Vol. II (London: Heinemann, 1967), p. 119.
4   For a description of the prewar demands of the ministry see R. Lowe, 'The Ministry of Labour, 1916–1924: a graveyard of social reform?', *Public Administration*, vol. 52 (1974), pp. 415–38.
5   *Parl. Papers 1922*, Vol. ix (Cmd 1581), pp. 141–60.
6   Two vacuous Liberal orators (Macnamara in the early 1920s and Ernest Brown in the late 1930s) were separated by well-meaning but ineffectual Conservatives (Montague Barlow, Steel-Maitland, Betterton and Stanley) and two statutory trade unionists (Shaw and Bondfield). The appointment to the post of the first woman Cabinet minister in 1929 and a Liberal nationalist in 1935 might be taken as a measure of the ministry's lowly status.
7   B. B. Gilbert, *British Social Policy 1914–1939* (London: Batsford, 1970), p. 307.
8   In 1920 a new Permanent Secretary was appointed to inquire (unbeknown to his minister) into the administrative need for the ministry. His reply that (apart from the political danger of abolishing a 'Ministry labelled "Labour"') there was a sufficient volume of coherent administration to justify a ministry of Cabinet status permanently convinced the Treasury. AC 25/4/37, Austen Chamberlain Papers, Birmingham University Library.
9   In 1939 the Permanent and Third Secretary (Sir H. Wilson and Sir A. Barlow) and the principal assistant secretary in charge of the social services division (F. N. Tribe) had had lengthy careers in the ministry. For their wartime importance see Bullock, *The Life and Times of Ernest Bevin*, Vol. II, p. 119.
10 For Beveridge's dismissal, see J. Harris, *William Beveridge* (Oxford: Clarendon Press, 1977), pp. 230–1. For the peculiarities of Askwith, see R. Lowe, 'Review article', *British Journal of Industrial Relations*, vol. 13 (1975), pp. 115–20.
11 88 *House of Commons Debates* 5 s., 18 December 1916, col. 1172.
12 I. Macleod, *Neville Chamberlain* (London: Frederick Muller, 1961), p. 61.
13 H. M. D. Parker, *Manpower* (London: HMSO, 1957), p. 17.

14   GT 1825, 20 August 1917, CAB 24/24.
15   F 17/5/12, Lloyd George Papers. The concordat is in LAB 2/297/ED 39023/12, Ministry of Labour Papers, Public Record Office, London.
16   A. Fitzroy, *Memoirs*, Vol. II (London: Hutchinson, 1925), p. 660.
17   GT 644, 26 April 1917, CAB 24/12.
18   Churchill's phrase in Lloyd George papers, F 8/2/49.
19   See, for example, their letter to *The Times*, 26 July 1917. For Thomas's refusal of the ministry, see J. H. Thomas, *My Story* (London: Hutchinson, 1937), pp. 44–5.
20   G. R. Askwith, *Industrial Problems and Disputes* (London: John Murray, 1920), pp. 443.
21   GT 5792, 26 September 1918, CAB 24/64. The author was Austen Chamberlain who, as Neville's half-brother, had no cause to love the ministry.
22   For a fuller discussion of the civil war see Lowe in *British Journal of Industrial Relations*.
23   LAB 10/399. The staffing constraints on the Chief Industrial Commissioner's Department were such that in 1914 seven officials were available to handle eighty-eight conciliations and arbitration cases, in 1918 only thirty to handle 2,681.
24   WC 440 (1), 4 July 1918, CAB 23/7. The resolution of the Coal Controller's dispute (which took five months) had occasioned the first authoritative Cabinet statement on industrial relations procedure, the Barnes-Milner memorandum, GT 2194 A, 4 October 1917, CAB 24/27. Its reaffirmation after the 12½ per cent fiasco is recorded in GT 2772A, 27 November 1917, CAB 24/23 and WC 317 (1), 7 January 1918, CAB 23/5.
25   GT 56, February 1917, CAB 24/6. WC 462 (3), 21 August 1918, CAB 23/7.
26   MUN 5 – 346 – 300 – 2, Ministry of Munitions Papers, PRO.
27   *Lord Riddell's War Diary* (London: Nicholson & Watson, 1933), p. 265.
28   A. Griffith-Boscawen, *Memories* (London: John Murray, 1925), p. 207. Fitzroy, *Memoirs*, Vol. II, p. 642.
29   Butler, *Confident Morning*, p. 124.
30   See, for example, GT 1825, 20 August 1917, CAB 24/24 and LAB 2/427/HQ 262.
31   In one town, for instance, the only place with sufficient flat surfaces for signing on the unemployed was the local graveyard (Minlabour, vol. 14, 1, 1960). The Treasury also sited the central unemployment insurance records office at Kew on a site liable to be flooded and where, on one notable occasion, dogs were found swimming amongst the stamps which had been washed from their cards. Planners continue to triumph. The site is now occupied by the Public Record Office.
32   *This Month's Work*, vol. 1, no. 10 (1919). The forthrightness of J. B. Adams, the general manager, was legendary. Churchill, keen to appoint him in 1909 owing to his Antarctic adventures, was not discouraged when to the inquiry about what impressed him most about Beveridge's book *Unemployment*, Adams replied 'the price'.
33   *Parl. Papers 1920*, Vol. xxv (Cmd 1069), p. 265, paras 9 and 16.
34   *Parl. Papers 1919*, Vol. xxx (Cmd 305), p. 201, paras 12 and 41; AC 25/4/37, Austen Chamberlain Papers.
35   T.1/12610/24460/1920, Treasury Papers, PRO.
36   R. Lowe in *Public Administration* (1974).
37   See R. Lowe, 'The erosion of state intervention in Britain, 1917–24', *Economic History Review*, vol. 31 (1978), pp. 278–81 for the attack on trade boards. The mere existence of industrial relations staff was held to discourage trade unionists

from accepting the 'hard facts' of industrial life and so their number was cut by 87 per cent between 1919 and 1924.

38 See particularly LAB 2/213/L156/1904.
39 *The Times*, 6 September 1916.
40 See especially Harris, *William Beveridge*, p. 195; N. Whiteside, 'Welfare insurance and casual labour: a study of administrative intervention in industrial employment 1906–1926', *Economic History Review*, vol. 32 (1979), pp. 507–22; R. Davidson, 'The Board of Trade and industrial relations', *The Historical Journal*, vol. 21 (1978), pp. 571–91; J. Hinton, *The First Shop Stewards' Movement* (London: Allen & Unwin, 1973), ch. 1.
41 C 16/4/4, Lloyd George Papers; W. H. Beveridge, *Power and Influence* (London: Hodder & Stoughton, 1953), p. 162.
42 TUC, *Annual Report*, 1916, p. 185.
43 LAB 2/218/ML 1132/1917. Askwith's formation, after his dismissal from the civil service, of a Middle-Class Union to defend the small property owner against the 'extreme demands of labour' provided telling confirmation of TUC suspicions.
44 E. Halevy, *The Rule of Democracy* (London: Benn, 1961 edn), p. 447.
45 95 *H.C. Deb.* 5 s., 28 June 1917, col. 596.
46 LAB 2/218/ML 1132/1917. The following quotations are from LAB 10/399 (deputations on 23 November and 21 September 1917).
47 The five reforms were representation on the Committee on Production, cancellation of the proposed extension of unemployment insurance, greater trade union involvement in the running of employment exchanges and legislation to facilitate the extension of trade boards and trade union amalgamation. Hodge's reaction to the fifth demand was 'the Labour Party should be asked for a print and then I could ask the War Cabinet to adopt it'. LAB 2/218/ML 1059/3.
48 P. B. Johnson, *Land Fit for Heroes* (Chicago: Chicago University Press, 1968), p. 472.
49 LAB 2/218/ML 1059/3.
50 CP 68, 5 November 1919, CAB 24/92.
51 LAB 10/399 (deputation on 21 September 1917). The society was the Iron Moulders' Association.
52 LAB 10/64.
53 WC 614A, 14 August 1919, CAB 23/15.
54 C. G. Dennys to F. Tribe (1919, no date), Tribe Papers, private possession; quotation by kind permission of Dr C. R. Tribe. The postwar orthodoxy of the ministry can therefore be contrasted to the prewar unorthodoxy of the Board, one of whose socialist recruits (C. E. M. Joad) was simultaneously receiving smuggled diamonds to pay the expenses of the Russian trade mission. See F. Meynell, *My Lives* (London: Bodley Head, 1971), p. 121.
55 LAB 2/213/ML 2161. Griffith-Boscawen, *Memories*, p. 207.
56 LAB 10/64.
57 The ministry's own phrase in CP 285 (27), 19 November 1927, CAB 24/189. Terry Rodgers has confirmed that the Allan Smith papers provide evidence of Sir Robert Horne's collusion in the setting up of the NCEO.
58 GT 7361, 28 May 1919, CAB 24/80.
59 G. J. Wardle (the ministry's future parliamentary secretary) in 93 *H.C. Deb.* 5 s., 14 May 1917, col. 1430; the reference to social control was inevitably by an academic, Henry Clay, in LAB 2/212/ML 12177.
60 See, for example, Harris, *Beveridge*, pp. 258–9 and Beatrice Webb's diary, 25 May 1924, Passfield Papers, British Library of Political and Economic Science, The London School of Economics.

61 The government experimented with the Committee of Civil Research and the Lord Privy Seal's office (1929–31), for example. All reform programmes, such as Mosley's, also started with administrative reorganisation. See R. Skidelsky, *Politicians and the Slump* (Harmondsworth: Penguin, 1970 edn), pp. 195–8.

62 See Lowe in *Economic History Review*, section 4.

63 LAB 2/454/ML 2574/8.

64 See, for instance, R. Lowe, 'The failure of consensus in Britain: the National Industrial Conference 1919–21', *The Historical Journal*, vol. 21 (1978), pp. 703–4.

65 LAB 2/231/ED 28232/5; T.1/12594/23571. The extension of unemployment insurance is a good example of a policy battle fought within a department in a rapidly changing political and industrial environment. To the old Board of Trade Employment Department decentralisation was anathema. The new Headquarters Departments defeated it in principle in February 1919, but the complexities of the industrial structure and mass unemployment rendered 'contracting out' unworkable.

66 LAB 2/254/ML 12475/2. Beveridge was a late convert to this philosophy. As he wrote in *Power & Influence* (1953), p. 102: 'unreasoning rejection of industrial discipline even in war however dangerous in itself is perhaps the last ditch against totalitarian rule'.

67 See H. E. Dale, *The Higher Civil Service* (London: Oxford University Press, 1941), p. 94 and M. Hill, *The Sociology of Public Administration* (London: Weidenfeld & Nicolson, 1972), p. 104. This issue has recently been raised, and obscured, by K. Middlemas, *Politics in Industrial Society* (London: Deutsch, 1979).

68 R. Davidson, 'Social conflict and social administration', in T. C. Smout (ed.), *The Search for Wealth and Stability* (London: Macmillan, 1979), p. 194.

6

Bureaucrats and Businessmen in British Food Control, 1916-19

I

The Ministry of Food that was set up as a result of the Cabinet crisis of December 1916 bore, superficially at least, all the hallmarks of the new Prime Minister's personal philosophy of government. Headed by a Liberal businessman, it was staffed partly by a small nucleus of professional civil servants and partly by a much larger group of temporary administrators, drawn from retail trading, brewing, catering, agriculture, journalism, banking and finance. Over the next three years the ministry gradually established a monopoly over 85 per cent of the nation's food supplies, and in the financial year ending March 1919 registered a turnover of £900 million. All this was done with minimal expense to the taxpayer — in fact, accounts rendered by the ministry at the end of the war showed a modest profit of one-quarter of 1 per cent.[1] This experiment in state trading was interpreted by contemporaries in various conflicting ways: as a model for permanent state socialism; as proof that socialism could only work in conditions of dire national emergency; and as a landmark in that convergence of state and entrepreneurial interests which some historians have seen as a central theme of twentieth-century British history.[2] The vast range of the ministry's activities and the volume of its records make it impossible to explore such questions in detail here. The following essay will be mainly concerned with debates about the scope of state control provoked by the wartime food crisis, and with the widely varying and often conflicting contributions to those debates made by Whitehall civil servants and by businessmen drawn into government for the duration of the war.

II

At the outbreak of war in 1914 patterns of food production and consumption in Britain differed markedly from those in other combatant countries. More than 70 per cent of wheat and more than 60 per cent of meat eaten in Britain were imported from abroad.[3] Less than 10 per cent of the working population was engaged in agriculture – compared with over 40 per cent in France and over 37 per cent in Germany.[4] Since 1870 there had been a decline of 4 million acres in arable cultivation, and although there had been some expansion in meat and dairy farming, this had fallen far short of demographic growth.[5] By contrast, the retail distribution of food was a highly dynamic area of the economy, and probably no country in the world in 1914 had a more extensive and rationalised system of food marketing.[6] This balance between the interests of producers and consumers was closely reflected in prewar politics and public policy. Nowhere was the philosophy of free trade more deeply entrenched than in popular attitudes to food prices; and one of the major political battles of the 1900s had been waged over the issue of the cheap versus dear loaf. Alone among primary producers in advanced economies, British agriculturalists enjoyed no protection from tariffs; and government interference in the food trade was almost entirely confined to two peripheral areas – encouragement of scientific research through the Board of Agriculture, and enforcement of the laws against food adulteration.

The strategic dangers of Britain's dependence on foreign food had aroused some concern in the years before the war, and had been the subject of a Royal Commission in 1904–5. This Commission calculated that in the pre-harvest season national wheat reserves could fall as low as six-and-a-half weeks' supply (and readily available stocks to a mere one-and-a-half weeks' supply) and predicted that an outbreak of war would almost certainly be accompanied by inflation and panic buying.[7] Evidence from the Admiralty indicated that there was some doubt in naval circles about how far the navy would be able to maintain supply lines in wartime – and revealed also considerable disagreement among admirals about how much priority should, in fact, be given to defending the mercantile marine. These doubts and difficulties were, however, brushed aside in the commissioners' report. 'A blockade of the United Kingdom is said to be virtually impossible', they declared, 'so that this topic need not further detain us.'[8] Modern warships were not equipped for taking 'prizes', so there was little danger that food supplies would be treated as 'contraband of war'.[9] Profiteering by food traders was dismissed as 'well nigh impossible', and there was every hope that the interests of civilians would be protected by recent advances in international law.[10] Any attempt by the government to build up emergency supplies would be excessively expensive and ultimately self-defeating, since it would seriously disrupt normal channels of trade. The Commission's report concluded by recommending merely that the Board of Agriculture should improve its food statistics, and that in the event of war the government should maintain trade confidence by indemnifying shipowners whose vessels fell into enemy hands. With these two exceptions, strategic food policy was to be entirely subsumed under the two-power standard and Britain's command of the seas.[11] This extra-ordinary exercise in wishful thinking became over the next ten years 'the Bible and textbook of our rulers on the whole subject of food and raw materials in time of war'.[12]

Among combatant countries in 1914 Britain was therefore unique in having no arrangements for food production as part of her defence plans,[13] and this policy of official *laissez-faire* was retained almost without modification for more than two years of war. In the autumn of 1914 there was some pressure in parliament for state control of food supplies. But the Board of Agriculture confined itself to setting up a Consultative Committee and exhorting farmers to switch from meat to arable production; and the President of the Board of Trade, Walter Runciman, insisted that food supplies could best be maintained through normal commercial channels.[14] The only exceptions were made for freight rates and sugar. International shipping freight rates were fixed by the government from the outbreak of war. Sugar supplies, which before the war had come mainly from Germany and Austria-Hungary, were placed under the control of a specially con-stituted executive Royal Commission set up in August 1914.

Between 1914 and 1916, however, many factors conspired to under-mine the assumption that the war would not unduly disrupt normal supplies of food. Competition for supplies among the many belligerent nations sent prices soaring in world markets; and inflation was strongly reinforced by a rising home demand, caused by a decline in unemployment and rise in money wages. Requisitioning of ships for the transport of troops and munitions led to a serious shortage of cargo-space for imported foods. Moreover, the protection given by the Navy proved much less impregnable than had been hoped and many food cargoes were sunk in the German submarine attacks of 1916.

All these factors had serious repercussions on the supply and distribu-tion of British food. Although there seems to have been no overall deficiency, there were serious local shortages of particular commodities such as sugar and beer. Wheat prices rose by 80 per cent and meat by 40 per cent during the first twelve months of war.[15] Rising prices led to widespread suspicion that food was being hoarded and that speculators were operating in both home and international markets. They led also to serious social and industrial unrest — a factor that was to be of continuing importance in debates on food control throughout the rest of the war. Recent research has shown that the First World War brought substantial improvements in real incomes and nutritional standards for the British working class, particularly for unskilled labourers and for women and children.[16] But at the time these statistical trends were perhaps less obvious than other more immediate and irritating factors which seemed to suggest that workers were bearing a disproportionate share of the sufferings of war. Farmers and middlemen were believed to be making vast profits out of conditions of scarcity; retailers were accused of setting aside sugar and other luxuries for their wealthier customers and there was much resentment at growing middle-class consumption of what had previously been seen as cheap working men's foods.[17] While bread queues lengthened there appeared to be no shortage of fodder for hunters, race-horses and polo ponies; and class relationships can scarcely have been eased by the fact that while grain for brewing was extremely scarce, port, champagne and sparkling wine consumption went soaring up — port becoming, according to one food historian, 'the staple drink of the middle-class war worker' for the rest of the war.[18]

Since the start of the war there had been spasmodic pressure from the labour movement for state control of food prices; and in June 1915 a committee under Lord Milner advised the first coalition government to adopt a much more interventionist policy, by compelling farmers to plough up their grasslands and by fixing a minimum price for homegrown wheat.[19] Not until the midsummer of 1916, however, was there serious support for state control within official circles. In June 1916 the minority report of a Board of Trade committee on prices called for drastic action against profiteering; and the Board's permanent staff became increasingly critical of their President's policy of unrelenting non-intervention.[20] In August a much publicised report from the Royal Society estimated that average per capita food consumption was no more than 5 per cent above the nutritional minimum and pointed out how slight was the margin for maldistribution of supplies.[21] After the poor harvest of 1916 the demand for a more positive food policy became one of the main spear-heads of attack on the Asquith coalition.[22] A major political scandal began to rage on the issue of spiralling prices, and criticism of government inertia came from right across the political spectrum, from Lord Milner, Winston Churchill, George Barnes and H. M. Hyndman. In response to such pressures a special Wheat Commission was set up in October 1916, to co-operate with other allied governments in wholesale purchasing of wheat. A month later an extension of the Defence of the Realm Acts gave the Board of Trade special powers over food supplies; and a new ministerial post of Food Controller was created to wield these powers.[23] These measures came too late, however, to avert the collapse of the Asquith coalition. In the reconstruction of government in December 1916 the Food Controller became the head of a new specialised department of state, the Ministry of Food.

III

The new ministry started work over Christmas, December 1916, in a very grand suite of offices in Grosvenor House lavishly decorated by Rubens.

Lloyd George's choice as Food Controller was Lord Devonport, the owner of a retail grocery chain and a partner in Kearley and Tonge, one of the biggest tea importers in the Port of London. His parliamentary secretary was Captain Charles Bathurst, a gold medallist of the Royal Cirencester Agricultural College, whose main function in the new ministry was to represent agricultural interests. The ministry's official staff in its early days fell into three main groups. A contingent from the Board of Agriculture was headed by the new Permanent Secretary, Sir Henry Rew, an experienced civil servant who had close connections with the farming community. Rew had a very high reputation as a statistician, and had served as secretary to the Milner committee on food supplies in 1915. A second group came from the Labour Department of the Board of Trade, headed by William Beveridge, the inventor of labour exchanges and one of the most dynamic administrative reformers of the prewar period. Thirdly, there was a group of businessmen from various branches of commerce and industry, who had volunteered their services, mostly without pay, for the duration of the war. Brewing was represented by Hugh Paul, distilling by Walter Roffey, retail tailoring by William Burton, catering by Arthur Towle and Isidore Salmon, the latter a director of Lyons' Corner Houses. Outstanding among the business group were Sir Alan Anderson, a director of the P. & O. Shipping Line and Sir John Beale, a director of the Midland Bank, who was the personal friend of leading politicians like Reginald McKenna and Bonar Law and had wide connections both in the City and in the manufacturing industry.

The new ministry appeared to be a strong team, and there was a widespread public expectation that it would rapidly solve the problems of scarcity and high prices. This expectation was shared by the leading Board of Trade representatives in the Ministry of Food, Beveridge and Stephen Tallents. Beveridge had been an advocate of statutory food control since the outbreak of war; and in December 1915 he drew up an ambitious programme for the new ministry which included state purchasing of imports, fixing of prices, prohibition of luxury consumption and far-reaching measures of food rationing both voluntary and compulsory.[24] It soon became clear, however, that the Lloyd George government once in office was no more prepared for drastic measures of food control than its predecessor under Asquith,[25] and this diffidence was shared by the heads of the new ministry. Bathurst and Rew effectively sheltered the farming community from demands for state regulation; and this period saw an intensification of what Lloyd George later called the 'junkers' strike' — the refusal of the owners of large estates to plough up their grasslands for wheat.[26] Devonport himself greatly preferred moral exhortation to measures of coercion. He made it clear that he regarded all civil servants as 'molluscs' and that his main concern was to preserve the existing channels of retail trade.[27] He had 'a profound suspicion of all educated men', and insisted on doing an excessively large part of the ministry's work himself, including routine trifles.[28] During the early months of 1917 he infuriated Beveridge and the Board of Trade contingent by refusing to allow them to press ahead with plans for compulsory rationing. Instead he tinkered with a large number of trivial and largely futile measures — such as 'meatless days', registration of pickled herrings, and rules prescribing the size of bread rolls.[29] His officials, 'itching to establish the indispensable local machinery for rationing', found themselves instead drafting 'letters of reply to householders in trouble with servants' and to 'clergymen concerned as to the propriety of parish teas'.[30] Not until May 1917 did Devonport submit to the Cabinet a proposal for compulsory rationing, and even then he asked only for approval of rationing in principle, rather than commitment to a specific scheme.[31] During this period, however, the voluntary approach to food control was increasingly overtaken by events. Public anger against shortages, and particularly against the sugar famine, grew more intense; and the government became increasingly concerned about the political capital being made out of food shortages by militant shop-stewards and other critics of the war. A nationwide inquiry into the causes of industrial unrest found that high food prices and resentment against hoarding were the most potent causes of discontent in every part of the country.[32] Lord Devonport's timid policies were increasingly denounced in Parliament and the press and he resigned on 30 May. Lloyd George first offered the post to Robert Smillie, the president of the Miners' Federation who on 24 May had led an angry deputation on food shortages to Downing Street. But Smillie declined the offer and the post was taken by Lord Rhondda, a South Wales coal-owner with wide business interests in Britain and North America.

Lord Rhondda like Lord Devonport was a Liberal businessman, but he soon proved to be Lord Devonport's antithesis in virtually every other way. Unlike Devonport he was a man of considerable personal charm and moral stature; and unlike Devonport he had a strong grasp of economic theory and 'an almost insatiable love of economic argument'. He was a disciple of the economist Stanley Jevons, and like Jevons he combined a firm belief in rational economic man with an equally firm belief that certain economic functions could and should be undertaken by the state.[33] Almost alone among politicians of the day he appeared to take seriously the problem of inflation and as soon as he was appointed Food Controller he brought the issue of rising prices before the War Cabinet.[34] He came to the Ministry of Food determined to 'make a clean sweep and to start again',[35] and one of his first acts was to reduce the power within the ministry of the agricultural interest. Sir Henry Rew was replaced as Permanent Secretary by Ulick Wintour, who had been a brilliant though controversial success in the War Office as director of army contracts; and

Captain Bathurst was succeeded by John Clynes, a Labour MP who had been one of the severest critics of government inertia. As an ex-mill-worker and leader of one of the largest general trade unions, Clynes was widely regarded as a spokesman not merely for organised labour but for the poorest and least skilled section of the industrial working class.

From the start Rhondda was given much wider powers than Devonport, and he used those powers not to deal with trivia but to develop an ambitious and all-embracing economic policy. His responsibilities included not merely the Ministry of Food, but co-ordination of the food policies of the Board of Agriculture, the Wheat and Sugar Commissions and the British delegates to the Inter-Allied Food Authorities.[36] Moreover, unlike Devonport he established a very close rapport with his permanent officials — to such an extent that many of them in later years looked back on Rhondda as the model of what a departmental minister should be. From the point of view of a vigorous and dynamic administrator like Beveridge he was the ideal political superior 'because he trusted absolutely his chosen subordinates', and delegated to them wide discretionary and decision-making powers.[37] 'You can use my authority as you think necessary', he told them, 'but do be careful to let me know exactly what you have said'.[38] He continued to bring in outside business experts, arguing that their co-operation was essential for maintaining public confidence, but he used them mainly as technical advisers, leaving planning and policy-making mainly to the permanent officials.[39] He also appointed a Consumers' Council, consisting mainly of trade unionists and co-operators, to represent both the 'unorganised consumer' and the 'organised working-class'. To supervise rationing and price control he set up throughout the country fifteen regional commissioners and hundreds of local Food Control Committees, representing workers, farmers, traders and co-operative organisations. Moreover, he soon realised that rationing and price control were pointless unless the government could prevent the drying up of supplies. In June 1917 he dispatched to North America a food mission of ten trade experts to buy up meat on behalf of the British government, and this was the prelude to a general policy of bulk purchasing of imported foods.[40] In the home market flour mills, milk distribution and livestock markets were brought under direct public control; and a guaranteed minimum price for wheat was introduced for farmers to induce them to plough up their grasslands — the latter with only limited success.[41] Further demands from farmers for excessive guaranteed meat prices were firmly resisted by Rhondda as 'blackmail' and 'bluff'.[42] One of his major political victories was the introduction of a bread subsidy in September 1917 — a victory that was won in the face of bitter Treasury opposition,[43] but that did much to defuse the atmosphere of political unrest. In spite of these ambitious measures, however, Rhondda adhered as far as possible to the pragmatic principle that 'existing channels of trade' should be maintained. Large areas of food control, such as the marketing of oils, fats, butter and meat, were exercised not directly by the ministry but by quasi-autonomous associations of tradesmen set up at the ministry's instigation, 'whose transactions never entered into the accounts of the Ministry at all'.[44] The machinery of state food control was superimposed upon existing commercial patterns of production and distribution, and Rhondda went to great lengths to accommodate both large and small traders and to disrupt as little as possible the normal methods of supply.[45]

Detailed accounts of Rhondda's direction of food policy were left by no less than five of the ministry's administrative staff — Beveridge, Frank Coller, Professor Gonner, E. H. Lloyd and E. F. Wise[46] — all of whom agreed in seeing Rhondda as one of the most unqualified political successes of the First World War. Beveridge in his official history ascribed the dynamic style of Rhondda's administration partly to Rhondda himself and partly to the brilliance of Rhondda's chosen confidant, Ulick Wintour.[47] In private correspondence, however, Beveridge painted a rather different picture; there he claimed more credit for other officials — particularly for himself, Stephen Tallents and E. F. Wise.[48] The accuracy of this private account is to a certain extent borne out by the evidence of the ministry's records. That Wintour was a man of charm, lucidity and impeccable good taste is clear from everything he wrote, and it was undoubtedly he who was responsible for the grand structural simplicity of the ministry's central organisation;[49] but his substantive contribution to food control policies seems to have lain mainly in promoting co-operation between the different Allied governments.[50] The initiative in more tedious and intransigent questions such as rationing seems to have come mainly from the second rank of officials such as Beveridge, Wise, Tallents and Coller. It was a plan worked out by Tallents and Beveridge that eventually disbanded the sugar queues by withdrawing the discretion given to retailers and replacing it with a system of distribution through ration cards.[51] It was E. F. Wise, head of the Meat and Fats Division, who designed the arrangements for control of domestic livestock.[52] And it was Beveridge himself who, even before the retirement of Devonport, urged upon the government 'the elementary principle of economic administration... that prices could only be controlled if distribution was undertaken'.[53] Similarly it was Beveridge who devised the plan for central, regional and local rationing machinery — a plan combining 'central initiative with decentralised execution'[54] based directly on the system of labour exchanges that he had set up in 1910. It was a departmental committee under Beveridge that worked out the nutritional basis of rationing and devised special scales for workers in heavy industry, children of different age groups, and nursing and pregnant mothers.[55] In the autumn of 1917 it was Beveridge who insisted that if rationing was to be really effective it would involve more detailed regulation of private lives than had so far been contemplated[56] — by compelling all citizens from the king downwards to register with a retailer for every rationed commodity. Rhondda's role in all these activities was politics *pur sang,* rather than policy initiation.[57] Between May 1916 and May 1917 it was he who steered food control through the War Cabinet, against frequent opposition from the War Office and Treasury.[58] It was he who interpreted food policy to the press and public; and it was he who held in check potential conflicts between agriculturalists and tradesmen, between bureaucrats and businessmen and between different Whitehall departments. Not until a later period in the history of food control did the intensity of these conflicts, and Rhondda's strength and skill in subduing them, become fully apparent.

The question of rationing came to the forefront of wartime politics at the end of 1917. Compulsory rationing had been approved in principle before Devonport's resignation, but the War Cabinet had been extremely reluctant to impose specific rationing schemes — partly because it was feared that the bureaucratic controls involved would further excite social unrest and partly because reports from Germany suggested that rationing was inevitably accompanied by fraud and black marketeering.[59] By November 1917 Rhondda's measures had reduced average living costs by 8 per cent,[60] and members of the government were hopeful that general rationing could be avoided. During the winter of 1917–18, however, shortages of food were again intensified by the diversion of merchant shipping to transporting troops from North America. The police reported long food queues in many parts of the country, Smithfield market was closed for a week, and at a conference of labour organisations bitter attacks were made by working-class leaders on government policies in general and food shortages in particular.[61] Even more alarmingly, reports from France revealed that mass meetings had been held among troops behind the lines, demanding to know 'why, while they risked their lives for their country, she could not even manage to feed their wives and children at home'.[62] The War Cabinet, which had resisted the practical enforcement of rationing for so long, now began to press the ministry to introduce it with unrealistic speed — even though, as Rhondda pointed out, it required detailed advance planning and recruitment of a trained staff.[63] From November 1917 onwards two different rationing policies were pursued by the Ministry of Food — two policies which appeared to the outside world to be complementary but which in the context of departmental politics were in bitter competition with each other. At one level local authorities were encouraged by Stephen Tallents to introduce provisional schemes of rationing by local option; and at a higher level a Central Registration Clearing House under the direction of S. P. Vivian was set up to organise a national scheme, employing 600 new Whitehall staff and 6,000 local offices.[64] Throughout the winter months of 1917—18 Beveridge, Tallents and their assistants were working eighteen hours a day to implement rationing at both levels — recruiting staff, setting up new offices, printing ration cards, registering retailers and carrying out detailed local censuses of the whole population. A nationwide scheme for sugar rationing was introduced on 31 December. In February a general rationing order covering meat, butter, bacon and ham was issued for London and the Home Counties; and on 25 February a general meat rationing order extended the various local schemes to the whole country. The new system made an immediate impact on food distribution and on the attitudes of consumers, and by early March the number of people in food queues had fallen from 1,300,000 to less than 200,000 a week.[65]

The national and local rationing machinery was virtually complete by July 1918. It applied universally to sugar, meat, jam, butter, bacon, margarine and lard; and tea and cheese were rationed on a basis of local option. Food queues virtually vanished and a 'ruthless equalitarianism' was imposed on all classes — backed up by over 70,000 prosecutions and the levying of over £400,000 in fines.[66] In no other area of civilian life was rational bureaucracy imposed with such meticulous detail and comprehensiveness. Not perhaps surprisingly, however, these results were not achieved without controversy and conflict — political, administrative and personal. The ministry was locked in permanent combat with the Treasury — not so much over substantive items of expenditure, as over the Treasury's ambition to scrutinise all additions to Civil Service personnel.[67] There were frequent clashes with the Board of Agriculture about the proper balance between producers' interests and those of the nation at large.[68] The ministry was also in recurrent conflict with the War Office over control of supplies for the armed forces. During the food crisis of 1918 reports to the War Cabinet suggested that the generous food supplies available for home-based troops were a potent source of civilian resentment.[69] Rhondda, supported by Churchill and Austen Chamberlain, proposed that non-combatant troops should be included in general rationing — an arrangement that was opposed by the War Office, not on grounds of principle, but because of the jealousies and resentments likely to be caused by applying different food-scales to men living in the same barracks.[70] When in March 1918 Rhondda set up a special branch in the ministry to co-ordinate civilian and military food programmes, this provoked an explosion of rage and indignation from the Quartermaster-General of the Armed Forces, Sir John Cowans. No military body could possibly tolerate such civilian interference, wrote Sir John; 'I can only look upon this self-constituted body as redundant and unnecessary and I have instructed my officers accordingly.'[71] Rhondda got his way by appealing directly to the War Cabinet, complaining that Cowans's attitude 'shows a spirit which makes work impossible'.[72]

Conflicts of a rather different kind also occurred over the nature and scope of food control among the ministry's departmental officials. The Labour MP George Barnes reported to Lloyd George in March 1917 that the ministry included 'quite a number of smart men from other offices, most of whom have been troublesome in those offices and they cannot get on together in the Office of Food Controller'. Roberts's report was quite clearly motivated by a subconscious personal animus against some of the ministry's senior officials, particularly Wintour and Beveridge; but there was some substance in his observations on the department's 'lack of internal harmony'.[73] Much of the trouble centred on relationships with Sir John Beale, the ministry's most powerful and dynamic business representative. Since August 1917 Beale had been chairman of the Royal Commission on Wheat Supplies, where he had repeatedly made it clear that he wanted all state control to be as minimal and simple as possible.[74] Beale was a man who was used to making top-level decisions in a business organisation, and he rapidly established himself on a footing of equality with the food representatives of other Allied governments. Beale saw no reason why he should not buy and sell wheat without reference to the ministry; but Rhondda in May 1917 had laid down that the Wheat Commission, like all other aspects of food control, was to be the ultimate administrative responsibility of the ministry's Permanent Secretary.[75] This ruling brought Beale into recurrent conflict and personal rivalry with Ulick Wintour.[76] Similar conflicts surrounded the person of Beveridge — though these stemmed more directly from Beveridge's autocratic and abrasive personality than from his position within the administrative hierarchy. The intense strains involved in the imposition of rationing brought Beveridge to the edge of a nervous breakdown, and inflamed his never very harmonious relationships with certain departmental colleagues.[77] Beveridge's personal commitment to state control was far more total than that of most Whitehall officials, and in order to launch the rationing scheme he had ridden rough-shod over the views of many more cautious members of the ministry's staff.[78] He offended Charles Bathurst, now chairman of the Sugar Commission, by simply ignoring him;[79] and he clashed with the ministry's Director of Meat Supplies over delays in provision for large-scale cold storage.[80] A more serious clash took place between Beveridge and Sir John Beale. Beveridge's row with Beale is of some interest, not so much because of the substantive issue involved, but because it opened up a fundamental conflict of political philosophies. In March 1918 Beale reported a serious shortage of cereal supplies, and advised the Food Controller to give priority to production of bread.[81] Within the ministry this was taken as a sign that bread would soon have to be rationed; and after consultation with Rhondda and Wintour, Beveridge took the precaution of printing ration cards well in advance. This action provoked a violent protest from Beale, who accused Beveridge of wanting rationing and state regulation for their own sakes, and claimed that the mere printing of 'bread-tickets' would seriously undermine public confidence and morale. Beveridge in reply denied Beale's charges; but he argued that state control must be thorough, total and meticulously planned in advance if it was to be exercised at all.[82]

These various personal conflicts were held in check until the summer of 1918 by the fact that all parties concerned felt a strong sense of loyalty to Lord Rhondda. In July, however, Rhondda died, and almost immediately the balance of power in food control swung in the direction of the business representatives. Quite why this should have been so is a matter for conjecture. John Clynes, who succeeded Rhondda, can in no sense be seen as a pawn of business interests; but he was a much weaker minister than Rhondda had been and much more susceptible to Cabinet pressure. The increasing influence of businessmen in food control probably therefore merely reflected the increasing influence of business interests in the Lloyd George coalition. The first sign of change was the exclusion of Ulick Wintour. Rhondda was scarcely buried before Beale proposed to Clynes that control over all food imports should be transferred to a joint committee of the Allied governments, on which he himself would act as both chairman and British representative. As 'Director of Imports' he would have direct access to both the War Cabinet and the Food Controller, totally bypassing the Permanent Secretary of the Ministry of Food.[83] Wintour not unnaturally advised Clynes to reject this arrangement, arguing that such a committee would lack the technical competence to deal with major issues of food policy.[84] Wintour then went on holiday, and while he was away considerable political pressure was exerted on Beale's behalf. John Clynes was persuaded that only Beale could command the confidence of the Allied food authorities, and agreed that Beale should become both Director of Imports and chief executive of the new Inter-Allied Food Council. Wintour on his return reluctantly acquiesced in the curtailment of his authority; but Beale then refused to work with Wintour at all and demanded his dismissal. A plan drawn up by Beveridge attempted to reconcile the spheres of influence of the two men, but this again was rejected by Beale. Wintour at this point was forced to resign, and the War Cabinet then intervened in the person of the Chancellor of the Exchequer, Bonar Law, who gave the post of Permanent Secretary to Beale himself.[85]

After Beale's appointment questions of food control became increasingly bound up with plans for an Allied peace settlement. Beale himself saw domestic food policy as very small beer, and after November 1918 became permanently occupied with the food negotiations of the Paris peace conference. So far as Britain was concerned his main objective was to dismantle controls at the end of the war as rapidly as possible, and in particular to sell off the government's reserves of food at the top of the market before the anticipated postwar slump.[86] Beale resigned from the Ministry of Food in January 1919 to become one of the two British members of the Allied Supreme Council on Supply and Relief, and was succeeded as Permanent Secretary by Beveridge. Beveridge throughout the winter of 1918–19 argued for the continuance of a government-inspired Allied food programme, particularly for the relief of Eastern Europe; but when this was rejected he came to the conclusion that peacetime food control was politically impossible, and became almost as strong an advocate of decontrol as Beale himself.[87] Rapid decontrol had the support of the War Cabinet, and in June 1919 a Cabinet committee under Sir Auckland Geddes prescribed 'a policy of progressive and comprehensive decontrol', leading to a winding-up of the Ministry of Food by mid-November.[88] Decontrol proved, however, to have unexpected political complications. Contrary to official calculations, food prices remained high for more than a year after the war. The labour movement called for the permanent retention of certain controls; and postwar industrial unrest persuaded the Cabinet to retain price controls over the winter of 1919–20.[89] During the transport strike of 1920 the wartime machinery of distribution was again called into play to maintain essential supplies.[90] Moreover, decontrol met with opposition in some unexpected quarters. Farming interests, so long neglected in British politics, were happy to see the end of controls over production, but extremely reluctant to abandon the guaranteed prices that they had enjoyed since 1916.[91] Wholesale and retail traders were 'largely indifferent' to the question of whether controls were abandoned or maintained; but they had learned certain lessons from wartime conditions of trading – 'they had learned the value of combination... and they determined that the standard of a livelihood for the least efficient trader should set the pace of their profits, whether their activities were controlled or free'.[92] The experience of food control therefore accelerated the shift towards 'trustification' in the British domestic economy, and it significantly modified the almost hallowed belief in the virtues of competition that had prevailed in many branches of the food industry in the years before the war.[93]

IV

The Ministry of Food was dismantled early in 1921, though a residue of food control was transferred to the Board of Trade under the direction of Frank Coller and was not finally abandoned until 1925. In the scope and detail of its activities, if not in the ruthlessness of its methods, the ministry's empire in 1918 resembled that of a totalitarian state; and the degree of control exercised is all the more remarkable if set in the context of the almost total lack of food policy that prevailed down to 1916. In the early days of war critics of the government frequently contrasted the bumbling nature of English food production with the streamlined and coherent programme that had been put into force in Germany.[94] Yet in the long run the system of food control adopted in Britain was much more effective and comprehensive than that of the German Empire — one reason for this being that it proved much easier to control supplies in a country where so few of the population were engaged in primary production.[95] In spite of the uniformity of structure imposed, however, food control never ceased to be the subject of both practical and ideological controversy; and the question may be asked, did these controversies represent merely the different interests of the parties involved, or did they reflect a more abstract conflict, between detached political ideas? William Beveridge in his private correspondence and in the official history of food control hinted that one of the main sources of conflict was the clashing perspectives of businessmen and bureaucrats — a clash that arose from the former's pursuit of sectional self-interest and the latter's pursuit of a more objective ideal of the impartial administrative state. Beveridge was convinced that a man who had private interests in a particular commodity was inherently incapable of administering that commodity in the public interest — not because the man was necessarily feathering his own nest but because too close an involvement in one aspect of the market precluded a proper understanding of the market as a whole.[96] Such a lack of professional detachment, Beveridge believed, manifested itself in food control in numerous different ways — in Devonport's attachment to the interests of retail traders, in Bathurst's attachment to the interests of farmers, in Beale's refusal to accept the authority of Wintour and in the exertion of unseen partisan political pressures on Beale's behalf. This clash of administrative ideals was matched by a clash in administrative methods. In making decisions the businessman was 'secretive' and 'individualistic', whereas 'the civil servant aims at complete cooperation and openness'. The businessman was 'the lone hander' who 'when he comes into a department, asks that he may be relieved from the necessity of consulting anyone... and desires to refer papers only to the Minister'. Moreover, erosion of bureaucratic control led to 'scandals and extravagances' in public expenditure; 'hustle, regardless of expense', became the policy practised by 'businessmen spending for the first time the money of other people instead of their own'.[97] All these deviations from standard Whitehall practice Beveridge viewed as both inefficient and constitutionally improper.[98] 'Not only the last Government, but the whole of the Civil Service is out of office', he wrote in January 1917, 'and much of the subordinate government of the country is in the hands of amateurs.'[99]

Beveridge's interpretation of the conflicts over food control has a measure of plausibility about it, but analysis of the inner workings of wartime food policy suggests that it was both disingenuous and inadequate in certain important respects. It was disingenuous because Beveridge's own claim to embody reified political impartiality cannot be taken at its face value. Beveridge himself only eight years earlier had been brought into government as the personal adviser and quasi-political nominee of a Liberal minister, and had only later become an established permanent official. Beveridge's liberalism was not of a 'party political' variety, but it was sufficiently strong for Frank Coller to describe Beveridge's permanent secretaryship as 'the period of Reform Club rule'.[100] Moreover, by no means all Whitehall administrators shared even a notional commitment to the ideal of the impartial state; Board of Agriculture officials quite openly promoted the interests of farmers and thought that it was quite right and proper that they should do so.[101] Secondly, Beveridge's interpretation is inadequate because, although clashes between businessmen and bureaucrats *were* on occasion undeniably important, there were at the same time many examples of successful co-operation between the two groups – and many conflicts that could *not* be accurately explained in these terms. Beveridge himself, for example, had no difficulty at all in working with Lord Rhondda – and Rhondda's relationship with Wintour was based on day-to-day correspondence and exchange of ideas of the most frank and harmonious kind.[102] Differences of approach to policy among the permanent officials themselves were at least as marked as differences between administrators and businessmen; and, as the contrast between Devonport and Rhondda suggests, businessmen themselves in no sense shared a single political or administrative point of view.

Conflicts over food control must therefore be at least partly explained in a more personal though less tidy way; and Beveridge's outlook cannot be taken as representative of administrators as a whole. Indeed, Beveridge's approach to food control was untypical in several important respects. Beveridge, for instance, was a passionate disciple of the principle of 'thorough'[103] – a principle that was shared by Lord Rhondda, but was little short of anathema to the ministry's first Permanent Secretary, Sir Henry Rew. 'The sort of critic whose watchword is "thorough", wrote Rew scathingly, 'and whose favourite adjective is "drastic", will never understand why the Government did not at the outbreak of war immediately take control of all food supplies and put the country on rations. He will always maintain that this would have settled the food problem at once, and we should have had no more trouble. Of course, in the nature of things he cannot be contradicted, he can only be disbelieved.'[104] Similarly, Beveridge maintained that state control was an all-or-nothing process, and that half-measures and compromise merely reinforced the problems they were designed to solve.[105] But his successor, Frank Coller, thought that food control at times overreached itself and that there was considerable value in 'the half-way house between inaction and control'.[106] Coller, like Beveridge, had been a professional barrister and had a double first in Greats from Oxford, but two more contrasting personalities can scarcely be imagined − Coller being a Catholic, a primaeval conservative and a man of gentle, 'cheerful' and 'sagacious' mien who liked to judge policies according to 'the moral rule of right and wrong'.[107] Whereas Beveridge constantly generated friction, Coller was the master of an irony so subtle that it was quite invisible to its victims, including Beveridge himself. While Beveridge stormed at businessmen as 'freaks', 'grocers' and incompetents, Coller merely remarked that they 'had a fine sense of spaciousness, they were accustomed to live in large houses and spend lots of money; they were, above all, addicted to foreign travel, which we were not'.[108]

Different again from Beveridge, Rew and Coller was Ulick Wintour, the ministry's second Permanent Secretary. Wintour appears to have had no personal philosophy of public administration except that of creaming off the ideas of his staff and carrying out the policies of his political superior. A Wykehamist, an aesthete and an old China hand, Wintour was a man of cosmopolitan and aristocratic connections. Like Sir John Beale, he was used to getting his own way and had something of the grand manner; and it seems to have been the basic similarities between Beale and Wintour, rather than any fundamental clash of perspectives, that led to the rivalry between them. Both of them were administrative pragmatists, both of them were personally ambitious in the area of international rather than domestic food control, and both of them expected to confer with departmental ministers and foreign governments on equal terms. Moreover, it was not only Beale who wanted to get rid of Wintour. Beveridge himself recalled that John Clynes 'for one reason or another... never felt comfortable with Wintour' − an unease perhaps explained by the immense gulf between their social backgrounds. After his resignation Wintour spent a year as Controller of His Majesty's Stationery Office, then married a French countess and retired for the rest of his life to a villa in Antibes.[109]

Other examples may be cited of personal and departmental attitudes that cut across Beveridge's division between businessmen and permanent officials. Beveridge himself, for instance, was intellectually much closer to Lord Rhondda than to many of his official colleagues, in that he combined a belief in free market economics with a 'devotion to the idea of State action in social reform'.[110] E. H. Lloyd, who was by no means a militant individualist, thought that civil servants had many lessons to learn from private traders − not least that 'there is a point where uniformity and consistency become incompatible with the freedom and initiative on which success and efficiency depend'.[111] Stephen Tallents worked amicably with Sir John Beale − even though he differed from Beale on certain substantive issues of policy.[112] But, as mentioned above, Tallents came into headlong conflict with a fellow-official, S. P. Vivian, on the issue of local versus central rationing − a conflict that involved 'one of those battles to the death' and led to Vivian's eventual withdrawal from the ministry.[113] The collision between Tallents and Vivian was partly a clash of personalities. But this masked at a more fundamental level a clash of administrative philosophies, since Tallents was a dedicated pragmatist whereas Vivian, who was known in Whitehall as 'Morant's little Sylvester', was an exponent of the *a priori* administrative functionalism currently being preached by Sir Robert Morant and Sidney and Beatrice Webb.[114] In terms of overall policy, some at least of the ministry's senior officials privately thought that far too much emphasis was being laid on bureaucratic control over food supplies, and far too little on the equalisation of resources through progressive taxation.[115] Perhaps closest to Beveridge in administrative approach was Frank Wise, head of the Meat and Fats Division, and subsequently a British representative on the Inter-Allied Food Council. Wise, like Beveridge, was an aggressive and impatient spirit, convinced of the 'danger and impossibility of half-measures' and harshly contemptuous of self-interest, timidity and caution. 'He was constantly taking risks, doing unprecedented things, defying the precedents, incurring the disapproval of his colleagues, butting in and suggesting improvements, shortcircuiting the established routine, and stretching the authority given to him to its extreme limit ... he was a thruster; a man of action; an adventurer who took a creative artist's delight in a successful piece of organisation.' To Beveridge, Wise was a living refutation of Lloyd George's view that professional civil servants were less adventurous and less imaginative than members of the business community. Yet Wise himself by no means shared all of Beveridge's beliefs. Unlike Beveridge he was converted to socialism by his experiences of wartime public administration. Whereas Beveridge in 1919 became a strong advocate of decontrol, Wise argued that food control should be retained as the first instalment of a postwar collectivist state; and he spent the rest of his life trying to develop trading relationships between Britain and Soviet Russia.[116]

V

The above discussion has attempted merely to pick the lock of the iron cage of bureaucracy constructed by British food controllers between 1916 and 1919. Doubtless further research into the inner recesses of that cage would reveal a more complicated picture — as would research into the *terra incognita* of the records of private traders and into the attitudes of businessmen who were not absorbed into the structure of the state. Nevertheless, it is clear that controversies over food control were based on a spectrum of beliefs and interests considerably more complex than is suggested by a simple division between administrators and private traders. E. H. Lloyd, writing five years after the Ministry of Food was dismantled, suggested that the most successful wartime administrators were neither typical businessmen nor typical officials but 'a new class of professional administrator' who combined the perspectives of both.[117] Lloyd's conclusion is an interesting one, particularly as it anticipates the fashionable conclusions of some more recent historians, but it does not explain why the new model army of dynamic administrators does not appear to have survived the end of the war. More appropriate perhaps than either Lloyd's or Beveridge's analysis was Frank Coller's suggestion that food administrators could be divided into 'adventurers' and 'mandarins' — the former comprising both businessmen and bureaucrats who were prepared to take risks, the latter comprising those in both camps who preferred to do nothing. In Coller's view Sir Henry Rew was the model mandarin, Ulick Wintour the archetypal adventurer.[118] Such an analysis is clearly too personal and too idiosyncratic to take account of the many changes in economic and administrative structure brought about by wartime food control. But it is a useful reminder of the limitations of rationalistic concepts of bureaucracy, of the complexity of relationships between public administration and the market place, and of the diversity of interests and political philosophies embedded in the modern state.

Notes: Chapter 6

1 Ministry of Food, *Financial Report with Appropriation Account for the year ending 31 March 1918*, pp. 1–3 (1919, Cmd 191); *Provisional Trading Account for the year ending 31 March 1919* (1919, Cmd 286).
2 J. R. Clynes, *Memoirs, Vol. I, 1869–1924* (London: Hutchinson, 1937), p. 294; W. H. Beveridge, *British Food Control* (London: Oxford University Press, 1928), ch. XVI; E. M. H. Lloyd, *Experiments in State Control at the War Office and the Ministry of Food* (Oxford: Clarendon Press, 1924), pp. 394–5; for a recent statement of the convergence theme, see Keith Middlemas, *Politics in Industrial Society. The Experience of the British System since 1911* (London: Deutsch, 1979).
3 Thomas Hudson Middleton, *Food Production in War* (Oxford: Clarendon Press, 1923), p. 87.
4 Calculated from B. R. Mitchell, *European Historical Statistics 1750–1950* (London: Macmillan, 1975), pp. 155, 156, 163.
5 R. Henry Rew, *Food Supplies in Peace and War* (London: Longman, 1920), pp. 21–2.
6 P. Mathias, *Retailing Revolution* (London: Longman, 1967), esp. ch. 10.
7 *Royal Commission on Supply of Food and Raw Material in Time of War, First Report, Vol. I* (1905, Cd 2643), pp. 15–16, 35.
8 ibid., pp. 22, 30–1.
9 ibid., pp. 22–6.
10 ibid., paras 112, 162, 148. The commissioners did note that a caddish person called Field Marshal von Moltke had renounced all adherence to international law; but they appeared to be largely indifferent to the possibility of war with Germany, their main concern being war with Russia or the USA.

11 ibid., pp. 58–63. These conclusions were not fully endorsed by all the Commission's members, several of whom wrote dissenting memoranda, criticising the report's optimism and complacency. Discussion of the strategic questions raised by the Commission continued in various government departments down to the outbreak of war, though with little practical outcome; see David French's essay, 'The Rise and Fall of "Business as Usual"', Chapter 1 above.
12 Frank H. Coller, *A State Trading Adventure* (London: Oxford University Press, 1925), p. 4.
13 ibid., p. 10.
14 Middleton, *Food Production*, ch. 4, pp. 104–7; Beveridge, *British Food Control*, p. 23.
15 Rew, *Food Supplies*, p. 45.
16 J. M. Winter, 'The impact of the First World War on civilian health in Britain', *Economic History Review*, 2nd series, vol. XXX, no. 3 (1977), pp. 496–500.
17 *Commission of Inquiry into Industrial Unrest*, report for the North East division, 12 July 1917 (1917, Cd 8662).
18 A. R. Prest, *Consumers' Expenditure in the United Kingdom 1900–1919* (Cambridge: Cambridge University Press, 1954), pp. 83, 87; Coller, *State Trading*, pp. 137–8. Coller ascribed the rise in port consumption to the compulsory release of fine wines from bonded warehouses in November 1917 – a measure imposed by the government with a view to discouraging consumption of spirits. But port drinking steadily increased during the first two years of war and reached the highest level on record in 1916. Whether port was in fact so exclusively a middle-class beverage as Coller assumed is perhaps open to question. Further research might reveal that the rise was caused by female munition workers discovering the pleasures of port and lemon.
19 Coller, *State Trading*, p. 12.
20 *Departmental Committee on Prices*, Minority Report, 22 September 1916 (1916, Cd 8358); W. H. Beveridge Papers, British Library of Political and Economic Science, The London School of Economics, London.
21 *Report of the Physiology (War) Committee of the Royal Society on the Food of the United Kingdom* (1916, Cd 8421).
22 J. O. Stubbs, 'Lord Milner and patriotic labour 1914–18', *English Historical Review*, October 1972, p. 720.
23 Beveridge, *Food Control*, p. 245.
24 'Heads of action for food supplies department', c. 15, December 1916, Vol. IV, p. 20, Beveridge Papers.
25 Beveridge, *Food Control*, pp. 45–6.
26 *War Memoirs of David Lloyd George*, 2 vols (London: Odhams Press, 1938 edn), Vol. I, pp. 783–4.
27 Coller, *State Trading*, p. 37.
28 MS. notes on 'Wartime in Whitehall', Lady Beveridge Papers, BLPES, LSE, London.
29 *Orders made by the Food Controller under the Defence of The Realm Regulations* (1917–18, Cd 8432–8969), *passim*.
30 Beveridge, *Food Control*, p. 46.
31 War Cabinet Minutes, 7 May 1917, MAF 60/108, Ministry of Agriculture, Fisheries and Food Papers, Public Record Office, London.
32 Commission of Inquiry into Industrial Unrest, *Summary of the Reports of the Commission* by G. N. Barnes, 17 July 1917 (1917–18, Cd 8696).
33 *D. A. Thomas, Viscount Rhondda*, by his daughter and others (London: Longman, 1921), pp. 29–30, 244, 289–90.

34 Lord Rhondda to David Lloyd George, 13 July 1917, F/43/5/30, David Lloyd George Papers, House of Lords Record Office, London.

35 W. H. Beveridge to A. S. Beveridge, 17 July 1917, IIa, Beveridge Papers.

36 Personal papers of U. Wintour, 27 June 1917, MAF 60/53.

37 W. H. Beveridge to A. S. Beveridge, 7 July 1918, IIa, Beveridge Papers.

38 *D. A. Thomas, Viscount Rhondda*, p. 254.

39 Lord Rhondda to U. Wintour, 7 August 1917, MAF 60/53. E. F. Wise, 'The history of the Ministry of Food', *Economic Journal*, vol. XXXIX, no. 156 (1929), pp. 570–1.

40 Coller, *State Trading*, p. 53; Beveridge, *Food Control*, pp. 118–19.

41 Farmers were statutorily obliged to plough up poor grasslands under the Corn Production Acts of 1917 and 1918, but these Acts were never successfully enforced because of bitter opposition in the House of Lords. The Food Controller's powers in this area appear never to have been fully asserted. In May 1917 Rhondda's brief from Lloyd George appeared to include authority over production as well as distribution and consumption; but it is significant that in the official history of food production, Thomas Hudson Middleton's *Food Production in War*, Rhondda's name never once appears.

42 Lord Rhondda to U. Wintour, 7 August 1917, MAF 60/53.

43 Minutes of War Cabinet meeting, 19 July 1917, MAF 60/54.

44 Sir William Beveridge, *The Public Service in War and Peace* (London: Constable, 1920), pp. 23–4, 58–9.

45 Beveridge, *Food Control*, ch. 5.

46 i.e. Beveridge's *British Food Control*; Coller's *A State Trading Adventure*; Lloyd's *Experiments in State Control*, Sir Edward Gonner, 'Lord Rhondda at the Ministry of Food', *D. A. Thomas, Viscount Rhondda*, pp. 249–62; E. F. Wise, 'The history of the Ministry of Food', *Economic Journal*, vol. XXXIX, no. 156 (1929), pp. 566–71.

47 Beveridge, *Food Control*, pp. 51–3.

48 W. H. Beveridge to Christopher Addison, 9 November 1923, IIb, Beveridge Papers; ibid., Ib 23, 'A day of encounters' by W. H. Beveridge, 26 April 1955.

49 Beveridge, *Food Control*, pp. 64, 253.

50 U. Wintour to J. Clynes, 11 September 1918, MAF 60/53.

51 Beveridge, *Food Control*, p. 44.

52 ibid., pp. 142–3.

53 E. F. Wise, 'Ministry of Food', p. 567.

54 Beveridge, *Food Control*, p. 335.

55 Report by the Departmental Committee on Rationing and Distribution as to *Scale of Rations*, January 1918, MAF 60/108.

56 Notes on the History of Rationing by W. H. Beveridge, MAF 60/109.

57 Beveridge, *The Public Service in War and Peace*, p. 11. Beveridge saw Rhondda as presenting a striking contrast in this respect to other members of the new school of businessman ministers, most of whom 'became, in varying degrees, their own principal officials'.

58 Rationing; Memoranda and Decisions, Cabinet Papers, MAF 60/108.

59 Minutes of War Cabinet meetings, 30 May and 28 November 1917, MAF 60/108; Coller, *State Trading*, pp. 54–5, 63.

60 Coller, *State Trading*, p. 113.

61 Beveridge, *British Food Control*, p. 205; Edward George, *From Mill-Boy to Minister. The Life of the Rt. Hon. J. R. Clynes, MP* (London: T. Fisher Unwin, 1918), p. 72.

62 Clynes, *Memoirs*, pp. 235–6.

63 'Compulsory rationing. Further memorandum by Food Controller', 24 January 1918, MAF 60/108.
64 Notes on the History of Rationing by Mr W. H. Beveridge, n.d., MAF 60/109; Stephen Tallents, *Man and Boy* (London: Faber, 1943), pp. 240–2.
65 W. H. Beveridge to A. S. Beveridge, 6 March 1918, Beveridge Papers; *The Times*, 15 March 1918.
66 Beveridge, *Food Control*, pp. 234–40; Clynes, *Memoirs*, p. 223.
67 Coller, *State Trading*, p. 169.
68 Lord Rhondda to U. Wintour, 7 and 8 August 1917, MAF 60/53; correspondence with Board of Agriculture about control of fish, MAF 60/54.
69 Minutes of War Cabinet, 30 January 1918, MAF 60/108.
70 Minutes of War Cabinet, 15 February and 18 March 1918, MAF 60/108. Lloyd George in his *War Memoirs*, Vol. I, p. 791, ascribed the high morale of British troops to the fact that, whereas the German army was rationed in 1917, the food of British soldiers was never cut 'by a single ounce...a single protein, calory or vitamin'. But this claim is not entirely borne out by Ministry of Food records (see Minutes of War Cabinet, 7 December 1917 and 15 February 1918, MAF 60/108).
71 Sir John Cowans to U. Wintour, 8 March 1918, MAF 60/53.
72 ibid., Lord Rhondda to D. Lloyd George, 14 March 1918; U. Wintour to Sir John Cowans, 21 March 1918.
73 G. Barnes to D. Lloyd George, 11 March 1918, F/4/2/25, Lloyd George Papers.
74 Sir John Beale to W. F. Burton, 29 June 1917; memorandum by Beale, 12 August 1917, both MAF 60/54.
75 Personal papers of Wintour, memorandum of 27 June 1917, MAF 60/53.
76 U. Wintour to J. Clynes, 30 May 1918, MAF 60/53.
77 W. H. Beveridge to A. S. Beveridge, 27 January 1918, IIa, Beveridge Papers; *D. A. Thomas, Viscount Rhondda*, p. 238; Wise, 'Ministry of Food', p. 566.
78 *D. A. Thomas, Viscount Rhondda*, p. 239.
79 W. H. Beveridge to Sir Charles Bathurst, 4 April 1918, IV 27, Beveridge Papers.
80 W. H. Beveridge to Annette Beveridge, 3 May 1918, IIb, Beveridge Papers.
81 Memorandum by the Royal Commission on Wheat Supplies for Consideration by the Food Controller, 11 March 1918, IV 27, Beveridge Papers.
82 Sir John Beale to W. H. Beveridge, 19 March 1918; W. H. Beveridge to Sir John Beale, 20 March 1918, both IV 27, Beveridge Papers. For a more detailed account of this dispute, see José Harris, *William Beveridge: A Biography* (Oxford: Clarendon Press, 1977), pp. 242–3.
83 J. R. Clynes to U. Wintour, 3 September 1918, MAF 60/53.
84 U. Wintour to J. R. Clynes, 11 September 1918, MAF 60/53.
85 W. H. Beveridge to J. R. Clynes, 13 September 1918, MAF 60/53; note by Wintour on the correspondence with Mr Clynes which preceded his retirement from the Ministry of Food, 28 September 1918. W. H. Beveridge to A. S. Beveridge, 13 and 14 September 1918, IIa, Beveridge Papers.
86 Coller, *State Trading*, p. 203.
87 Inter-Allied Commission on Relief of German Austria, Interim Report by British Delegate (Sir Wm Beveridge) to the Earl of Reading, 17 January 1919, F97/5/1, Lloyd George Papers; 'International food control', by W. H. Beveridge, June 1919, E. H. Lloyd Papers, BLPS, LSE, London.
88 Ministry of Food, Report for the month ending 15 June 1919, Lloyd Papers.
89 W. H. Beveridge to A. D. Hall, (25?) July 1919, IV 20, Beveridge Papers.
90 Coller, *State Trading*, pp. 231–7.
91 Middleton, *Food Production*, p. 292; Coller, *State Trading*, p. 239.
92 Coller, *State Trading*, p. 239.

156   WAR AND THE STATE

93 Wise, 'Ministry of Food', p. 569.
94 74 *H.C. Deb.* 5s., cols 629–31.
95 On the problems of German food distribution, see Gerald D. Feldman, *Army, Industry and Labor in Germany 1914–1918* (Princeton, NJ: Princeton University Press, 1966), pp. 283–91.
96 Beveridge, *British Food Control*, pp. 335–6.
97 Beveridge, *The Public Service in War and Peace*, pp. 6–8, 18, 37.
98 W. H. Beveridge to A. S. Beveridge, 13/14 September 1918, IIa, Beveridge Papers.
99 W. H. Beveridge to A. S. Beveridge, 14 January 1917, Beveridge Papers.
100 Coller, *State Trading*, pp. 206–7.
101 On the strong sympathies that prevailed between farmers and administrators in the Food Production Department of the Board of Agriculture, see Middleton, *Food Production*, pp. 291–2; A. D. Hall to W. H. Beveridge, 26 June 1919, IV 20, Beveridge Papers.
102 Personal papers of Wintour, MAF 60/53.
103 *D. A. Thomas, Viscount Rhondda*, pp. 220–1.
104 Rew, *Food Supplies*, pp. 63–4.
105 Beveridge, *Food Control*, pp. 341–2.
106 Coller, *State Trading*, pp. 227, 290.
107 Clynes, *Memoirs*, p. 291; Coller, *State Trading*, p. 203.
108 Notes of conversations with A. S. Beveridge, 30 December 1916 and Spring 1917, Beveridge Papers; Coller, *State Trading*, p. 170.
109 Lord Beveridge, *Power and Influence* (1953), p. 144. Wintour was 'promoted' from the Ministry of Food to being Controller of HMSO, from which he resigned after a year.
110 *D. A. Thomas, Viscount Rhondda*, p. 289; Harris, *William Beveridge*, p. 471.
111 Lloyd, *State Control*, p. 389.
112 Tallents, *Man and Boy*, p. 234. Paper by S. Tallents, 20 August 1917, MAF 60/54.
113 Tallents, *Man and Boy*, pp. 240–2.
114 For information about Vivian I am grateful to Mr Stephen Stacey. An exactly similar conflict had arisen between Tallents and Beveridge on the one side and Morant on the other over the issue of 'functionalism' in employment policy in 1910 (Harris, *William Beveridge*, pp. 161–5).
115 Rew, *Food Supplies*, pp. 89–91; Lloyd, *State Control*, pp. 288–9.
116 Beveridge, *Food Control*, p. 149; Wise, 'Ministry of Food', pp. 566–71; E. H. Lloyd Papers, folder on Frank Wise.
117 Lloyd, *State Control*, pp. 393–5.
118 Coller, *State Trading*, pp. 67, 76, 169.

7

Winding Down the War Economy: British Plans for Peacetime Recovery, 1916-19

Historians' attempts to explain the 'erosion of state intervention' in the British economy following the First World War continue to take their bearings from R. H. Tawney. It was principally Tawney who in 1943 defined the issues in his now classic analysis, 'The abolition of economic controls, 1918–1921'. Here, Tawney brilliantly diagnosed the previous generation's failure to draw peacetime policies from the findings of its own wartime 'experiments in state control' as well as from the manifest evidence of need for state direction of economic development.[1]

A general review of Tawney's perspective reveals, among other things, a tone that is hortatory. Tawney wrote, after all, in the midst of a second great war with even more thoroughgoing state controls, and he meant to instruct his readers on the lessons of the earlier conflict and the transition that followed it. Still fresh in his readers' memories were interwar Britain's social and economic ills, which Tawney believed were largely the result of government policies that were permissive rather than organising, directing and even managing. Because the state had organised, directed and even managed sectors of the economy during the last years of the First World War, the historical problem as Tawney saw it was to determine why the state beat a hasty retreat from the economy in the reconstruction period, even in the face of manifold indications that a 'return to normalcy' of the 1913–14 economy was not possible. What Tawney discovered was that attempting to revert to the 1914 state had also been undesirable; that the origins of the retreat lay in an uncircumspect government that made 'no attempt to survey the problem [of the fate of controls] as a whole, to inform itself and the public as to the merits and defects of different war-controls, or to discriminate between those whose utility had ceased and those which could with advantage be retained'. As the government was 'without any general view, it was ready to be pushed'. And those who pushed – businessmen, bankers and Treasury officials – Tawney believed, did so 'in one direction', towards prewar, orthodox economic policy. So goes Tawney's line of thought.[2]

Despite the passing of nearly four decades and the opening of government records and private papers, the writing of the history of the postwar transition still retains Tawney's outline. Working from these more recently available materials, students of the period have mostly amended Tawney's details and refocused his questions to sharpen particular issues, with the result that we can now see individual ministers, civil servants and bankers shaping and unshaping policy. Tawney's successors, while retaining his outline, have however both narrowed and shifted his original focus: whereas the principal tension Tawney identified was between a feckless government and the mullahs of economic orthodoxy, more recent scholars find the focus of tension to be within government itself.[3] As they have particularised the issue, Tawney's successors have left the impression that possibilities of major innovation were even more possible than Tawney believed. In this connection, however, we should be cautious about generalisations from studies which magnify particular issues; they often threaten to lose to the periphery the broader context and, with it, the congeries of forces at play.

There are, however, yet more fundamental limitations than this in the work done since Tawney: real historical debate with Tawney's general outline and key assumptions has yet to take place, and, even though materials pointing up their limitations have been available for more than a decade, Tawney's assumptions remain unchallenged. Paul Barton Johnson's book on the Reconstruction Ministry is an example.[4] Whereas Johnson shows us that extending state intervention into peacetime was not only considered but virtually settled upon, he fails to mention (as Tawney had failed to do before him) that these plans arose from considerations not of social amelioration or economic development, but of *national security*. For whatever reasons, decontrol as a function of national defence policy falls outside Tawney's scope, and this omission is significant. The failure to mention national security considerations heightens Tawney's emphasis on government fumbling. As he defines the issue, the government lacked sound reason for decontrols and so, in his phrase, it followed the course of least resistance, 'trimmed its sails, and ran before the storm' of indignant demands for decontrol.[5] That this storm may have appeared to the helmsmen to be of hurricane proportions has not been considered. And here whether the government should have decontrolled is not the issue (the point is not a moral one). Instead, the significant questions yet unanswered are these: why did the government initiate the 'bonfire of decontrols'; what were its reasons; had it anticipated doing so; what for the government were the chief contingencies determining the fate of controls, and how did it prepare against them?

It should be mentioned here that, without access to their records, Tawney could not have known what the War Cabinet thought the outcomes of the war might be. By delimiting his inquiry so as to ignore national security planning, he did not entertain the possibility that these considerations lay at the centre of economic policy and that security needs had been expected by the government to remain important even after hostilities ended. In this context, it should be remembered that at least until the summer of 1918 the War Cabinet did not expect the general collapse of Germany. If we examine government thinking more broadly, we may see that what looked to Tawney like government's first real reflection on the question of extending state intervention may, instead, be a change of gears consequent upon a sudden shift in the nature of the central problem for the peacetime economy.

The conventional practice of beginning the study of decontrol in 1918 or 1917 has exaggerated the importance of social and economic issues which emerged as control problems of government only late in the war. By entering the story of reconstruction late in the war, one finds the focal issues are industrial efficiency, peace and democracy; employment; housing; the shorter-term issues of priorities and allocations during reconversion. But this diverts us from the origin of reconstruction planning, from the overriding issue which initiated planning and remained until 1918 its essential motivation. So, if we extend our period backwards to the first years of the war to consider reconstruction in its earlier manifestation, when the German problem was unarguably the focal point of plans for the postwar economy, we begin to see economic policy planning shaped by the constraints of national security. Notwithstanding the picture we get from the vantage-point of 1917–18 – when radical politics and a struggle over manpower can be seen to force the government to extend its postwar agenda – it was actually the German problem which earlier had not only prompted reconstruction planning, but also gave form and direction to that planning. The defeat of the 'British revolution' of social and economic reconstruction was only secondarily the result of the reassertion of orthodox economic thinking in 1919: the primary cause was the unexpected collapse of Germany in 1918. For four years the prevailing assumption had been that Britain would face an economically strong Germany when the war ended; here was the nexus of Britain's recovery problems. Germany's sudden collapse in the closing months of the war removed the politically strongest, least vulnerable, justification for the expanded state; it removed the prop which would have sustained the programme of state-initiated economic development. Thus, decontrol looks very different if we examine it not as the cause of interwar problems, but instead as the result of collapsing wartime expectations. In this light, the consequences of Britain's 'total victory' appear ironic, indeed.

Expected Outcomes and Contingencies

During the four years of the war, intensive discussions took place, plans were laid and commitments were undertaken surrounding the anticipated outcomes of the war, and upon the expected conditions at the cessation of hostilities. The most important of these conditions (in the order in which they appeared as dominating expectations) can be identified:

(1) It was first anticipated that at war's end Germany would be strong enough economically to undertake a major export push to recover its markets lost during the war. Businessmen and some government officials in France, Belgium and Great Britain were inclined to believe that the Germans would be able to undermine the recovery efforts of Entente producers by underselling them.

(2) Later it was thought that Germany would seek a compromise peace using her vast territorial gains as a bargaining asset. This outcome would leave the Entente beginning peace in firm control over the economic resources (raw materials, shipping, sea coal, and so on) which Germany required for recovery. In this case, the British state's prolonged control of the economy would be required for diplomatic efforts at enlisting Germany's co-operation with a peace settlement.

(3) Later, however, it was thought that peace would find Britain facing scarcities of essential goods and services, including raw materials and shipping, in which event 'chaos' (the common description) would ensue without continued state control over distribution.

(4) Finally, more as an addition than an alternative view, it was thought that peace would find Britain unable to absorb 4·175 million military men and munitions workers. Without the exercise of control for some system of priorities co-ordinating demobilisations — joined together with a distribution system for goods and services working by the same principles of incremental restarting — labour unrest would be severe and economic depression nearly certain.

All of these conditions at one or another time lay at the centre of postwar economic planning as it took place during the war years. In the face of these expectations, planners evolved a series of strategies which required the extension of state organisation and direction to ensure national security.

The relative transience of this series of expected conditions in no way reduced their influence or significance. In the process of looking at each condition and its anticipated realisation in turn, everything that happened thereafter would be seen as a consequence of that condition, and policies would be designed to meet it. Even abandoned expectations left a potent legacy in the plans and preparations they had initiated or affected. Indeed, each inquiry prompted by the sequence of expectations above acquired a life of its own, turning up new justifications and widening its scope, and so transcended the outlook that produced the inquiry in the first place.

Like most economists of the time, the government took a narrow, short-term view of the developing relation of the state to industry and trade. Both lacked the tools of understanding that would have been required to prescribe that relationship and, because of this, the gap between the agenda of planners and the policies of government was often very wide indeed. In this connection (and recalling how very recently state economic planning had become a function of government), it seems that the planning that did occur for the postwar economy could not be correctly termed inadequate. It may even be contended that the state, having underestimated the difficulties of adapting the economy to the exigencies of war, then swung to the other extreme (chiefly in the Reconstruction Ministry) and exaggerated the difficulties of the economy's adapting back to peacetime conditions. Certainly that would have been the judgement of the demobilisers and decontrollers in 1919.

While the periods of actual control are familiar, those of planning for peacetime are less so. As has been outlined here, the country's needs that were to have been met by state initiative were redefined several times during the war according to calculations about the relative postwar conditions of Germany and Britain. In addition, changing expectations about the way conflict would be broken off, and changing expectations about the availability and accessibility of materials required for rebuilding a peacetime economy, also redirected planning. This shifting outlook actually falls easily into distinct periods, the first of which corresponds to the last year of Asquith's government.

Before 1917

In the final year of the Asquith government, the first phase of Britain's planning for postwar economic policy was generated and directed by apprehensions about the ability of British trade to recover in the face of an expected economic onslaught from Germany. The early manifestation of this concern can be found in December 1915 (actually three months before Asquith formally appointed a Reconstruction Committee), when Walter Runciman requested each department head to examine recovery problems and report his findings to a central committee, as yet unnamed.[6] Runciman's request followed two months of questioning by Members about the government's intentions for trade recovery and, specifically, about Britain's response to the enemy's announcement of a *Zollverein* for postwar Central Europe.[7]

But, during this period, pressure for a government statement came from beyond Parliament as well. By the time of Runciman's action, the business community, with the Executive Council of the Chamber of Commerce in the lead, had already begun campaigning for a government declaration.[8] This campaign gained some support because the business community's confidence in the state had been shaken by recent evidence of failure — both by generals and politicians. Moreover, the business community had come to believe that the Germans would shift armed conflict to an economic plane after peace, and that against the state-sponsored efforts of German enterprise, Britain's trade would suffer badly. With the war seemingly no closer to a decision and the derangement of the economy running well ahead of government measures to bring order, there was widespread doubt that Britain would ever achieve so decisive a victory that Germany would be unable to retaliate with a postwar economic offensive. And while such defeatist sentiment was not directly expressed, it was unmistakably there, frequently expressed as apprehensions about the postwar German economy.[9]

Whereas part of business apprehension was fixed on expected outcomes, these expectations found root in prewar German practices which came to light in 1915 when the Foreign Office evidenced a 'new awareness' of Germany and its methods of aggression. This new awareness perceived German enterprise abroad as the cat's paw of the aggressive German state, and saw evidence that expansionist objectives of the state had been pursued through the private channels of German commerce, industry and finance. H. W. Carless Davis quotes one senior official at the Foreign Office as saying: 'While British trade was pure and simple, German trade was a wheel, and a most important wheel in the German war machine.'[10] In this view of things, July 1914 had marked merely a shift from 'peaceful penetration' to overtly hostile aggression. And, while V. H. Rothwell has written that there existed no concrete evidence that Germany would launch a 'trade war' after the shooting stopped, fear of one was so general as to threaten the government and prompt planning for postwar recovery.[11]

Not all those favouring an aggressive, anti-German economic policy did so for security reasons. Runciman was particularly suspicious of the Tariff Reformers' role in this campaign, and for this reason he tried to stop it. In January 1916 he told the House that Germany was a 'beaten nation' whose manufacturers were cut off from necessary supplies, whose markets were drying up and who, in the end, would be able to recover economically only very slowly. Moreover, he argued Europe's need for German recovery and, therefore, Britain's interest in avoiding putting up obstacles to that end.[12] As well, he released evidence — a report by business advisers to the Board of Trade — to demonstrate that the government was studying trade recovery. But Runciman's efforts failed. There followed an exodus of Free Trade Businessmen from the old fiscal policy. Beginning with the London Chamber of Commerce, and then Birmingham and then Leeds, all voted for resolutions supporting prohibitions on postwar trade with the enemy.[13] They were followed by other Chambers. And, just prior to a national meeting of the Chambers in February, the citadel of Free Trade fell; the Manchester Chamber voted by a margin of two-to-one against its own board of directors' resolution affirming Free Trade in the absence of 'unmistakable proof of the absolute necessity of a change to a protective policy'.[14] The national meeting of the Chambers only served to reaffirm regional support for the use of tariffs for anti-German purposes.[15]

While one direction taken by Britain's anti-German commercial groups was economic protectionism, another was a customs union or *Zollverein* among the Entente members. It was in this latter direction that the government, unable to hold back the storm, finally bent in March.

Asquith took two steps. In March he finally appointed the Committee (Reconstruction) which Runciman had urged upon him four months earlier. Asquith's second step was to permit Runciman and his French counterpart, Etienne Clémentel, Minister of Commerce, to meet and prepare agenda and resolutions for an Allied conference on economic policy. The eventual result of this meeting was the Paris Economic Resolutions which enjoined the Entente allies to take special measures to prevent Germany's resuming 'peaceful penetration' and regaining access to foreign supplies of raw materials. And although the Entente plan was addressed to the *Zollverein* announcement by the Central Powers, it was less ambitious – this despite Belgian and French efforts.[16]

The resolutions the Entente finally did propose divided wartime into three periods – the war, postwar transition and 'thereafter' – and prescribed certain steps for each. For the war, the signatories pledged to work towards common blockade policies. For the transitionary period (understood to last between six and eighteen months) the Allies pledged to preserve wartime regulations – a modified form of the blockade – to give Allied recovery a head start and to exercise pressure against Germany to make good the damage it had done to occupied territories. Finally, for the peacetime thereafter, the 'permanent' measures (lasting as long as five years) to be taken were to make the Allies independent of Germany for essential raw materials, industrial products, finance and commerce. The Entente allies also agreed to establish transportation, post and telegraph services that were independent of the enemy states and to co-ordinate among themselves the registry of patents, trade marks and copyrights.[17] An important qualification insisted upon by Asquith was that each signing nation would pursue these ends in the manner appropriate to commodities involved and without prejudice to each nation's fiscal policy.[18] On 2 August 1916, referring to 'the lessons the war has taught us' and to the need to 'be flexible enough' to adapt to 'changing conditions and unforeseen circumstances', Asquith put to the House his reluctant endorsement of the resolutions.[19] Here was the first important government commitment made during the war to enlarge the state's peacetime role in the economy. The resolutions reflected British policy and embodied the fundamental principles underlying economic recovery planning. And their effect was immediate and direct.

As the clamour for economic security had produced the Reconstruction Committee, the signing of the Paris Resolutions yielded the (Balfour of Burleigh) Committee on Industry and Trade after the war. When Reconstruction first met in March at the height of the storm of anti-German economics, Bonar Law had recommended a non-parliamentary committee of acknowledged experts to survey the prospects and propose policy for postwar industry and trade.[20] However, Asquith did not name a committee until July; that is, after the Paris economic conference had given some definition to postwar policy and had effectively ended Asquith's opportunities for further temporising. In its charge, the committee was directed to consider commercial and industrial policy 'with special reference to the conclusions reached at the Economic Conference of the Allies...'[21]

In the two interim reports made before Asquith's fall, the Balfour of Burleigh Committee recommended prohibitions on trade with the enemy 'for the "transitionary" period after the War'.[22] Later, in the committee's Final Report made at the end of 1917, the committee (as Tawney observed) recommended extending some state economic controls into peacetime. The premise underlying this advice was the need for economic security, the case for which had been stated by the Paris Resolutions. Indeed, the Final Report was written as if the resolutions themselves reflected British policy. And while the committee's Final Report documents the temper and preoccupations of the closing months of 1917, with its appreciation of state initiative for social amelioration, nevertheless its overriding concern with positive state action is, as might be expected, economic security for British industry and commerce principally *vis-à-vis* Germany.[23]

The same concern, bordering almost upon obsession, is reflected in the terms of reference Runciman gave to the Board of Trade committees appointed in the immediate aftermath of the Paris economic conference.[24] Composed of civil servants and business representatives, these committees were charged with the task of investigating the likely postwar position of shipping, shipbuilding, textile trades, engineering, the iron and steel trades, the coal industry and the electrical trades, 'especially in relation to International Competition'. The committees were to report on measures 'necessary or desirable in order to safeguard [the prewar] position'. Whereas the war had initially seemed a commercial bonanza for Britain (Germany and Austria had had to stop an estimated £600m. exports to Entente and extra-European markets), by 1916 Britain's expansionist dreams had faded to fears about even holding on to the volume of trade equal to that before the war.[25] Thus the fears of the German challenge as expressed in the Paris Resolutions instigated reconstruction planning and infected the expanding network of that planning's structured inquiry. So, like Runciman's Board committees on trade before them, Balfour of Burleigh's sub-committees had expanded their assigned study of such specific, transitional matters as demobilisation and resettlement, into a larger plan to prepare Britain against the economic battle looming in the post-Armistice period. And, thus, it is no exaggeration to say that the Paris Resolutions guided the Reconstruction Committee's (and later, the ministry's) approach to the study of state assistance to British industry. To be sure, in the war's final few months, Reconstruction's interest in industrial efficiency turned increasingly on its connections to social issues (where, for example, productivity growth was seen to be needed to sustain the much higher wartime wage levels and to generate higher tax revenues required for the housing, education and other social reconstruction measures). And yet, prior to the summer of 1918, the government's chief interest in economic efficiency was as that efficiency might serve such security aims as the Paris Resolutions had identified.

Because the Paris Resolutions not only stimulated but also channelled early reconstruction planning, and continued to have direct influence on preparations for peacetime, one might wonder at the relative lack of attention given to them. J. A. Spender's judgement is typical. In his life of Asquith, he described the resolutions as having merely 'antiquarian' interest.[26] To be sure, looking back from the postwar decades, the resolutions must have seemed the remote sentiments of a moment, and the issues distant from those of interwar Britain. And even within the war years themselves, the resolutions seem to belong very much to an earlier phase, when France and Britain were in charge, and before the Americans entered and Russia collapsed. Because President Wilson would not join the United States to the resolutions, American entry into the war vitiated their international force. So did reservations about them, filed in 1917, by Serbia, Russia, Japan and Italy.[27] But all of this did not render them nugatory. Nor did the government give up its efforts to convince the Americans to adhere to the resolutions. Until the autumn of 1918 those efforts continued, with the principal emphasis on administrative benefits rather than punitive effects. And, of greatest long-term significance, the resolutions themselves continued to the war's end to figure prominently in all principal assessments of industrial and commercial policy; the expectations they represented and the security aims invested in them were principal causes of the birth and death of economic reconstruction.

The advent of the Lloyd George government in December 1916, while it had a decisive influence on the organisation, scope and leadership of Reconstruction, did not essentially change the operative assumptions about the war's outcome. Even so, initially, postwar planning was pushed to the side; the new government was so strong that trade concerns could be ignored for a time to allow the government to concentrate on the war. When Lloyd George did turn his attention to postwar planning, his earliest act was to reconstitute the Reconstruction Committee. For his new membership, he sought amateur reformers — persons with ideas — and advanced thinkers who could be counted on to broaden the scope of inquiry to include more extensive considerations of social amelioration.[28] But, seven months later, the streamlined executive detached itself from the Reconstruction Committee by creating for it a new ministry. The result was a burgeoning and, yet, more systematised process of postwar planning working apart from real political power and so from the routine concerns of the powerful.[29] By these changes Lloyd George freed Reconstruction planning from the constraints imposed by Asquith and Runciman who had regarded postwar economic policy defensively — almost exclusively in narrow political terms. (For example, their real concern with the Paris Resolutions, as expressed in private, lay in fighting the conclusion that customs duties were the only feasible way of favouring the trade of the allies and of restricting that of Germany.[30]) Lloyd George, no less diffident about the politics of fiscal policy, was none the less able, because of his reorganisations, to stand rather apart from the politics of postwar planning. In 1917 the Paris Resolutions did not lose their central place, but as the dimensions of postwar economic planning expanded, they had a correspondingly diminished part of Reconstruction's attention; that is, until the preparation of an economic offensive in the autumn.

Although the new government inherited its predecessor's premises about the German peril to British recovery, the cumulative effects of an increasing state intervention and of the process of planning itself pressed that government towards expanding the state's responsibility for the organisation and direction of the economy. Producers responded to this development: as the political arena seemed very largely to have replaced the marketplace as the arbiter of economic activities — a condition which Asquith, Runciman and McKenna had deplored and resisted — producers were rather naturally drawn to the state and into the process of planning its postwar activities. Once producers, themselves eager for state protection, witnessed the state cracking the door to protection by adopting extraordinary measures for guarding commerce and industry against the expected 'trade war', producers burst through that door to claim need for special protections against all foreign competition. In 1917 the Board committees Runciman had appointed for reviewing the likely postwar condition of leading trades in the light of the expected trade war became scenes of an energetic scramble for special protections. Concern about the competition of enemy states dropped by the wayside as industry spokesmen on each committee adduced instead arguments and evidence supporting special consideration of their trade against all foreign rivals after the war. So, for example, the textile trades sought privileged access

to Empire and Allied raw material sources; the iron and steel trades
wanted the domestic market shielded by tariffs and special anti-dumping
duties; the engineering trades committee, while making no recommendation
on tariffs, urged anti-dumping legislation and a commitment from public
purchasing bodies to 'buy British'.[31] It should be noted that the candid
self-criticism of early 1915, when the Board's commercial intelligence
inquiries into Germany's prewar success had characterised British industry
and commerce as ill organised, inefficient and obsolescent, had now in
1917 all but disappeared.[32] None of the later Board committees justified
its recommendations on the grounds that British industry or commerce
was weak; each now argued that German success was the result of government aid (special railway rates, for example) or of dishonest or unfair
practices (dumping, for example). The exceptional measures that these
committees recommended for the protection and promotion of Britain's
major industries and trades were, in the reports, justified by the coming
'trade war' or, more generally, by the postwar danger of the German
economy.[33]

These investigations, then, actually opened to producers their most
direct and extensive opportunities for participating in postwar planning
of production and its circumstances. In addition, the investigations reflect
a turning in businessmen's attitudes away from prewar ideas about the
state's role which we know from other sources to have varied from
industry to industry and to have been rather ambivalent even among
producers most aggressively seeking protection. It seems that, generally,
producers were prepared to relinquish certain freedoms of action if state
controls were necessary (in the event that Germany was not decisively
defeated). As for exporters who expected difficulties recovering their
foreign markets, the government encouraged them into channels which
seemed to lead to a Department of Overseas Trade and possibly further
reconstitution of the Board into a Ministry of Commerce and Industry.[34]
Certainly the government did not discourage them from imagining that
after the war there would be government departments whose chief duties
would be trade promotion and industrial development. However, as was
found in the Farington and Hyde Committees (that proposed the Department of Overseas Trade and reforms of the Board of Trade) producers
and traders had profoundly ambivalent feelings about the state.[35] Although
eager for state protection and assistance, businessmen's support was
inconsistent, and always tempered by their suspicion that any assistance
given also supplied the government with levers for control.

Preparing against an Indecisive Outcome

While postwar planning proceeded in its newly created and burgeoning
structure, the War Cabinet quietly discussed economic policy from a new
perspective: the idea of an economic offensive. For reasons which we

need not explore here, by August 1917 the War Cabinet had come to have profound doubts about the Entente's chances of a decisive military victory. This led them back to the Paris Economic Resolutions in search of potential economic weapons to contain and possibly to outmanoeuvre an unbroken Germany. The result was the development of an economic offensive whose purpose was twofold: to give to the Entente leverage in bargaining for peace; and to give the Entente a mechanism for fostering their recovery at the expense of Germany's. The decision to prepare an economic offensive strategy, taken by the War Cabinet on 20 August, begins the next period of planning for state intervention. As with the early period, the underlying intent of second-stage planning was still 'to prepare Britain for the presumed Armageddon with a competitive and powerful Germany'.[36] The new initiative was, however, prompted by a sharper, more compelling expectation about the war's outcome; one which moved the government beyond the generalities of the Paris Resolutions to concrete measures of extending state controls over the economy.

In August 1917 pessimism pervaded the War Cabinet. Reports from the Western Front were grim; Venice seemed threatened; Russia was on the verge of anarchy. Only the war at sea went well. Although the idea of an economic offensive may be dated earlier, in this climate of gloom the War Cabinet was easily prepared for conversion to the idea by the zeal of Edward Carson. Preparation for an economic offensive was already well advanced by 20 August as the record of the War Cabinet's meeting of that date discloses.[37] At that meeting two distinct, though not clearly distinguished, probable endings to the war were considered. In one case, the unbroken and unbowed adversaries would strike a deal. And in the other, the Entente would 'fall back on a passive defensive' and 'rely upon the blockade to bring about the collapse of the enemy, just as often occurred in the case of a siege'. Raising the first probable outcome, Lord Robert Cecil recounted a conversation with Etienne Clémentel (French Minister of Commerce), who was then visiting London, in which the minister had outlined proposals for tightly organising Allied control over the 'principal essential raw materials of the world'. The aim was to render access to them a 'bargaining asset in the eventual peace negotiations'. Before being permitted to acquire raw materials, Germany would first have to relinquish territorial gains. The idea of using the Allies' (which meant chiefly Britain's) economic leverage — something that now seemed feasible since Cecil's Blockade Ministry had imposed a tight, effective rationing on European neutrals' imports — was attracting the thoughts of others as well. For example, John Whitley, Speaker of the House, had advanced a scheme similarly calling for state control 'of a great many articles of prime necessity, such as tungsten, jute, vegetable oils, etc.', for an attempt to force Germany to come to terms, and to withhold these and other materials for twenty years if Germany refused. There was yet

another scheme for using sea coal for similar purposes. In the other outcome considered possible, one in which there would occur so complete
a stalemate that the Entente would fall back on a passive defence and wait
out the blockade's strangulation of the enemy, the War Cabinet discussed
whether men would be released from military service, as presumably
would some goods and services, in order to allow Britain a head start on
recovery.[38] Obviously French and British political leaders were casting
about for economic means of doing what apparently the generals could
not.

Although neither Lloyd George nor Bonar Law believed economic
weapons could deliver a real victory, that line of thinking was given
institutional life and translated into actual measures for extending state
control. The War Cabinet appointed a committee led by Edward Carson,
'which, without prejudice to the effective continuance of the existing
Economic Offensive, should consider the whole question with a view to
their recommendations being utilized as the basis of further consultations' with the Allied governments.[39]

The role for the economic offensive, as proposed by Carson, included
both propaganda and bargaining-leverage elements; this plan would com-
plement the work of the blockade and simply extend the principle into
the peace-negotiation phase of the conflict. By economic offensive
preparations, Carson wrote, Britain and her Allies might 'convince
Germany that the longer the war continues the worse will be her commercial prospects after the war'.[40] British intelligence believed that German
commercial opinion, already alarmed by the prospects of *post bellum*
economic sanctions, might be moved by threats such as these to put
pressure on German military authorities.[41] But, to be effective, these
threats could not be empty; the economic offensive would have to 'prepare for the Allies a sound economic foundation to serve as a basis for
negotiation when serious peace projects are being discussed'.[42] This was
necessary because, as Carson wrote, 'when serious peace negotiations are
begun we shall almost certainly find that the enemy is in possession of
large tracts of allied territory and that economic concessions to Germany
will be all we have to offer in exchange'.[43] Such were the scenarios drawn
during the gloom of 1917, and it was from these forecasts of the war's
end, then, that preparations arose for an economic offensive – a plan
whose measures not incidentally followed many of the particular commitments made as early as the Paris Resolutions.

During the winter and early spring of 1918, when the offensive began
to take definite form (though not just as its designers intended), it encountered opposition in Parliament, where suspicions were raised concerning
the government's intentions. Because the government disclosed neither
their general aims nor the relationship of specific legislation to (as yet
unstated) postwar economic policy, these suspicions were not dispelled.

One source of misunderstanding was not entirely remediable: although Carson and his committee had actually set aside the intention of preparing for a 'trade war',[44] British propaganda kept the threat alive in order to keep pressure on the enemy. In February Philip Snowden put before the house Labour's opposition to such a *post bellum* commercial conflict and, thereby, affirmed Labour's support for the third of Woodrow Wilson's Fourteen Points (proscribing recriminatory actions against postwar Germany). While the opposition of the Labour Party and of the American President did not stop British 'trade war' propaganda, it may have tempered the effectiveness of the threats, and certainly it encouraged the government to replace the aggressively titled offensive with a less controversially named body.[45]

Not all opposition resulted from misunderstanding. Some who opposed the government's determination to arm itself with powers to control trade during the postwar transition believed this step was unwise when taken out of the context of a larger inquiry into the overall questions of postwar economic policy. Voices of organised business interests and of suspicious Free Traders joined Labour in opposing a 'trade war'. The particular objections of business centred on the government's attempt at securing state controls over British exports. For their part, Free Traders regarded the economic offensive in the same way many had looked on the Paris Resolutions: as a potential cat's paw of protectionism. Together, business spokesmen and Free Traders effectively held up the Imports-Exports Bill, a legislative cornerstone of the offensive introduced by Albert Stanley in November. Their opposition caused the government to withdraw the bill temporarily.[46]

In January 1918, however, the War Cabinet decided they should reintroduce the bill – this time without any accompanying general policy statement.[47] Still by spring this had not been done, although in April Bonar Law reiterated before the House the government's intention of introducing the bill and acknowledged that there had been 'many protests' from 'important sections of the community'. He added that this was a common experience. In May Albert Stanley, responding to a question from Edward Carson, told the House again that the bill was to be brought back, and in August Bonar Law again reiterated the same promise before the Commons, this time agreeing that a general statement of government policy should precede discussion of the bill. But it was not until December, when the government was preparing for the General Election, that the government's policy was stated; by then the circumstances were so altered that the issue of the Imports-Exports Bill was moot.[48]

It would be mistaken to conclude from the fate of the Import-Exports Bill either that anti-German economics declined significantly in popularity or that Britain did not continue to regard preventative measures against the resumption of German 'economic penetration' as essential. Other legislation had a relatively easy passage — for example, the Non-Ferrous Metal Industry Bill, 'to restrict temporarily the persons who may engage in business connected with certain non-ferrous metals and metallic ores'. Presented by Stanley in November 1917, the bill received the Royal Assent in February. Its opponents objected to the principle of licensing the access to trade; they contended that the bill would protect incompetence (particularly in the spelter industry); and they argued that Woodrow Wilson's speech in reply to the Pope's Peace Proposal meant that America would oppose the measure.[49] But such preventative steps — ones which merely excluded Germans — had adequate support. So also easily passed was the Trading with the Enemy (Amendment) Act that denied Germans re-entry to the closed German banks in Britain.[50]

As popular as these two bills was another economic offensive measure derived from the Paris Resolutions: this denied to Germany the benefits of most favoured nation status. As early as the summer of 1917, the French government had indicated privately its intention, based on the Paris Resolutions, to withdraw MFN status from Germany and to prepare for organising an Allied trade bloc.[51] Renunciation of commercial treaties was similarly urged on the British government by the Federation of British Industries when, in October 1917, it sent a delegation to the War Cabinet to argue this position.[52] Without renunciation, the terms of Britain's trading arrangements with any ally or neutral would most likely, if that neutral extended MFN status to Germany, apply equally to that neutral's trade with Germany.[53] So, with Germany and Belgium reciprocating MFN status, for example, Belgium's waiving of import duties on British machinery would, assuming Belgium and Britain reciprocated MFN status as well, oblige Belgium to confer similar advantages to the importing of German machinery. While Robert Cecil contended that renunciation by Britain and her Allies was essential for the rebuilding of Belgium, clearly very much more was involved.[54] The government had expected to have the power to suspend MFN clauses by provision of the Imports-Exports Bill, but when that became stalled and when in April the government learned (from the newspapers) that the French government had renounced its commercial treaties, the British government was constrained to declare its own position.[55] Two weeks later, Bonar Law told the House that Britain was reviewing its commercial treaties with an eye to freeing its hand for making arrangements with its Allies and for peace negotiations.[56] Still a final decision concerning renunciation was held up. The War Cabinet and the 1918 Imperial War Conference had first to settle basic questions about extending preferential treatment to Britain's Allies as well as to its Empire.[57] When the War Cabinet finally decided not to extend preference to Britain's Allies, but instead to 'have careful regard to' their 'interests', Dominion support of MFN renunciation was declared the very next day (July 18). Forthwith, the government decided in favour of renunciation and made that decision public.[58]

Because these steps, by which the government attempted to give life to the economic offensive, were the chief ones actually taken publicly to prepare against the postwar economic transition, they kept the matter of recovery focused on the German problem. And, despite the press reports on Germany's deteriorating material condition – particularly following the flurry of peace resolutions in the summer and autumn of 1917 – the undefeated enemy remained in British eyes a potent threat to economic recovery. However, within Reconstruction and the Foreign Intelligence Department of the Foreign Office there had already begun a shift in thinking away from emphasis on the German problem and towards a broader conception of Britain's difficulties, in which Germany was a contingency in the overarching problems of scarcity.

This new outlook emerged in a paper prepared by Edwin Montagu, secretary to the (about-to-be-superseded) Reconstruction Committee in July 1917. Written for Albert Stanley, Montagu's assessment of 'post-war commercial policy in the light of recent events' argued that not Germany *per se* but the likelihood of worldwide scarcities made joint Allied control over supply and distribution essential. Germany would not be in a position to disrupt the economic transition: 'To put it at its lowest, many months must elapse before German manufacturers will be able to produce on a large scale for export or to compete as previously with their rivals in the markets of the world.' So, for example, the prospect of Germany's dumping manufactured goods, which had been 'held to be a danger' at the time of the Paris economic conference, was no longer considered by Montagu a likelihood in the summer of 1917.[59] Sir Ernest Pollock, controller of the Foreign Trade Department, writing in June, reflected on the possibilities of a trade war against Germany; like Montagu, he understood Germany to be incapable of launching a postwar commercial battle against British recovery.[60] Indeed, according to Montagu, 'the chief element' in economic planning in 1917 'is a probable world-shortage for some time to come in important raw materials and food-stuffs, accentuated by the recent bad harvests of last year and by the increasing shortage of shipping'. Montagu concluded, as did Pollock from a different perspective, that the circumstances called for 'concerted action' among the Allies for the short-term purpose of making 'skilful use' of their economic power, and so to give them leverage to influence 'the enemy both during the War and in any peace negotiation'. Beyond that, the interest of Britain and her Allies was 'not so much to defend themselves against German aggression as to provide co-operatively rather than competitively for their own post-war needs'.[61]

In the succeeding twelve months, this understanding of the postwar recovery problem came only gradually to prevail in the government. Early among those moving to Montagu's view was Christopher Addison, newly appointed Minister of Reconstruction, who was then, together with Montagu and Albert Stanley, appointed to the Economic Offensive Committee. And it appears that they influenced Carson's thinking, as they made of the committee a 'sounding board' for their viewpoints and reconstruction proposals.[62] They seemed to have cooled Carson's ardour for a 'trade war' and diverted him from the issue of protectionism. They encouraged Carson instead to pursue their common interests in postwar materials controls. Thus, it seems, it was under their influence that the focus of the economic offensive shifted from Germany as the chief danger to British recovery, towards the more diffused menace of world shortages and dislocations. The committee agreed on one thing, however. They all deplored the government's failure to follow up the Paris Resolutions (specifically, as those agreements informed the Balfour of Burleigh Committee recommendations on state control of trade), and they proposed the ill-fated Import-Export Bill as a first step towards national and Allied control over material distribution.[63] Evidently they intended that Germany's needs would be considered, but only after the needs of the Allies and neutrals had been secured, and only after peace had been made. The committee's strong recommendation that the government renounce most favoured nation treaties reflected their evolving strategy: Britain and her Allies had to free their hands before they could ration materials. In addition their report on the postwar prospects for raw materials, which the government took with it into its consultations with the Allies, made a strong case for controls.[64]

The Economic Offensive Committee was, thus, reaching beyond peacemaking and beginning to plan for commercial and industrial recovery; effectively this turned the economic offensive into a vehicle for planning reconstruction. Before June 1918, when it was superseded by the Economic Defence and Development Committee, Carson's group had begun plans (following recommendations of the Final Report of the Balfour of Burleigh Committee) to promote and safeguard 'key' industries, such as chemical dyes, for whose products Britain had depended on Germany before the war.

Carson was not entirely reconciled to motivational shifts which now focused attention on the viewpoint of the reconstructors. As he left the committee (and the War Cabinet) in January, he reiterated the view which stressed the German menace. For the reconstruction period, he stated, 'restrictions hardly less drastic' than those of wartime 'will be necessary', for 'In no other way can the country hope to escape from the perils of hunger, unemployment, social disorganization, industrial paralysis, and financial chaos.'

This challenge would not end with reconstruction; beyond it lay the renewed rivalry of Liberal Britain's nemesis. He warned the War Cabinet that 'British industry would be beaten in a stand-up fight against the organized state-aided efforts of Germany' if Britain continued to adhere 'rigidly to the old system of *laissez-faire* and refuses to learn the lesson that in modern commerce, as in war, the power of organized combinations pursuing a steady policy will speedily drive out of the field the unregulated competition of individual enterprise'.[65] It is in light of this belief that we should understand Carson's agreement with Addison that 'some co-ordinating authority, such as the Minister of Reconstruction', was absolutely necessary for British recovery, and that such a minister should be placed at the head of a Cabinet committee of real power which would represent the departments appropriate to direct the restructuring of commerce and industry. Six months later the War Cabinet, in belated response to Carson's urgings, created a co-ordinating authority for 'economic defence and development'. Thus, the path to economic security, its direction charted by anti-German economics, converged with the path to Reconstruction, its own direction having been initially charted by anti-German economics (and later marked out by radical Liberal social policy and diluted Fabian Socialism). So, what began in the summer of 1917 as a programme for putting pressure on Germany, first to cease hostilities and then to withdraw from occupied territories, had become a programme for national and Allied control of materials and a vision of a many-fronted drive for reforming the practices and reorganising the structures of British commerce and industry. The committee pushed the government, reluctant to act in the face of parliamentary suspicions about the fiscal or trade policy implications of the Economic Offensive Committee proposals, to take the first real steps for extending state controls selectively beyond the war. While its motives were mixed, the government's principal justification both in War Cabinet discussions and parliamentary debate remained economic security. In planning for the postwar economy, then, economic defence was the primary goal.

The Fear of Scarcity and the Threat of Crisis

When we consider the final period of wartime planning for postwar economic controls, which begins in the summer of 1918, security remains an important element, although now it no longer stands alone as the chief contingency. In fact, after August, considerations of security were nearly eclipsed by 'the fear of scarcity and the threat of crisis'; this because major changes were taking place in the government's outlook on the German problem. While, earlier, officials had tended to exaggerate the short-term resiliency of the German economy (and rather underestimated it for the long term), in the last six months of fighting the problem of the postwar German economy tended to recede into the background. Of course, this is not to say that the German problem had completely vanished from officials' agenda. On the contrary, at every turn in the inquiries into international, inter-Allied, or even national matters, planners continued to encounter the problem of Germany — whether in the plans for allocating raw materials and shipping or in discussions about the resumption of international banking. However, the German problem's singular influence on planning sharply diminished for reasons that may now seem obvious: for one thing, the failure of Germany's spring offensive raised British confidence — a complete victory over Germany was seen to be only a year or two (or possibly only months) away. In addition, new concerns arose to compete with matters on the government's ever-lengthening agenda. Sustained, systematic inquiries into supply and allocation; experience with the constraints of shortages; dislocations and price fluctuations; price-level differentials among countries; and an expanding awareness of the possibilities of social disorder turned up new contingencies which reduced the role of the German problem in planning for the postwar economy. Now, though with different motives in mind, planners nevertheless continued to anticipate the necessity of extending controls into peacetime. And, as in earlier periods, the continuation of the organising, directing and managing state was thought to be necessary because of particular conditions and circumstances that were expected to attend peace.

Thus to the government in the summer of 1918 the 'lessons' already drawn from the war were seen to address the more permanent danger posed by Germany, and in this form they continued to have an influence on postwar planning. These were the lessons discovered in 1915 and 1916 and applied by *every* successive inquiry into postwar policy: the Balfour Committee which had placed strong emphasis upon applying security considerations to policy on key ('vital') industries, dumping and imperial resources, among others; Lord Selborne's Commission on Agriculture, which had argued that food production was so vital to defence as to justify higher prices to British consumers from a neo-mercantilist policy aimed at greater self-sufficiency; and finally the Dominions Royal Commission, the Economic Offensive Committee and many lesser groups which had made their recommendations for protection and economic development framed by the commonly held assumption that the matter of economic security transcended the outcome of war.

Not even the apparent likelihood that Germany would be unable to thwart British recovery in the crucial first months of peace seemed to weaken the case for government action on the longer-term problem. Only five days before the Armistice, with virtually certain knowledge that Germany was in the throes of political and economic collapse, H. Llewellyn Smith, Permanent Secretary at the Board of Trade, could write of the war (in the past tense) and of its lessons: 'the war revealed to us fully the danger to which we had been exposed, of seeing vital industries penetrated and dominated by hostile alien influence, and great staple industries attacked and undermined and reduced to a position of dependence on foreign industrial cartels'.[66] The certainty of a decisive military victory did not preclude the need for the government to guide recovery, and so to strengthen Britain's economic security; otherwise, wrote Alfred Mond, echoing the judgement of others, 'it will be open for our beaten foe to secure a most dangerous revenge'.[67] Four years of planning based upon the wartime awareness of the connection between the outward reach of German economic power and the expansionary aims of the German state, and upon the assumption of a potent German challenge to Britain's economy following the war, were not suddenly reversed when those assumptions appeared to be exploded.

The British government's moment of recognition that Germany's straitened circumstances virtually ruled out a serious immediate economic challenge coincided with the planners' identification of the larger international problems (of materials, tonnage and finances) which stood between Britain and recovery. These understandings had an immediate and decisive impact on the government's disposition towards the advent of peace. We can see that impact in the manner in which the government considered extending its exercise of economic controls beyond the war. In August 1917 the War Cabinet had entertained the idea, albeit only briefly, of putting its military forces into a defensive posture and demobilising selectively to restart pivotal industries, thereby gaining a head start on Germany. Though impractical, the idea was indicative of recognisable assumptions about Germany's all-out push for resources and markets at the moment of peace, as well as assumptions about the probable strength of that push, and about the threat it presented to British recovery. This notion of stealing a march on Germany, which had its inception in the war's first months when the government promoted the idea that abandoned German markets opened a 'commercial bonanza' to Britain, was one of the earliest and most enduring desiderata. That this notion no longer appears in the minutes of the War Cabinet after the spring of 1918 is suggestive. To be sure, on the eve of the Armistice the Foreign Office was still pressing for the extension of controls on shipping and on the allocation of materials as part of an Allied effort to isolate Germany during peace-making. However, this strategy in its anti-German aspect was specifically diplomatic, anticipating as it did German resistance to Allied demands at the peace conference.[68]

In significant contrast to the objectives of the Paris Economic Resolutions, however, it was not among the aims of the October 1918 Foreign Office proposal that the Allies should isolate Germany. 'The moral [sic] of the German people is shaken, if not broken', the authors of the proposal wrote; therefore, the need to isolate Germany 'recedes into the background'. But 'as peace approaches the business community in this country is tending to become more apprehensive of continued government control, and to see in that control an obstacle rather than an assistance to the readjustment of trade and industry to peace conditions'. And yet, the authors, like the Ministry of Reconstruction and the Economic Defence and Development Committee (including even Joseph Maclay), believed in the principle of controls to allocate scarcities (tonnage, food and essential raw materials) according to their need and usefulness for reconverting the economy to peacetime. In practice, this led Britain to propose to the United States cooperative development of markets. In this plan American goods and capital would be advanced through British banks and financial institutions; contracts in Latin America and elsewhere would be divided so as to avoid competition.[69] However, the British interest in the application of this plan to the international economy encountered implacable American resistance in the final month of the war. Another effect the imminence of German defeat had upon British recovery plans can be seen in the Foreign Office's sudden acceleration (in September) of its efforts for postwar controls. Here the overriding concern about access to supplies was no longer how to *deny German access* as it had been at least through 1917; rather, it was how to *ensure British access*. Caught between dependence upon American loans *and* continental Allies who in turn depended upon British finance and supplies, Britain was acutely eager to improvise with the Americans some Allied machinery for postwar supply and distribution. Because time had become too short for 'elaborate detailed plans' the Foreign Office aimed at simply adding two new councils (raw materials and finances) to the three inter-Allied control agencies (transport, food and munitions) already in existence. In addition, the Foreign Office wanted to see a supreme economic board, consisting of Allied economics ministers, put in charge of all five inter-Allied control agencies.[70]

When the Armistice came, the British government had not yet found an inter-allied way out of the problem of scarcities; it was for this reason the government so hastily approved keeping the existing domestic control apparatus in place. A week later, Britain agreed to maintain its blockade of Central Europe, as provided in the Armistice agreement, and to join the Allies and neutrals in a general boycott on trade with the enemy.[71] And, while in February 1919 the Allies created a Supreme Economic Council, it was nothing of the sort Britain had wanted before the Armistice; it lacked executive power over supply and allocation. Nor did the United States extend further loans after 1918. These conditions all created a powerful economic incentive for the government to adopt policies which they believed would lead to a quick resumption of trade; in the absence of an inter-allied solution, only exports were seen as capable of containing the inflationary pressures of Britain's severe trade imbalance. Conditions would only grow worse as nations chased after scarcities, the government believed.

In the light of the foregoing discussion, it seems ironic that Germany would be a major issue in the General Election of December 1918. For, while the disintegrating German Empire had for the government faded as a major concern in recovery planning, the coalition was surprised to find campaign audiences responding only mildly to social and economic issues but enthusiastically to the talk of punishing the Germans and their Kaiser, and making them pay for the war. But then, astute observers might have anticipated this all along from the extraordinary popularity of the Economic Offensive with its narrowly exclusionary, anti-German measures.

Notes: Chapter 7

1   R. H. Tawney, 'The abolition of economic controls, 1918–1921' (1941) *History and Society: Essays by R. H. Tawney*, ed. J. M. Winter (London: Routledge & Kegan Paul, 1978), pp. 129–86. Tawney published an abbreviated version of the essay, under the same title, in *Economic History Review*, 1st series, vol. XIII (1943). Hereafter, references are to the fuller *History and Society* version. See also E. M. H. Lloyd, *Experiments in State Control* (London: Oxford University Press, 1924); S. J. Hurwitz, *State Intervention in Great Britain: A Study of Economic Control and Social Response, 1914–1919* (New York: Columbia University Press, 1949).

2   Tawney, 'Abolition of economic controls', *History and Society*, p. 149.

3   cf. Rodney Lowe, 'The erosion of state intervention in Britain, 1917–24', *Economic History Review*, 2nd series, vol. XXXI (1978); S. M. H. Armitage, *The Politics of Decontrol of Industry: Britain and the United States* (London: Weidenfeld & Nicolson, 1969).

4   P. B. Johnson, *Land Fit for Heroes: The Planning of British Reconstruction, 1916–19* (Chicago: Chicago University Press, 1968), p. 3.

5   Tawney, 'Abolition of economic controls', *History and Society*, p. 152.

6   Cabinet memorandum, 15 December 1915, CAB 37/139, Cabinet Papers, Public Record Office, London.

7   76 *House of Commons Debates*, 5 s., col. 387; 1766; 2220 (25 November, 13 December, 16 December 1915). 77 *H.C. Deb.* 5 s., cols 612, 646–8 (23 December 1915).

8   *Chamber of Commerce Journal*, vol. 33, no. 259 (November 1915); and cf. vol. 34, no. 260 (December 1915); vol. 35, no. 261 Annual Trade Review (January 1916), pp. 2, 24.

9   So commonly expressed are these apprehensions that they cannot be comprehended within a brief note. Readers are directed to the *House of Commons Debates*, *Chamber of Commerce Journal*, *The Times* and other sources revealing opinion for the closing months of 1915 and early months of 1916.

10   H. W. Carless Davis, *History of the Blockade: Emergency Departments*, HMSO, 1 June 1920, p. 183. Carless Davis is quoting a Confidential Print, 'Trading with the enemy correspondence'.

11   V. H. Rothwell, *British War Aims and Peace Diplomacy, 1914–1918* (London: Oxford University Press, 1971), p. 274.

12   77 *H.C. Deb.* 5 s., cols 1367–8 (10 January 1916). Runciman was responding to a resolution by W. A. S. Hewins that called on the government to consult with the Dominions about bringing 'the whole economic strength of the Empire' into the war effort (col. 1299). A useful discussion of protectionists' pressures

on Runciman may be found in R. E. Bunselmeyer, 'The cost of the war: British plans for the post-war economic treatment of Germany, 1914 to 1918', Yale University PhD dissertation, 1968, pp. 46–8.

13 *The Times*, 1 February 1916, p. 5.

14 *Chamber Journal*, vol. 35, no. 263 (March 1916), p. 89; and cf. *Monthly Proceedings* of the Associated Chambers of Commerce, no. 618 (March 1916), pp. 3ff., as cited in Bunselmeyer, 'The cost of the war', p. 49.

15 ibid., pp. 49–50 and cf. *Chamber Journal*, vol. 35, no. 264 (April 1916), pp. 112–13.

16 A text of the resolutions together with a memorandum about them is found in Box 143, W. R. Runciman Papers, University of Newcastle Library.

17 Bunselmeyer, 'The cost of the war', pp. 57–65, is a useful discussion of the final stage of the making of the resolutions.

18 'Memorandum on the Paris economic conference', Annex B, Runciman Papers, p. 143. Bunselmeyer argues that the Liberals actually divided over the Paris Resolutions 'both in 1916 and throughout the War', and so refutes Laurence Martin, *Peace Without Victory* (New Haven, Conn.: Yale University Press, 1958), who represented the Liberals as 'bound to interpret' such proposals as the resolutions as attempts 'by protectionists to reverse their pre-war defeat', pp. 69–70. Bunselmeyer, 'The cost of the war', p. 67.

19 85 *H.C. Deb.* 5 s., cols 333–42 (2 August 1916).

20 Reconstruction Committee, Conclusions (24 March 1916), CAB 37/145/13.

21 *Final Report of the Committee on Commercial and Industrial Policy after the War, 1917* (*Parl. Papers 1918*, vol. xiii, no. 239), Cd 9035, p. 4.

22 *Interim Report on the Importation of Goods from the Present Enemy Countries after the War, Committee on Commercial and Industrial Policy, 1916* (*Parl. Papers 1918*, vol. xiii), Cd 9034.

23 *Final Report of the Committee on Commercial and Industrial Policy*, chs. IV–VI.

24 *Report to the Board of Trade, Advisory Committee(s)*. These Parliamentary Papers (1918, vol. xiii) are as follows: Shipping and Shipbuilding (Cd 9092); Textile Trades (Cd 9070); Coal Industry (Cd 9093); Electrical Trades (Cd 9072); Engineering Trades (Cd 9073); Iron and Steel Trades (Cd 9071). As well, in March 1917, Munitions created an advisory committee to examine mineral resources, in November the Board chose one for the building industries, and the Treasury one for postwar financial facilities. Finally, in December, the Board appointed one to study the engineering industries. These Parliamentary Papers are, respectively, 1918, vol. xii (Cd 9184); 1918, vol. vii (Cd 9197); 1918, vol. x (Cd 9227); 1918, vol. vii (Cd 9226).

25 Among the many expressions of the belief in a commercial bonanza are *The Times*, 19 August 1914; *The New York Times*, 12 October 1914, p. 12; *Pall Mall Gazette*, 21 August 1914, as quoted in Ross J. S. Hoffman, *Great Britain and the German Trade Rivalry, 1875–1914* (Philadelphia, Pa: University of Pennsylvania Press, 1933); *Chamber Journal*, vol. 34, no. 249 (January 1915), p. 3; *Pall Mall Gazette*, 19 August 1914, as quoted in Keith Hutchison, *The Decline and Fall of British Capitalism* (Hamden, Conn.: Archon, 1966), p. 159.

26 J. A. Spender and Cyril Asquith, *The Life of Herbert Henry Asquith, Lord Oxford and Asquith* (London: Hutchinson, 1932), Vol. II, pp. 224–5.

27 Carl P. Parrini, *Heir to Empire: United States Economic Diplomacy, 1916–23* (Pittsburgh, Pa: University of Pittsburgh Press, 1969), ch. II; and cf. European Economic Alliances, National Foreign Trade Council, New York (September 1916).

28 Johnson, *Land Fit for Heroes*, pp. 32, 36–8.

29   ibid., pp. 32–3. Johnson emphasises the administrative, and touches on the political, consequences of department heads no longer, as with Asquith, sitting on the Reconstruction executive.

30   Runciman Papers, p. 143. See the exchange between Percy Ashley and Runciman over the matter of tariffs as a part of an Allied strategy for restricting Germany.

31   cf. note 24 above.

32   *Summaries of the Evidence taken by a Sub-Committee of the Advisory Committee to the Board of Trade on Commercial Intelligence in the Course of their Enquiry with respect to Measures for Securing the Position, after the War, of Certain Branches of British Industry, Parl. Papers 1916*, vol. xv.

33   cf. note 24 above.

34   'Report of a committee appointed to consider the question of the reorganisation of the Board of Trade', 9 August 1917, as in 'Reorganisation of the Board of Trade', 10 August 1917, *G* 163 CAB 24/4. D. C. M. Platt, *Finance, Trade and Politics, British Foreign Policy, 1815–1914* (London: Oxford University Press, 1968), p. 379; J. F. X. Homer, 'Foreign trade and foreign policy: the British Department of Overseas Trade, 1916–1922', University of Virginia PhD. dissertation, 1971), chs III and IV.

35   Homer, 'Foreign trade and foreign policy', chs II and III.

36   Johnson, *Land Fit for Heroes*, p. 96.

37   War Cabinet Minutes 220–3, 20 August 1917, CAB 23/3.

38   ibid.

39   War Cabinet Minutes 247–8, 9 October 1917, CAB 23/4.

40   'Memorandum on economic offensive, by Sir Edward Carson', 20 September 1917, *G* 156, CAB 24/4.

41   'Trade war' by Ernest Pollock, 27 June 1917, *GT* 1447, CAB 24/20.

42   'Economic offensive', *G* 156, CAB 24/4.

43   ibid.

44   Memorandum by Sir Edward Carson, 21 January 1918, *G* 190, CAB 21/108.

45   103 *H.C. Deb.* 5 s., cols 187–9 (13 February 1918). G. M. Young had warned of this in a letter forwarded to Lloyd George, F/1/4/5, David Lloyd George Papers, House of Lords Record Office, London. That the propaganda continued even in October is evident from Economic Defence and Development Committee, Memorandum 51, 21 October 1918, CAB 27/44.

46   War Cabinet Minutes 312–6, 3 January 1918, CAB 23/5.

47   ibid.

48   105 *H.C. Deb.* 5 s., col. 562 (18 April 1918); 106 *H.C. Deb.* 5 s., col. 3 (13 May 1918).

49   100 *H.C. Deb.* 5 s., cols 172–208; 1011–1132 (3 and 11 December 1917).

50   cf. War Cabinet Minutes 443–12; 444–9, 10 and 11 July 1918, CAB 23/7.

51   W. A. S. Hewins, *Apologia of an Imperialist* (London: Hewins, 1929), Vol. II, p. 138.

52   War Cabinet Minutes 248–13, 12 October 1917, CAB 23/4.

53   'Most likely' because, except in the unusual cases expressly stipulating to other arrangements, MFN status was understood among European nations to be unconditional.

54   War Cabinet Minutes 312–6, 3 January 1918, CAB 23/5.

55   ibid.; War Cabinet Minutes 401–1, 30 April 1918, CAB 23/6.

56   War Cabinet Minutes 413–11, 17 May 1918, CAB 23/6.

57   War Cabinet Minutes 431–11, 17 June 1918; 444–14, 11 July 1918; 446–6, 16 July 1918, CAB 23/6; 23/7.

58   War Cabinet Minutes 447–6, 17 July 1917, CAB 23/7, and cf. War Cabinet Minutes 448–2, 18 July 1918, CAB 23/7.

59 Reconstruction Committee, 'Memorandum on post-war commercial policy in the light of recent events', p. 121, 12 July 1917, BT 55/13, Board of Trade Papers, PRO, London.
60 'Trade war' by Ernest Pollock, 27 June 1917, *GT* 1447, CAB 24/20.
61 cf. note 59 above.
62 Johnson, *Land Fit for Heroes*, pp. 148–9.
63 ibid., pp. 97–8, 148–9.
64 War Cabinet Minutes 265–18, 5 November 1917; 283–17, 27 November 1917, CAB 23/4.
65 Memorandum by Sir Edward Carson, 21 January 1918, *G* 190, CAB 21/108.
66 'The Paris Resolutions in relation to free trade', H. Llewellyn Smith, 6 November 1918, F/2/6/2, Lloyd George Papers.
67 Economic Defence and Development Committee, Memorandum 18, 2 July 1918, CAB 27/44.
68 Economic Defence and Development Committee, Memorandum 51, 21 October 1918, CAB 27/44.
69 Parrini, *Heir to Empire*, pp. 41–50.
70 Economic Defence and Development Committee, Memorandum 51, 21 October 1918, CAB 27/44; Tom Jones, *Whitehall Diaries, 1916–25* (London: Oxford University Press, 1969), Vol. I, p. 67.
71 War Cabinet Minutes 501–7, 13 November 1918; 505–7, 21 November 1918, CAB 23/7.

Index

Aberconway Committee 120

Acts of Parliament: Defence of the Realm Act 2–3, 49, 96, 138; Defence of the Realm (Amendment Number 2) Act 22, 23, 26; Munitions of War Acts 49; Corn Production Act 73; Trade Boards (Amendment) Act 117; Trade Union (Amalgamation) Act 117; Trading with the Enemy (Amendment) Act 171; Non-Ferrous Metal Industry Act 170; Industrial Courts Act 119; Currency and Bank Notes Act 87

Adams, J. B. 120, 132(n.32)

Adams, W. G. S. 46, 52(n.3)

Addison, Viscount 6, 33, 37, 40, 41, 42, 43–4, 54(n.30), 65, 172–3, 174

Admiralty 8, 9, 12, 14, 18, 23, 25, 26, 27, 65, 68, 69, 71, 72, 89, 115, 136

Advisory Committee on the Diversion of Shipping 25

Aerial Operations Committee 68

Agadir crisis 8, 14, 16

agricultural interests 20, 136, 138, 139, 140, 143, 144, 147, 149, 154(n.41), 156(n.101)

Air Board 64, 69, 97

Allied (Entente) Powers 5, 8, 10, 16, 21, 22, 23, 74, 82(n.85), 89, 93, 142, 145, 146, 160, 163, 166, 168, 169, 171, 172, 173, 176, 177, 180(n.30)

Allied Purchasing Commission 93

Allied Supreme Council on Relief and Supply 147

American Committee 93

American Exchange Committee 95

American Society of Mechanical Engineers 50

Amery, Leopold 73–4, 76, 82(n.69 & n.75)

Anderson, Sir Alan 139

Armaments Output Committee 24

Arthur, Sir George 35

Ashley, Percy 180(n.30)

Askwith, Sir George 110, 111, 114, 115, 116, 123, 124, 126, 131(n.10), 133(n.43)

Asquith, Herbert Henry 2, 3, 5, 9, 14, 16, 17, 18, 22, 24, 25, 26, 33, 34, 36, 37, 40–1, 42, 54(n.26 & n.45), 57, 58, 59, 60, 61, 62, 63, 64, 67, 69, 70, 71, 72, 77, 78, 79(n.9 & n.10 & n.13), 161, 163, 164, 165, 166, 180(n.29)

Asquith Coalition government 22, 59, 62, 63, 64, 65, 78, 105(n.42), 105–6(n.42), 138, 139, 161

Asquith government 2, 3, 7, 34, 59, 65, 78

Austria 66, 137, 164

Baldwin, Stanley 96, 105(n.30), 109

Balfour, Arthur James 12, 34, 38, 58, 59, 60, 61, 63, 66, 79(n.10), 95

Balfour of Burleigh, Lord 164, 165

Balkans 60, 79(n.11)

Ballard Committee 8, 9

Banbury, Sir F. G. 103(n.7)

Bank of England 84, 85, 86, 87, 88, 89, 90, 93–6, 101, 104(n.19), 105–6(n.43), 107(n.77)

Bank Rate 86, 88–9

Baring, Cecil 36

Barlow, Sir A. 131(n.9)

Barnes, George Nicoll 65, 138, 145

Barnes-Milner Memorandum 132(n.24)

Bathurst, Captain Charles 139, 141, 145, 148

Beale, Sir John 139, 145–7, 148, 150

Beaverbrook, Lord (William Maxwell Aitken) 32, 33, 105(n.37)

Belgium (including Flanders) 8, 58, 71, 75, 160, 163, 171

Bethlehem Steel Corporation 35

Betterton, Sir H. B. 131(n.6)

Beveridge, William 5, 46, 110, 111, 122, 123, 131(n.10), 132(n.32), 134(n.66), 139, 140, 141, 142, 144, 145–6, 147, 148–51, 152, 154(n.57), 156(n.114)

Bevin, Ernest 118, 122

Black, Sir Frederick 44, 45

Blackett, Basil 89

Board of Agriculture 80(n.33), 136, 137, 139, 141, 144, 149, 156(n.101)